"Out and...
this book mak...   ...ly censored
documentary."

> —Robert Wade, co-screenwriter of
> *Casino Royale* and *Skyfall*

"Dr. Vince Houghton is smart—really smart—and doesn't suffer fools (or foolish plans) kindly. In *Nuking the Moon*, he hilariously skewers some of the military and intelligence community's weirdest, wackiest, and most outlandish plots, plans, and covert operations! From the story of the CIA's bugged kitty cat to tales of arming Chinese call girls with poisons, and blowing up the moon, it's a great read and highly recommended!"

> —H. Keith Melton, intelligence historian and
> coauthor of *Spycraft*

"Vince Houghton is a fresh new voice who will have you laughing out loud at some of the serious yet hysterical false starts in the history of the intelligence community."

> —Jonna Mendez, former CIA chief of disguise

"The Cold War wasn't just dangerous, it was also often bizarre, and sometimes even hilarious. Vince Houghton has put together an amazing compendium of schemes and plans that were once top secret—and for good reason. This is a compelling book, not only because of the light it sheds on a halfcentury of American secrets, but because it is a reminder that when human beings go to war—hot or cold—they can often be too clever for their own good."

> ...Nich...   ...*Expertise*

"These are amazing tales, and readers may, despite Houghton's research to verify each project, be left pondering whether the book will be shelved among works of history or science-fiction novels. Possibly, however, *Nuking the Moon* best belongs with political science to remind us that when national survival is believed threatened, desperation and innovation become kindred spirits that can make the otherwise unimaginable become real."

—Robert Wallace, former director of the CIA's Office of Technical Service and coauthor of *Spycraft*

"Houghton mixes humor and irony with an espionage historian's eye for detail to make *Nuking the Moon* both entertaining and informative. The litany of bizarre schemes and harebrained ideas had me continually asking, 'What were they thinking?' From ideas like the acoustic cat to synthetic goat poop, and so many ideas related to the use of atomic weapons, I would laugh out loud if it weren't so scary. As a CIA veteran, I'm just glad that my name can't be found in its pages."

—John Sipher, former CIA chief of station and lead instructor at CIA's clandestine training school

NUKING THE MOON

*And Other
Intelligence Schemes
And Military Plots Best Left
On The Drawing Board*

VINCE HOUGHTON

PROFILE BOOKS

First published in Great Britain in 2019 by
PROFILE BOOKS LTD
3 Holford Yard
Bevin Way
London
WCIX 9HD
www.profilebooks.com

First published in the United States of America in 2019
by Penguin Books
An imprint of Penguin Random House LLC

1 3 5 7 9 10 8 6 4 2

Typeset in Garamond by MacGuru Ltd
Design by Meighan Cavanaugh
Printed and bound in Great Britain by Clays Ltd, Elcograf S.p.A.

To Jon and Rae

CONTENTS

INTRODUCTION: LEFT ON THE DRAWING BOARD

This is a book about desperation.

It's a word that has been so overused and misused that it has lost much of its impact. Too many stories about some local sports team "desperate" for a win, or some housewives "desperate" for ... whatever that show was about. These pretenders have trivialized a word designed to be used only in the most extraordinary of circumstances. It should be a powerful word, reserved for the urgent and overwhelming feeling that one's life is at risk. It's for the truly existential threats (another misused word), to one's country, one's family, one's friends, or one's livelihood. When the stakes couldn't be higher and the options slimmer. To feel desperate is to believe there are no good options, that everything that has been tried, or could be tried, is destined for failure. Desperation leads us to consider ideas that would have been unfathomable under normal circumstances—because desperate people make desperate decisions.

This is also a book about innovation.

Creative thinking about how things work—and the possibilities of how things *could* work—has been the catalyst for the astonishingly dynamic technological transformation of the past hundred years. From the advent of lighter-than-air flight to hypersonic aircraft, from bolt-action rifles to electromagnetic railguns, from ENIAC to quantum computing, from one poor freezing soldier in a trench listening to intercepted wireless messages to the NSA's supercomputers collecting the metadata of billions—brilliant people with innovative ideas continue to shape our world, and do it exponentially faster than the generations that came before.

But when innovation and desperation meet, trouble will usually follow. If necessity is the mother of invention, desperation is the drunk uncle.

Every so often, we are surprised when one of these ideas actually pans out. The U-2 and SR-71 spy planes—some of the most innovative aircraft ever designed—were a result of American desperation to see inside the Soviet Union. Nuclear power, computers, the internet, modern textiles, and personal encryption were all born out of a nation's desperate fear to keep pace with an imposing rival. Much of that history has been written before. Countless books have been published about the remarkable and successful technology developed over the last century by governments for national security needs.

But this is not one of them.

Most history books are full of stories of things that happened; this is a history book about why things *didn't* happen.

Here we will take an expansive look at projects, missions, operations, and technology that were seriously considered, but didn't make the grade. Some were ultimately deemed too risky, expensive, dangerous, ahead of their time—or even certifiably insane. Others were canceled merely because they were overtaken by events: The atomic bomb worked, the war ended, the plans were captured, other technology superseded.

Generally, history books use events of the past to make powerful arguments about peoples' motivations, personalities, and states of mind. And rightfully so—this is part of what history books are supposed to do. But I contend that the evaluation of historical *events* is not enough. It can be just as important to investigate policies, decisions, and technologies that were considered at the highest levels, but then abandoned. The *intent* of historical actors can be (and I argue *is*) just as instructive and illuminating as the outcome of their policies.

"Outcome history" is the traditional way of viewing historical events, but it leaves much to be desired. It has severe limitations, primarily because its lessons are predicated on things that cannot be accurately quantified: fate, luck, misfortune, whatever you want to call it. If the D-Day invasion of Normandy had failed because of a freak weather system, or a lucky shot from a German soldier that took out a key American leader on the beach (or any number of other misfortunate scenarios), would we think any less of Eisenhower's plan? Using outcomebased history: yes. And therein lies the problem. Intent can be a very powerful tool for historians.

So leave your historical hindsight at the door. Ignore the fact that these policies, technologies, programs, and missions were scrapped before they became "real." The outcome really doesn't matter here at all. That's why this book scorns the counterfactual—the game of "what if"—vilifies it, mocks it mercilessly. The counterfactual is our enemy and it has no place here.

Instead, all of these stories should have you saying, "What were they thinking?" The best way to approach this book is with an open mind toward how the decision makers were approaching the problems facing them. In almost every case, those in power were *desperate* to do something (any-thing) to combat their adversaries. Thus, "What were they thinking?" is *exactly correct*—except I hope that you will be willing to truly embrace the question, and not see it as just a dismissive aside or a hasty pejorative. In all of these stories, very intelligent people were willing to do anything (or *just about* anything) to achieve or maintain national power. This resulted in extreme "outside the box" thinking—but not so extreme that it changes the fact that these were serious people making lifeanddeath decisions. Their *intent* is just as impor-tant as their actions, and that's why this task at hand matters: It offers a unique, unusual opportunity to put us (the reader, the historian) in the mindset of the historical figures, and to understand the unique and daunting challenges they faced.

In some cases, this gives us an unconventional perspec-tive on familiar figures. You might never see historic figures such as Winston Churchill, John F. Kennedy, Fidel Castro, Franklin Roosevelt, or even Carl Sagan the same way again. In other cases, these stories resurface fascinating figures left in the dustbin of history, who might be household names had their ideas panned out.

The book is organized into four parts, each with its own theme, but all full of stories centered on the desperation that was the product of the sheer terror of World War II, or the ideological fervor and suspicion of the Cold War. In each case, the originators of these ideas truly believed their very existence was at stake. And their desperation led to some … interesting choices.

Part I focuses on our furry and feathered friends from the animal kingdom. You know how when a movie uses animals—a *Babe the Sheep Pig*, a *Marley & Me*, a *Snakes on a Plane*—there's a disclaimer during the credits that says, "No Animals Were Harmed in the Making of This Film"? Well, that's not the case in part I. The animals in these stories were cut open, wired up, run over, set on fire, blown to pieces, dropped unconscious from thousands of feet, infected with biological pathogens, painted with caustic (and likely carcinogenic) paint, and shoved inside tactical nuclear weapons. All in the name of national security.

Part II centers on the secret world of covert and clandestine operations. The stuff that makes for exciting tales of espionage and intrigue: assassination attempts, special operations, secret missions, spies and spycraft, devious dealings, dastardly villains, doublecrossers, and deadly vixens. The fact that these operations never happened doesn't take anything away from the extraordinary plans developed for them. They are illogical, irrational, absurd, bizarre, ludicrous, and wild. But they are completely real.

Part III spotlights some of the most inspired and innovative technology of World War II and the Cold War. I'm talking about the *really* innovative stuff. The things so creative that they aren't just "outside the box," they are outside of the room, the building, the neighborhood, the city. Some of them were clearly ahead of their time. Some, we should hope, might *never* be in "their time."

Part IV takes things further. The development of nuclear weapons was, of course, the development of a new and novel technology. Yet it is disingenuous to consider the atomic bomb as "just another invention." The weaponization of nuclear energy was a watershed moment for the history of the Cold War. Humanity had created the most destructive technology in the history of the human experience, but in many cases we had no clue what to do with our newfound power. Do we use it just like any other weapon? Or do we reserve it for just the most extraordinary circumstances, or even depend on just the psychological impact of having the weapons at our disposal? Can we even find ways to use nuclear weapons for *good*? What are some of the most ridiculous and asinine things we can possibly do with nuclear weapons? These questions were under constant debate during the Cold War. Some were addressed, some still remain unanswered today. I will be focusing on the last one.

Finally, while my research for this book depended on serious research into primary and secondary source literature, archival resources, expert interviews, and broadranging scientific, intelligence, foreign policy, and national security policy perspectives, my primary reason for writing this book is to help you learn and have fun. And to have some fun myself. Because these stories are extraordinary. So pull up a chair, and sit back and relax.

We're going for a ride.

PART I

ADVENTURES IN THE ANIMAL KINGDOM

1

ACOUSTIC KITTY

Acoustic Kitty is not just one story, but rather *stories*. You see, there are two different versions of this tale.

The first version has all of the necessary and wonderful elements of successful drama: great characters, extraordinary spectacle, rising action, a climax that shocks and delights, and a denouement for the ages.

The second version is, well ... probably true.

But don't fret, the divergences between the stories are pretty trivial. The differences only make up a small part of the broader picture, and do nothing to change the most important, fundamental fact of the Acoustic Kitty story, which is:

The CIA tried to make a covert listening device out of a housecat.

People have been secretly intercepting communications for centuries. One of the most prominent historical examples is the French *cabinet noir*, run by Cardinal Armand Jean du Plessis, the Duke of Richelieu and Fronsac (Cardinal Richelieu of *Three Musketeers* fame) in the early seventeenth century. This "black room" or "black chamber" intercepted the letters of French citizens and foreigners suspected of conspiring against the king. The letters were secretly opened, read, resealed, and then sent to their intended recipient (who would never know what had happened in transit). More than one nefarious plot against king and country was foiled this way—and even some that hadn't yet reached the level of "nefarious." Richelieu didn't care if he trampled a liberty (or two). The protection of the crown was paramount: "If you give me six lines written by the hand of the most honest of men, I will find something in them which will hang him."

Skip ahead to the twentieth century, when the development of electronic communications inevitably lead to means for intercepting communications *with* electronics. Thus begins the age of the covert listening device—the "bug" or "wire." But 1940s and '50s listening devices hardly resembled the bugs from the movies, the ones where the hero gets the Mob boss to reveal where he's hidden the bodies, just before the cops bust in. Instead, they were soda-cansized monstrosities that could only be concealed in furniture or adequately large household appliances—lamps, comfy chairs, bookcases, and so on.

By the 1960s, some of the size issues had been resolved thanks to the natural evolution of electronics, but listening device technology still could not clear its most pressing hurdle: These bugs picked up everything. That might sound like a good thing. The more the better, right? No. When I say everything, I mean *everything*. A bug secretly placed on a park bench wouldn't just pick up the conversation of the people sitting on it. It would pick up dogs barking, birds chirping, traffic noise, cars honking, ambulance sirens, heavy footsteps, heavy breathing, etc., masking the conversation and wasting the time of the poor operatives whose job it was to try (futilely) to make sense of whatever cacophony was recorded on the tape.

Think of what it feels like to try to have a conversation at a crowded bar, a busy restaurant, or a deafening rock concert. Even though the musician onstage is shredding a face-melting guitar solo, you and your friend can nevertheless have a reasonably understandable conversation. Sure, you are screaming into each other's faces from two inches away, but you can still make out what your friend is saying. This is because humans (and many animals) have a structure inside our inner ear known as the cochlea, and this is where something called transduction takes place—the conversion of energy from one form to another. In this case, the cochlea transduces sound waves into electrical impulses that our brains perceive as sound. Most importantly, this process allows our brain to differentiate between different kinds of sounds—we can focus on our friend's offer to go to the bar, as we are simultaneously inundated with 120 decibels of heavy metal mayhem.

In the 1960s, the engineers working for American intelligence tried, in vain, to develop an artificial cochlea for use in covert listening devices. After a time, they realized that the technology of the day was inadequate for such an ambitious undertaking. And who can blame them? The cochlea is ridiculously complicated, so much so that we didn't really understand its form and function until the late 1950s/early 1960s. Housed inside the cochlea is something called the basilar membrane, on which are found thousands upon thousands of hair cells, called stereocilia. The stereocilia at specific locations react to specific frequencies of sound. Low frequencies are picked up by certain hairs, while high frequencies stimulate others. This is why some people with mild hearing loss can no longer hear very high- or low-pitched sounds—the stereocilia for those particular frequencies have been damaged, but the rest of the cochlea is good to go.

Understandably, this level of complexity was beyond the capabilities of even the world's greatest scientists and engineers of the 1960s—and the CIA had some of the very best, many of whom worked in a division that is today known as the Office of Technical Service (or OTS, at the time called the Technical Services Division, or TSD). The intricacy of the cochlea is the result of millions of years of evolution, while inventors and engineers of the time had just finished perfecting the Etch A Sketch, felttipped pens, AstroTurf, acrylic paint, and the audiocassette tape. We were still a couple of years away from the handheld calculator, electronic fuel injection for cars, and the first artificial heart (which, although way more important to us than the cochlea, is far less complicated). So give them a break. They did their best with what they had.

It's at this point that some scientist in CIA's TSD—unfortunately (for us, though perhaps fortunately for him) his name has been lost to history—decided to go in an entirely different direction. Instead of killing themselves trying to make an artificial cochlea, why didn't they take something that already has a perfectly well-functioning cochlea, and turn it *into* a listening device?

And thus, Project Acoustic Kitty—that is actually the official title—was born. But we aren't *quite* ready to tell the rest of the story. It wasn't, on the face of it, quite as crazy a plan as it first appeared. Along with the CIA's Office of Research and Development (ORD), the scientists and engineers of TSD understood the very real potential usefulness of a feline secret agent. In many major cities, cats are ubiquitous. They come and go as they please, and no one thinks twice about a lone cat taking a stroll in a public park. Or even sliding through the gates of an embassy compound. It's the perfect cover for a perfect clandestine operation.

But as we all know, cats can be difficult customers. They tend to do whatever they want, when they want, and how they want, regardless of human pleading, soft cooing, bribery with treats, or even threats. They are famously impossible to train, or even herd. Of course, the scientists and engineers at TSD and ORD understood this as well, but they had real reason to think that recent developments in brain science had paved the way for an attempt at the seemingly impossible. Part of this renaissance in neuroscience was a result of the natural progression of scientific discovery that defined the early to midtwentieth century. This is a time in history where science was redefining our understanding of, well, everything.

Part of it was due to the CIA's own inhouse research. For the decade and a half leading up to Acoustic Kitty, the CIA had been pushing the envelope of what was "possible"—from applied science, to technology, to medical research, to even the parapsychological, much of this under the broad auspices of a program known as MKULTRA.

MKULTRA earned its welldeserved notoriety due to experiments in "mind control," testing a bevy of hallucinogenic drugs, most notably LSD, on both witting and unwitting test subjects. Further criticism has been targeted at the program's research and manufacture of what can only be described as biological and chemical weapons for CIA operational use in assassinations and other "executive actions." But what many people don't realize is that MKULTRA was actually multiple programs—about 150—under the single umbrella of the code name, and many of these subprojects had nothing to do with biological toxins, chemicals, or psychedelic drugs. Admittedly, we have no idea about most of the subprojects that made up MKULTRA. We only really know about a handful of them. The majority of the MKULTRA documents were (deliberately) destroyed decades ago, and unless someone kept a secret copy somewhere, we will never know the full extent of this particular chapter of the CIA's history.

We *do* know that at least two of the subprojects centered on the use of electronic brain stimulation and the control of animals. According to a CIA report in late 1960, one of these, Subproject 94, demonstrated the "feasibility" of electronic implants and the behavioral manipulation of "several species" of animals. There is no specific mention of cats, but the results of the experiments were enough to spur on "development of future Agency applications." One of these "applications" is the feline hero of our story, Acoustic Kitty.

Remember when I said there were two versions of this story? Up to this point, the stories are more or less the same. Here, however, is where they begin to veer off in vastly different directions. We'll take them one at a time, and then bring them back together at the end—which is, as far as anything that matters, essentially the same for both. The middle? Not so much.

The first version comes courtesy of Bob Wallace, who was the director of the OTS in the late 1990s and early 2000s.

Bob briefly wrote about Acoustic Kitty in his book *Spycraft*, and even though I've read this book several times, I always try to get more out of him in person. On several occasions I've asked Bob about Acoustic Kitty, and his response is basically the same each time: a sardonic grin, a sly chuckle, and then a look of resigned acceptance when he realizes that I'm not just going to go away. I also think that Bob would much rather talk about some of the extraordinary accomplishments of TSS/TSD/OTS. But I don't want to talk about their integral part in the development of the U-2 spy plane, which first saw service in the 1950s, but was so revolutionary it still flies today, or their role in the rescue of six American diplomats from Tehran after the ouster of the shah (dramatized in the movie *Argo*). I want to talk about cats. According to Bob, the CIA's scientists and technicians understood from the getgo that this project firmly fell into the "high risk" category. Inserting electronics into a living organism was not as routine as it is today (this is several years before the first heart transplant). Living bodies are not welcoming spaces for electronics. They are hot and they are wet. They have natural defense systems, which fight against foreign intruders. Through millions of years of evolution, the cat has been designed to specification. Everything inside a cat is there for an important biological reason. There's not a whole lot of extra room for implants, wires, and batteries. It wouldn't do the CIA much good if the cat listening device worked to perfection but it blew its cover—or damaged its equipment—by constantly clawing or licking at itself, or if it couldn't walk straight because it was laden with the extra weight of the CIA's electronics package.

With this in mind, the CIA did all it could to ensure the

humane treatment (relatively speaking, of course) of the test cat, a gray-and-white female of undocumented breed. A professional veterinarian, working in a clean, sterile operating environment within an animal hospital, conducted the procedure. A threequarterinch audio transmitter, developed by TSD and an outside contractor, was embedded at the base of the cat's skull. You know the loose skin just below the head of a cat, where you (or its mother) can pick it up and carry it around without causing it any pain? The perfect place for the audio transmitter. The small, wirelike microphone was—of course—placed in the ear canal, to allow for easy and fluid conduction of sound.

The antenna, made of very fine wire, needed to extend beyond the insulated inside of the cat for it to work effectively. But it couldn't just stick straight up into the air. To ensure it remained hidden, it was woven into the cat's fur, down along her spine.

After the operation, Acoustic Kitty was placed inside a recovery area, as the CIA techs anxiously waited for the anesthesia to wear off. Once back on her feet, the cat was put through a series of tests. To the scientists' and technicians' satisfaction, the microphone worked as advertised, and provided a usable signal. However, there were other issues. Despite their best efforts at training the cat to move consistently according to mission, results in this area were "inconsistent" and the operational utility of Acoustic Kitty was "questionable," even after several weeks of exercises and tests. For some reason (obvious to anyone who has ever interacted with a cat), the CIA was having trouble training a cat to behave. Because the results failed to improve, and the CIA was hesitant to deploy its new robocat in an operational environment without a guarantee of some level of practical control, the project was ultimately scrapped.

Ambitious, yet sensible. Pushing the outside of the envelope, but not taking things too far. Walking the line, but not falling over. If this was the only version of the story, it wouldn't be in this book.

But it isn't.

Version two of the Acoustic Kitty story comes from Victor Marchetti, former special assistant to CIA Director Richard Helms in the mid to late 1960s, and coauthor of the book *The CIA and the Cult of Intelligence*. As his book title suggests, Marchetti became disillusioned with the Agency, and perhaps this attitude influenced the version of Acoustic Kitty he provides. So take this with a grain, or a pound, of salt. It might be utter nonsense. But it's one hell of a story.

According to Marchetti, Acoustic Kitty can be summed up in a single word: a "monstrosity." However, Marchetti's and Bob's versions of the creation of our wired cat hero don't really diverge all that much, excepting the fact that Marchetti says Acoustic Kitty's tail was used as the audio antenna (I'm assuming he meant they strung the wire through, or on top of, its tail, but he isn't specific), and that it was a male cat, and not a female. The real differences in the stories come when we turn our attention to the training, testing, and—according to Marchetti—a realworld operational dry run in an actual living, breathing urban environment.

The testing and training process was slow, but ultimately fruitful. Acoustic Kitty would follow commands, negotiate obstacles put in its way by the scientists, and accomplish the short missions (walk from here to there, stop on command, sit over there, and so on) that would progressively get harder and more complicated. The only hiccup was something they probably should have seen coming: Cats, from time to time, need to eat. Acoustic Kitty would be plugging along during testing, but then get hungry and wander off in search of food. And that's where the MKULTRA experiments with electrical brain stimulation in animals come into play. Obviously, the CIA couldn't have its invention disappearing in the middle of a mission to look for some Whiskas, so the vets and techs went back in and rejiggered Acoustic Kitty's wiring, turning off its natural instinct to seek sustenance. After a successful second surgery, and equally successfully followon testing, Acoustic Kitty was now ready for its full-scale field test.

Marchetti never provided a detailed, minute-by-minute account of the first (and only) CIA field test of Acoustic Kitty. He told us the ending, but that's all. But this is how I think it played out:

As I imagine it, the field test takes place on a sleepy street somewhere in Northwest Washington, DC. The CIA techs parallel park their spy van along the street, directly across from one of the many public parks scattered throughout the city. Maybe their van is just plain and white. Maybe it has "Bob's Plumbing" or "Phil's Handyman" or "Flowers by Irene" painted on the sides in an effort to establish a plausible cover. Inside the van, the two CIA techs are surrounded by 1960sera technology: blinking lights, knobs, switches, buttons. Monitors that project the feed from a handful of clandestine cameras line the top of the interior. These will allow for the CIA to watch the test from every angle. As one of the techs takes Acoustic Kitty out of its cage and makes sure everything is where it's supposed to be, the other turns the knobs, flicks the switches, and pushes the buttons that activate the Agency's newest top secret listening device. The cat is placed on the asphalt, and the tech points to two men, deep in conversation, sitting on a bench in the park.

To the surprised satisfaction of the CIA techs, Acoustic Kitty goes straight for the men on the bench—no hesitancy, no deviation, no stopping to search for food. A beeline to the target. It's not hard to imagine what might have been going through the techs' heads: *This is going to make my career. I'm going to be promoted, get a raise. Maybe I can take that vacation at the beach this year. Maybe buy a boat. Or a motorcycle! The sky's the limit.* And as they watch our feline heroine cross the doublepainted line in the street, pride swells up in them. This is fifty small steps for a cat, but one giant leap for mankind.

But here's what we do know from Marchetti's version of the story. Only feet away from the safety of the curb, Acoustic Kitty was run over by a taxi.

No promotion. No raise. No boat. No Harley. Just the indignity of having to scrape the still-sparking Acoustic Kitty off the pavement, before the Soviets—or worse, the *Washington Post*—find out what the CIA was up to.

No matter which version of this story we believe we are fairly confident we know the ultimate outcome of the project. The CIA left a paper trail. In a heavily redacted document, entitled "[Redacted] Views on Trained Cats [Redacted] for [Redacted] Use," the CIA gave its verdict. Although the report acknowledges the "remarkable scientific achievement" in training cats to move short distances, and that the work done on this project over the years "reflects great credit on the personnel who guided it, particularly [Redacted] whose energy and imagination could be models for scientific pioneers," the CIA decided the program was not practical, and Acoustic Kitty was scrapped for good.

Or was it?

AND THEN WHAT?

Evidence from the last decade suggests that some people think the Acoustic Kitty program may never have ended—or maybe it ended in the United States but was continued by one of her allies. Newspaper headlines from around the world provide the proof: "Iranians Arrest 14 Squirrels for Spying"; "Shark 'Sent to Egypt by Mossad'"; "Hamas Arrests 'Israeli Spy' Dolphin"; "Hezbollah: We Have Captured an Israeli 'Spy Eagle' in Lebanon"; "Saudi Arabia 'Nabbed Israeli-Tagged Vulture for Being Mossad Spy'"; "Turkey Clears Bird of Spying for Israel"; "Abbas Accuses Israel of Using Wild Boars against Palestinians."

And my favorite, non-Israeli headline: "Police in India Nab a Pigeon, Suspect Fowl Play from Pakistan."

This trend has become so prevalent there is an entire Wikipedia page dedicated to "Israel-related animal conspiracy theories." Really. Look it up.

It's impossible to trace the roots of these stories directly to the doorstep of the CIA and the Acoustic Kitty program, and as a historian I am loath to confuse correlation with causality, *and*, of course, it is obvious that a not insignificant amount of antiIsraeli sentiment is fueling this craze—but it's hard not to see a clear lineage from the laboratories and operating rooms of the CIA to the poor "Mossad" secret squirrels rotting away in an Iranian jail cell.

Finally, let's talk about the cochlea, because that's where

this all started. Today, we are still not able to fully replicate the intricacies of this complex organ, but we are getting close. A device known as a cochlear implant can replace some of the function of damaged or inoperable hair cells (the stereocilia) by artificially converting sound into electrical impulses that the brain can detect. The quality of sound isn't perfect, but technology continues to develop each and every year.

There is no concrete (read: declassified) evidence that the CIA experiments in aural engineering and neuroscience had a direct impact on the cochlear technological milestones of today. But maybe (just maybe) the civilian scientists working to help cure the hearing impaired are, in some way, continuing the work of CIA scientists and engineers back in the 1960s.

I'd love for that to be true.

Acoustic Kitty wouldn't have died in vain.

(If she died in the first place.)

2

OPERATION CAPRICIOUS

But the man had hereditary tendencies of the most diabolical kind. A criminal strain ran in his blood, which, instead of being modified, was increased and rendered infinitely more dangerous by his extraordinary mental powers. Dark rumours gathered round him in the university town, and eventually he was compelled to resign his Chair and to come down to London. He is the Napoleon of crime, Watson. He is the organizer of half that is evil and of nearly all that is undetected in this great city. He is a genius, a philosopher, an abstract thinker. He has a brain of the first order.
—Sherlock Holmes describing Professor James Moriarty in
"The Final Problem"

This is a story about poo. Goat poo. Specifically, synthetic goat poo.

And a lot of it.

Stanley Lovell was a chemist, and a very good one. Like many patriotic Americans, he signed up to contribute when the United States joined the Second World War. His talents and skills were immediately recognized by Dr. Vannevar Bush, the director of an American wartime agency known as the National Defense Research Committee (NDRC), who assigned Lovell to help the Quartermaster Corps design innovative chemical solutions to common military problems posed by a truly global war. Some of these would include how to make grommets (like an eyelet on a shoe or tarp) out of plastic instead of metal (to save the metal for other uses); or how to make moldproof tents, shoes, leggings (etc.), which are particularly necessary in Pacific jungle environments; or to figure out a way to make ponchos suitable for desert warfare, where it can be frigidly cold in the night, but blazing hot during the day.

This was immensely important work. It would help to win the war. Lovell was making a contribution.

But he was bored.

Fortunately for him Dr. Bush was now helping to recruit scientists for another organization. A secret one. Full of spies—and the people who would develop the technology to help those spies win the war. One day, Bush came to his new employees with a seemingly simple thought experiment:

> You are about to land at dead of night in a rubber raft on a Germanheld coast. Your mission is to destroy a vital enemy wireless installation that is defended by armed guards, dogs and searchlights. You can have with you any one weapon you can imagine. Describe that weapon.

Lovell couldn't just say "tactical nuclear weapon" (which would be my knee-jerk reaction if asked that question today, but alas, they hadn't been invented yet), so he spent about a week concocting his answer. His response hinted at his future aptitude for dirty wiles and clandestine shenanigans. He submitted:

> I want a completely silent, flashless gun—a Colt automatic or submachine gun—or both [technically this would be cheating—Bush said *one* weapon]. I can pick off the first sentry with no sound or flash to explain his collapse, so the next sentry will come to him instead of sounding an alarm. Then, one by one, I'll pick them off and command the wireless station.

Quite devious for a chemist. And it was enough to get Bush's attention. Shortly afterward, Lovell was told to report to an address in Northwest Washington. It was there that he first met William "Wild Bill" Donovan: lawyer, politician, the most decorated soldier in American history, and the director of the newly formed intelligence agency the Office of Strategic Services (OSS).

Donovan kept it simple: "You know your Sherlock Holmes, of course," he said. "Professor Moriarty is the man I want for my staff here at OSS. I think you're it."

Donovan continued, "I need every subtle device and every underhanded trick to use against the Germans and the Japanese—by our own people—but especially by the underground resistance groups in all occupied countries. You will have to invent all of them, Lovell, because you are going to be my man." As Lovell described in his memoir, Donovan was really telling him, "Throw all your normal law-abiding concepts out the window. Here's a chance to raise merry hell. Come, help me raise it."

Lovell had found his war. He was in.

Bill Donovan was a firm believer in the power of science to help win the war. He thought the side that most effectively and efficiently applied science and technology to intelligence and combat operations would have the decisive edge. As a result, in October 1942, only four months after the creation of the OSS, Donovan formed the OSS Research & Development unit (OSS/R&D), and put Lovell in charge. OSS/R&D had a number of responsibilities: camouflage; chemical, mechanical, and electrical implements; documentation forgery; disguise; drugs, toxins, and lethal weapons; secret writing; chemical and biological warfare defense … and offense. And, of course, the devious special weapons, spy gadgets, and devices.

The unit had some smashing successes … and some dismal failures.

Some of the lowlights:

1. A cat bomb, based on the undisputed premises that (a) cats always land on their feet and (b) hate water. The plan was to hang some poor cat in a harness from the bottom of a bomb, with some kind of device that allowed said cat's movements to guide the bomb as it fell. If you dropped it in the vicinity of a naval target (such as a German battleship), then the cat's natural instinct would be to think, "Oh no, I'm falling into water. I hate water, so let's try to land somewhere dry. Like that German battleship over there." And then BOOM. Of course, this was a ridiculous idea for a number of reasons. But perhaps the most important

one was that during experimentation, the test cat became unconscious (and thus ineffective) during the first fifty feet of the fall. We don't actually know if the harness/steering apparatus would have worked, since the cat passed out before that technology could be fully vetted.

2. The OSS learned that Hitler and Mussolini would be holding a war conference at the Brenner Pass, located in the Alps between Italy and Austria. Lovell proposed an "attack which they cannot anticipate." He was probably right—had it succeeded, they quite literally wouldn't have seen this one coming. Lovell's plan called for smuggling in a vase of cut flowers to be placed on the table between Hitler and Mussolini. In the vase's water would be an odorless, colorless chemical derivative, which would seep into the two tyrants via their eyeballs. Hitler and Mussolini (and anyone else in that room) would be permanently blinded as the chemical atrophied the optic nerve, rendering it irreversibly nonfunctional. But that was only part one of the plan, and it's surprisingly the less absurd part. Part two required the assistance of the pope—despite the Vatican being officially neutral during the war—who would issue a papal bull stating that God himself had smitten the two leaders for their evil ways. In other words, asking the pope to lie. Unfortunately for Lovell, the plan fell apart when the war summit was moved to Hitler's private railway car, surrounded by some of his best troops. The OSS was good, but not that good.

3. Working from quaintly old-fashioned—and

completely ridiculous—gender stereotypes, Lovell and his team saw Hitler's penchant for violent mood swings and poor emotional control as evidence that he was "definitely close to the malefemale line." The plan involved spiking his food with female hormones, to push him over the gender edge, making his mustache fall out and his voice turn soprano. They even supplied one of his gardeners with the drugs and a satchel full of money as payment for the operation. Apparently it didn't work—or perhaps more likely, the gardener took the money and then quietly threw the drugs away.

4. Another plan called for arming Chinese call girls with poisons or toxins to use against high-ranking Japanese officers who utilized their services. Simple enough, right? The catch was that the poison's delivery system needed to be almost invisible, since these women didn't have the means to conceal anything in what they were(n't) wearing. (You can probably figure out on your own how they solved that problem …) And then the weapon, which was based on the highly lethal botulism toxin, was successfully smuggled into Japanese-occupied China. But nothing happened. No high-level Japanese officers were killed, and the OSS was baffled as to why. Only later would they learn that their OSS contacts in Asia, performing their due diligence, decided to test the botulism on donkeys before giving it to the Chinese prostitutes. To their dismay, the weapon didn't work. The donkeys survived (and in fact seemed completely oblivious that they'd been poisoned), so the OSS

contacts in Asia assumed the weapon was ineffective and scrapped the mission. What they didn't know: Botulism is so lethal it will kill almost everything on earth … except for donkeys, which are one of the few living creatures immune to the toxin. Whoops.

These are just some of the unusual hijinks of the OSS/R&D unit. But the crème de la crème of unconsummated insanity was an operation known as "Capricious." For Stanley Lovell, this was the high point of his time as the OSS's Professor Moriarty.

It's interesting to think that in a war in which tens of millions of people were killed in almost every manner possible—conventional munitions, disease, starvation, genocide, civilian and military purges, and, of course, atomic bombs—nations would be hesitant to use a type of weapon because they thought it wasn't ethical. And although the United States formed a committee to research the utility of biological pathogens in the war (the Merck Committee, named after its chairman, Dr. George Merck, president of Merck and Company), there was little appetite among the American leadership to go beyond the casual "thinking about things" phase. President Roosevelt was vehemently opposed to the use of germ warfare, and military leaders such as George Marshall and Bill Donovan thought it was an immoral way to fight a war (bullets and bombs only, like God intended). The normally composed and erudite Vannevar Bush was known to say all manner of unspeakable things any time the topic was raised.

As long as the war was going well, biological weapons were

off the table. Any conversation about their use was a non-starter. Any longterm planning for their production was a waste of time. They were simply not to be.

As long as the war was going well.

In November 1942, America got its first taste of combat against the German troops in North Africa led by General Erwin Rommel. And America got thwacked.

It was a bitter pill to take, and a sense of panic began to set in throughout the corridors of the Pentagon. Thousands of American soldiers were killed, wounded, or missing; hundreds of vehicles were destroyed; and there were abject failures at every measurable level of military metrics—command, training, logistics, air support, joint operations, combined arms. Even things as seemingly simple as basic map reading were apparently too onerous for America's green troops (and their just as inexperienced commanders).

Adding injury to injury, large numbers of Germany's best and most battletested troops were flooding into Spanish Morocco. Francisco Franco's Spain was nominally neutral, but he was a fascist and highly sympathetic to the Axis cause. Clearly these German troops were entering Morocco with the consent—and maybe even the cooperation—of Franco's government. This could be a frightening omen for things to come. What if Spain formally joined the Axis? Spanish Morocco could become a staging point for hundreds of thousands of German troops, who could then cut off the vital supply lines to Allied forces who were trying (perhaps now in vain) to dislodge Germany from the African continent.

Something drastic had to be done, and so they turned to Lovell, their evil genius. Now that the handcuffs were off, germ warfare could be the answer to the Allies' problems in North Africa.

The best covert action tends to be *covert*. I know that sounds obvious. But there is covert, and then there's COVERT. Say you are at war with country X, and you secretly infiltrate a team deep inside enemy territory to blow up a bridge. That's technically covert action. Your team got in and wreaked havoc—but there is no question that it was your guys who did the damage. They might have covertly made their way in and out of the war zone, but they made a lot of noise along the way.

Now let's look at scenario number two. You aren't technically at war with another nation, but you are worried they are developing a nuclear weapons program that could shift the balance of power in an important region. As a response, you set up a covert action to slow down their technological progress. Maybe (hypothetically, of course) you insert a computer worm into the systems that control one aspect of this technological development. Perhaps that worm does its job, and your rival's nuclear weapons program is set back several years. No one *knows* who was behind this cyber attack, but there are few countries that have the means, motive, and opportunity to pull this off. And you are one of them. You have what's known as "plausible deniability," and the mission resides safely within the defined parameters of a covert action. But it could be better ...

The perfect covert action takes place when your target doesn't even know he was the victim of an attack. When he assumes natural causes were the result of his bad fortune. When he isn't looking for someone to blame. Someone to punish. Someone to kill.

Stanley Lovell's mission was to execute the perfect covert action: a germ warfare attack against the Germans in North Africa without their knowing what hit them. This was more than a desire to be secretive. It was important to the Allies to maintain the moral high ground in the war, and to prevent the Germans from retaliating with their own biological attack.

One key aspect would be to employ a lessthanlethal strain of biological agent. The idea wasn't to kill all the Germans in the region—just to make them all *wish* they were dead. Hordes of sick soldiers might be chalked up to just bad luck; thousands of dead Germans, and someone is going to be asking questions. Imagine the worst stomach flu you've ever had ... then multiply that by an order of magnitude. According to Lovell, the germ cocktail OSS created contained "an assortment of bacteria from tularemia and psittacosis to all the pests known to the Four Horsemen of the Apocalypse." This would bring the German war machine in Spanish Morocco to a standstill. And when the troops came back, they'd be significantly demoralized.

Lovell set out to finalize his plans. His research of the region had uncovered several important facts:

1. There were more goats than people in Morocco.
2. Moroccan goats produced poo. A lot of it.
3. There were also a ridiculously large number of flies in North Africa. In the summer, they were *everywhere* in Spanish Morocco.
4. North African flies were particularly pesky. They flocked to the moisture from the eyes, noses, and mouths of humans.

5. Flies regurgitate what they've previously eaten when new food comes their way.

Each of these independently is a random fact. But taken together they crafted a recipe for a perfect germ warfare operation. If Lovell could lace the poop with biotoxins, the flies would provide the perfect vector to incapacitate the German army in Spanish Morocco.

But how do you *guarantee* the flies will be attracted to your particular brand of biotoxin-laced goat poop? The OSS wasn't going to leave this up to chance—Lovell had the answer. They would manufacture a synthetic variant of goat poo, with a pull so powerful that no fly could resist.

The only challenge that remained was to figure out how to deliver the synthetic goat poop to Spanish Morocco without being observed. After some brainstorming, Lovell decided that the only way to secretly introduce their concoction into the region was via airdrop.

It was then that one member of Lovell's team spoke up and identified a major kink in this plan. Most of the houses in Spanish Morocco have flat roofs. A whole lot of the goat poo would end up dropped on the roofs, and unless the OSS was also planning on developing a new genetically engineered variant of flying goat, it would be hard to explain how the poo got on the roof. Lovell pondered this problem, but had to concede this was a valid point. He finally responded, "The orders are to take out Spanish Morocco when ordered to do so, and if we do there'll be mighty few people inspecting rooftops." He, too, had a valid point.

Fortunately, the progress of the war intervened before Lovell could test his theory—and his synthetic dung. In the midst of development and testing, the OSS learned that the Germans were completely pulling their troops out of Spanish Morocco and redeploying them to the Eastern Front, to reinforce the effort to capture the Soviet city of Stalingrad. Hitler's illfated obsession with taking the city named after his nemesis saved the OSS, and by extension the United States, from being the only nation in the European Theater of World War II to resort to biological warfare.

AND THEN WHAT?

To witness the legacy of Stanley Lovell and the OSS Research & Development unit, one only needs to turn back to chapter 1 of this book. The CIA's Technical Services Division/Office of Technical Service is a direct descendant of OSS/R&D, and their official documents identify Lovell as their founding father. Of course, Stanley Lovell was responsible for more than Operation Capricious. He was a prolific leader whose team invented all sorts of useful technology and weapons to help the Allies win the war. In fact, the OSS built twenty-five different weapons that saw use during the war, from silenced pistols, to limpet mines, to "Beano grenades" shaped like baseballs—so that redblooded American boys could throw them more naturally—to "Aunt Jemima," an explosive powder packaged in Chinese flour bags. They also developed tools and techniques that resistance fighters, guerrillas, and saboteurs used to combat the Germans and the Japanese. Much in the same way, TSD/OTS invented, tested, and built hundreds of gadgets to help the CIA fight the Cold War, and continue to invent, test, and build helpful technologies today.

But if you want to read about those, you bought the wrong book.

PROJECT X-RAY

During World War I, President Woodrow Wilson created the Naval Consulting Board (NCB) and appointed Thomas Edison as its chairman. This makes a lot of sense, since the NCB was supposed to be the premier institution for the analysis of new technologies during the war—who else would you want leading it other than the nation's greatest inventor? The NCB consisted entirely of engineers, save for a single scientist—a physicist. When asked why he had chosen the scientist for the board, Edison told Wilson, "We might have one mathematical fellow in case we have to calculate something out."

The board's primary mission was to screen inventions submitted by industry and private citizens. It had limited success. Out of 110,000 inventions submitted to the board, only 110 had enough promise to be evaluated with any detail. Only one went into actual production during the war. The NCB was a tough audience. Edison himself came up with almost fifty wartime inventions. Not a single one was accepted by the Navy.

During World War II, things were markedly different. In

June 1940, the United States created the National Defense Research Committee (NRDC), under the leadership of Dr. Vannevar Bush, former dean of the MIT School of Engineering and, since 1938, chairman of the National Advisory Committee for Aeronautics (the predecessor to NASA). Its mandate was to "coordinate, supervise, and conduct scientific research on the problems underlying the development, production, and use of mechanisms and devices of warfare." With this mission, the NDRC coordinated national research resources, created new facilities for military research, and conducted groundbreaking work on innovative technologies that could help win the war. In 1941, the NDRC became the Office of Scientific Research and Development (OSRD). Today, it is easy to conflate "science" and "technology," or "research" and "development," as though they always belonged together, like two sides of the same coin. But this wasn't the case before World War II. It was the OSRD, also under the leadership of Dr. Bush, that took basic scientific research and brought it together with the practical, development stage: for instance, by taking esoteric physics concepts about splitting atoms and chain reactions and making them go boom.

Government science did some enormously impressive things during the Second World War, but this didn't mean that civilian scientists, engineers, inventors, and other patriotic (and entrepreneurial) Americans were not sending in their best ideas. Like they did in World War I, enterprising would-be inventors flooded the government with thousands upon thousands of innovations to help the good guys win the war.

Most of them, as you might imagine, were ... terrible. But one can also imagine that in the mass of paper sent in to the government by enthusiastic civilians, some good ideas got lost. Maybe tucked into the piles of submitted documents was an invention that could have changed the course of history. Something that could have made us live longer, feel better, live healthier, save the environment, end war, cure cancer.

And perhaps if the US government hadn't been spending millions of dollars and vast quantities of resources trying to work out how to turn bats into flaming balls of flying explosive terror, we might have found it.

Dr. Lytle Adams was a dental surgeon from the small town of Irwin, Pennsylvania. Like many Americans, Dr. Adams heard of the Japanese attack on Pearl Harbor on the radio, while he was on vacation in New Mexico.

Adams was not your ordinary, runofthemill dentist, though. He was also a fairly accomplished inventor. After the war, he had an idea for a fried chicken vending machine. That kind of genius doesn't come around every day.

In 1930 he filed a patent for what he called a "Ship to Ship, Ship to Shore, and Shore to Ship Air Mail Transfer System and Apparatus." The invention allowed for expedited mail delivery at a time when sending a letter overseas could take weeks, since much of the mail traveled via ship rather than plane. With Adams's invention, you could shave a couple of hours off the transit time. It might not sound like much, but his idea was deemed good enough to be awarded patent number 1,973,244 in 1934. Though never implemented on a large scale, Adams's air mail delivery system merits a place in history because it got him an introduction to First Lady Eleanor Roosevelt, who was given a demonstration by the inventor himself. Adams was also a licensed pilot, and he flew Roosevelt around in his own plane to show off his invention.

It's hard to imagine that kind of thing happening today, but perhaps Roosevelt and the security team were disarmed by Adams's unassuming appearance. He is described by one contemporary as a "jolly-looking little man" who "looked like Santa Claus without a beard, cherubic and ruddyfaced, small and plump—his white hair stood out in wild disarray, and small, round piggy blue eyes never seemed to blink, but sparkled mischievously."

But he had grand ideas. When Adams heard the news of the devastation at Pearl Harbor, he was driving back from a trip to Carlsbad Caverns, home to what is believed to be the world's largest bat colony. At that point, something in his inventor's mind clicked:

1. The United States has access to thousands (maybe millions) of bats.
2. Japan is a country of cities and towns filled with houses made of paper and wood.
3. Bats love to fly into the attics, eaves, nooks, and crannies of whatever shelter is available. In Japan, that would mean the attics, eaves, nooks, and crannies of paper and wood houses.
4. If we could affix a small bomb to the bats ...

On January 12, 1942, just a little over a month after Pearl Harbor, Adams put his idea in writing to the president of the United States. In his letter, which begins, "I attach hereto a proposal designed to frighten, demoralize, and excite the prejudices of the people of the Japanese Empire," Adams lays out his scheme for the destruction of Japan. "The ... lowest form of animal life is the BAT, associated in history with the underworld and regions of darkness and evil. Until now reasons for its creation have remained unexplained."

He continues, "This lowly creature … is capable of carrying in flight a sufficient quantity of incendiary material to ignite a fire." At last, "If the use of bats in this allout war can rid us of the Japanese pests, we will, as the Mormons did for the gull at Salt Lake City, erect a monument to their everlasting memory."

Mad though this all sounds, Dr. Adams had friends in high places, in particular the president's wife. She made sure FDR saw the letter, and after reading it, he sent a quick note to William Donovan. At the time, he was known as the Coordinator of Information, and the director of an office of the same name whose job was to collect, analyze, and disseminate intelligence information.

FDR to Wild Bill: "This man is *not* a nut. It sounds like a perfectly wild idea but is worth looking into."

President Roosevelt had spoken, but that didn't mean Donovan needed to do the "looking into" himself. The first chance he got, he dumped the idea straight on the lap of the NDRC. It was their problem now.

Meanwhile, Dr. Adams was a man on a mission. He traveled to Harvard University's Psychoacoustic Laboratory to meet with scientists to refine his plan. There, he met Donald Griffin, who was at Harvard working on improving military communications equipment. He was also one of the world's leading bat experts. Griffin discovered what many of us would later learn about bats in the third grade: Bats don't see very well, yet they can successfully move around using sound reflected off objects in their way. Griffin called this acoustic form of navigation "echolocation."

That made him the perfect advocate for Adams, someone who could give legitimacy to this wild scheme. And as it turns out, he actually thought Adams's plan had a chance to work. In April 1942, he wrote his own letter to the NDRC in support of the project. "This proposal seems bizarre and visionary at first glance, but extensive experience with experimental biology convinces the writer [Griffin] that if executed competently it would have every chance of success."

"Executed competently." For most of the stories in this book, that's an ominous phrase.

When I first encountered this story, I assumed that attaching a bomb to a bat would be a cruel but simple task. But according to people who actually know things about bats—like Griffin—it's not that easy. There are about a thousand species of bat, and very few of them were appropriate for the mission. For instance, there's a bat in Thailand that is so small it could land on your fingertip. And if you're planning a trip to the Philippines, you might run into the giant flying fox bat and its sixfoot wingspan. Good luck sleeping after that.

North America's largest bat is the mastiff, which could potentially carry a one-pound stick of dynamite with its twenty-two-inch wingspan. The problem is there are not enough of them. The most common bat is the mule-eared bat, but it was probably too fragile to handle the rigors of the mission.

The Goldilocks choice—the one that was just right—was the Mexican free-tailed bat. Although it's light (it weighs only one-third of an ounce), it can fly while carrying up to 18 grams, and there were *millions* of them in the southwestern United

States. In just two caves in Texas, Ney and Bracken, scientists estimated there were twenty to thirty million Mexican free-taileds. This was enough to bomb most of Japan into ashes, and still have a couple of million bats left over.

While the bat search was under way, the NDRC assigned the task of developing the incendiary device to Harvard organic chemist Dr. Louis Fieser. An accomplished chemist who was twice considered for the Nobel Prize in Physiology or Medicine (in 1941 and 1942) for his work on the structure of vitamin K, Fieser was now using his genius to develop weapons of war. One of his inventions would become both an important warfighting tool for decades and a source of controversy and dissent: napalm.

Fieser and his team of chemists at Harvard invented synthetic napalm in 1942 (the first tests were held on a football field behind Harvard Business School). Napalm is a mixture of petroleum (usually gasoline) and a gelatin agent. This allows it to burn very hotly, and to stick to whatever objects it encounters (buildings, vehicles, people). The chemistry of napalm lets it pack a huge punch at a relatively light weight. Fieser built an inflammable celluloid case filled with napalm that weighed, along with the igniter, 17.5 grams.

All that was left to do was test it.

The first test of the bat bomb concept took place in May 1943 at Muroc Dry Lake in the Mojave Desert of California. Muroc, now called Rogers Dry Lake, is now known as a legendary location for postwar aviation. It later became the home of Edwards Air Force Base, where American fighter jock test pilots pushed the "outside of the envelope" and challenged the limits of what could be done in the air (Chuck Yeager was at Edwards when he became the first human to break the sound barrier in 1947). Until the early 1990s, Muroc served as a landing field for the Space Shuttle.

The Muroc bat tests did not go well.

To get the thirty-five hundred bats that the team had captured at Carlsbad Caverns to the California desert, the animals were placed in refrigerators that artificially forced them into a state of hibernation. This was a necessary step—the bats needed to be docile for transport. The idea was to allow for enough time for them to wake up.

But the team miscalculated. During a test drop from a B25 bomber flying at only five thousand feet, many (if not most) of the bats failed to come completely out of hibernation. Gravity works on bats much in the same way as it works on everything else. And while bats have wings, they can't fly if they are asleep.

Fortunately, no one in power attended the Muroc tests. If they had, there might never have been a second one.

But there was a second test, and this one went much better than the first. Or maybe much worse. You be the judge.

For test number two, the bat squad was moved to an operational Army Air Force base in Carlsbad, quite near to the caves that were home to the test subjects. They still needed to force the bats into hibernation, but the close proximity would allow for a shorter duration, and the team hoped this could help them to better control the experiment.

And it worked. Sort of. Many of the bats in the Carlsbad experiment woke up!

But it was a particularly warm summer day in Carlsbad, and so the team miscalculated again. The bats woke up too quickly, and dozens escaped before they could be put on the test aircraft—but not before they had been fitted with their incendiaries, which were controlled by a timed ignition.

The good news is that several of the bats flew straight to the constructed test village, designed to simulate a Japanese town, and burned it to the ground.

The bad news is that other bats flew to the operational airfield—and its hangars, and control tower, and barracks, and offices. Because the project was so secret, the team did not have firefighters on hand—this would have looked too conspicuous. Even the commander of the Carlsbad base was not in the "need to know," so when he showed up with his fire team, he was prohibited from entering *his own facility*. He—and everyone else—just had to wait and watch the airfield burn.

The base commander was not amused. And apparently neither was the Army. Shortly after the Carlsbad test, the Army decided to cancel the project. Fortunately for Adams and his team, a Marine general by the name of Louis DeHaven had quietly observed the Carlsbad test (unbeknownst to Adams). DeHaven was not principally concerned with the damage that had been done to the Army airfield. He saw the potential in the program's concept and convinced the Navy to pick it up. Up until then, the program hadn't developed to the point at which it had been given a formal name. Most everyone was just calling it the "Adams Plan." The Navy decided to give it one: Project XRay.

The first Navy tests for Project XRay began in December 1943. Some were successful, but it soon became clear that a more powerful incendiary device would be necessary before the bat bombs could be combat-ready. For the next round of testing, scheduled for August 1944, new and more powerful incendiaries were planned for what would be a full-scale bomber test—the closest yet to actual operational conditions.

But as quickly as the Navy had given Lytle Adams's dream a second chance, they pulled the rug out from under Project XRay. By this point, the program had already cost an estimated $2 million (the equivalent of about $30 million today), but when the Chief of Naval Operations (CNO), Fleet Admiral Ernest King, heard that the project would not be ready until mid-1945 (at the earliest), he immediately canceled the operation. "It [has] been decided to terminate the XRay project. This has not been based on any shortcomings of the incendiary and time units developed by NDRC, but rather upon the shortcomings of the fundamental idea and the opportunity of getting sufficient reliable data in order to plan a timely operation." In essence, just because they *could* do it didn't mean it was a good idea, especially given the timeliness of winning a war threatening the very notion of democracy.

As CNO, King was well briefed on a new and secret weapons system also scheduled for mid-1945: the atomic bomb. He assumed that the bomb would have a much better chance to end the war. So why waste time, physical and intellectual resources, and money on a plan whose success could at best be considered a long shot? Project XRay was scrapped.

AND THEN WHAT?

As you might expect, Dr. Adams was devastated when his program was canceled. Seemingly, it wasn't so much a desire for personal glory as a firm conviction in his idea. Until his death at the age of eightyseven, he believed that Project XRay, if it had been allowed to mature to fruition, would have caused more damage than even the two atomic bombs. He also argued that the war could have been won with far fewer

Japanese civilian deaths. Although his bat bombs would have set Japan ablaze, he maintained, innocents would have had the time to evacuate areas before they were consumed by the inferno (time that atomic bombs did not provide). What we know today about the firestorms created through the conventional bombings of Tokyo and other Axis cities makes this a dubious claim. But we are now in the realm of the counterfactual.

After the war, Adams shifted to other inventive pursuits. He had an idea to reseed part of the desert with pelletized seeds sprayed from his airplane. And, of course, fried chicken.

Donald Griffin only spent a short time with the project, but later would seriously question his role in what he considered the unethical weaponization of animals. He continued to make his name in the field of biopsychology, contributing to the understanding of animal thinking and consciousness. He coined the term "cognitive ethology," which dealt with the scientific and objective observation of the influence of awareness and intention on the behavior of animals. (In other words, how do animals think, what do they believe, are they rational, how well do they process information?) In his obituary in the *New York Times*, Griffin was credited with what he might have considered to be the ultimate compliment: He was "the only reason that animal thinking was given consideration at all." One shudders to imagine the final thoughts of an explosiveladen bat emerging from induced hibernation to blow up an airplane hangar.

Louis Fieser continued to develop high explosives and incendiaries. His most famous invention, napalm, was fitted into bombs that were produced by the tens of millions, and still has considerable effect on war to this day. But Fieser was more than just one invention. He was a true polymath. A prolific writer of books (the most interesting titled *Arson, an Instruction Manual*) and articles/research papers (over three hundred in his career), he conducted cancer research and worked on chemotherapy efficacy, aromatic chemistry, steroids, and a bunch of other things like carcinogenic hydroquinones, napthoquinone antimalarials, and other things that neither I nor my spellcheck understand.

Finally, Project XRay lived on in one more way. Pieces of its design were used for Project Orcon, an equally perplexing plan by famed psychologist B. F. Skinner to train pigeons to fly guided bombs against the Germans. The pigeons would be trained not to fly with bombs attached like Adams's bats, but rather to peck at a control screen, steering the weapons into strategic military targets.

But that's a story for another day.

4

PROJECT FANTASIA

The Allied strategy for winning World War II in the Pacific Theater of Operations was relatively simple: Capture a key island in the western Pacific and use it as a launching point for the invasion of another island (and so on). Eventually this will lead you all the way to the main islands of Japan (Japan is an archipelago, so "islands," not "island"), and victory. The socalled islandhopping campaign, also known as "leapfrogging," was quite successful. More than a few historians have argued that this strategy, coupled with the destruction of the Japanese merchant fleet (effectively cutting off the nation from military supplies and even basic goods), would have ended the Pacific War even without the introduction of the atomic bomb.

But success came with a heavy price: some military analysts predicted that as many as a million Americans could be killed trying to invade the Japanese main islands. This is probably an unrealistically high number, but it would be hard for anyone to argue—at the time or today—that an invasion of the main islands would not have caused an unacceptably high number of casualties.

The problem was that the Japanese refused to quit. In most cases, to a man, they refused to surrender. They fought to the death, for Japan and for their emperor, taking with them scores of Allied soldiers, sailors, and airmen.

Clearly, something had to be done. Even a successful invasion of Japan would quickly become a Pyrrhic victory if hundreds of thousands of men were sacrificed to the cause.

Of course, something *was* being done. In laboratories, institutes, and universities across the United States some of the greatest American, Allied, and immigrant scientists and engineers were developing technologies that would radically and permanently redefine warfare. And we're not just talking about atomic weapons here. Progress was being made across the board in radar, cryptanalysis (codes), rocketry, jet propulsion, materials engineering, thermodynamics, battlefield medicine, statistical analysis, chemistry of explosives, industrial production capabilities, early stages of computer science, and exploding bats—to name just a sampling.

While some scientists and engineers toiled on projects focused on the physical world—the guns, bombs, aircraft, ships, tanks, and related technologies of war—others investigated ways to use the human mind as a weapon. Psychological Operations (or "PsyOps") have, in one form or another, been used in warfare for all of recorded history, but this concept truly reached maturity during the Second World War, when organizations such as the Office of Strategic Services realized that PsyOps could constitute a significant force multiplier—a way to dramatically increase the effectiveness of Allied troops in the face of a determined and relentless enemy.

OSS director William Donovan was a major proponent

of PsyOps. Within OSS, he formed the Morale Operations Branch in 1943 to target both the general population and the military forces of the Axis powers. In a speech he gave shortly before the Morale Branch was founded, Donovan explained his rationale:

> In this war of machines, the human element is, in the long run, more important than the machines themselves. There must be the will to make the machines, to man the machines, and to pull the trigger. Psychological warfare is directed against that will. Its object is to destroy the morale of the enemy and to support the morale of our allies within enemy and enemy occupied countries.

At a different point in the speech, he was more succinct: "When you strike at the morale of a people or an army you strike at the deciding factor, because it is the strength of their will that determines the length of wars, the measure of resistance, and the day of final collapse."

In the war against the Germans, Donovan and the OSS Morale Branch put this concept into play, deploying tactics aimed at sowing fear and distrust among the Nazi soldiers. They tried to undermine the German soldiers' will to resist, to inspire feelings of war weariness and convince them of the futility of continuing their struggle against impossible odds. Part of this effort consisted of a dedicated propaganda campaign, in which demoralizing leaflets or flyers were dropped over enemy positions. Some of them showed German soldiers who had died in horrible ways, with captions like "His children will miss him" or "More than he bargained for." Others had graphics of seriously wounded or maimed German troops, and the captions "An Iron Cross and a wooden crutch" or "He never saw the fatherland again" (to accompany a blinded soldier). The OSS supplemented these by sending falsified death notices to the families of deceased German soldiers. Some of them said that their sons/husbands/fathers had been killed at the hands of a German doctor, while others claimed that Nazi Party officials had looted the bodies as their loved ones took their last breaths.

But the one that really sets the standard for devious propaganda was a campaign known as the "League of Lonely War Women." Developed by the only woman on the propaganda staff of OSS's Morale Branch, Corporal Barbara Lauwers, the League of Lonely War Women was a stroke of absolute genius. Here's how it went down: Leaflets were dispersed among the German troops, seemingly the product of German leadership. The text held an alluring promise. If a soldier cut out the heart at the bottom of the page and wore it on his lapel while home for some rest and recuperation, a local "member" of the League of Lonely War Women would approach him and offer some … companionship. According to the leaflet, "The dreams you had at the front, and the longings of your lonely nights, will be fulfilled." The problem, of course, is that the only women back in the rear—and the only women who could be "members" of the league—were the girlfriends and wives (and maybe daughters) of fellow soldiers on the battlefield. This wasn't spelled out explicitly, but the German soldier wasn't stupid. They knew what it meant. Ouch.

But we began this story in the Pacific, and that's where we now return. OSS PsyOps in the war against the Japanese mirrored those against the Germans in Europe. There was propaganda. There was disinformation and deception.

There was a general messing with the minds of adversaries. And then there was almost the operation known as Project Fantasia—one of the most extraordinary attempts to use the human psyche against an opponent in battle. It taps into deep-seated fears and religious beliefs and superstitions, and demonstrates (not for the first or last time) the breadth of the racism, ethnocentrism, and general disregard of Japanese culture held by many, if not most, of the top American military, intelligence, and political leadership. It might have been one of the most ridiculous examples of America's perceived sense of cultural superiority. It might have been one of the most embarrassing operations of World War II. Thankfully, we never got the chance to find out.

Phew.

Project Fantasia was the brainchild of a man named Edgar Salinger, who by all accounts seemed to be a pretty decent guy. He started his career in the importexport business in Tokyo in the years leading up to World War I, and then served in the Wilson administration as a member of the US Tariff Commission. After World War II, he worked to help refugees of the war, and was active in the relief and rehabilitation of displaced persons. He was a sophisticated man of the arts, an accomplished cellist who spent his later years collecting American and antique Asian art while directing the Art Center in Dorset, Vermont. His nephew was John F. Kennedy's press secretary, Pierre Salinger.

His 1971 *New York Times* obituary lists all of these, and mentions his time serving in the OSS psychological warfare division—but doesn't mention Fantasia. That's not at all surprising, really. These kinds of operations were closely guarded when they actually *happened*. Fortunately for Salinger's reputation, Fantasia was scrapped before it had a chance to do lasting damage.

To understand Fantasia, we have to take a step further back. Way back, to the sixth century, when the religion of Shintoism was first founded in Japan (or seventh, or eighth—depending on what source you check, and how you define the "beginning"). Shinto (literally translated as "the way of the gods") is deeply rooted in Japanese traditions. In fact, from 1868 to 1945, it was the official state religion of Japan, and Shinto priests became state officials, religious buildings/shrines received governmental support, and the religion was used to create a national identity (read: extreme nationalism) under the guidance of the emperor, who was considered a Shinto deity in human form. The tightknit relationship between Shinto and the Japanese state ended with the defeat of the empire at the end of World War II, but the cultural influence of many aspects of Shintoism continues today. Many people in modern Japan who don't formally identify themselves as Shintoists still participate in some Shintobased practices or rituals.

If you have been to Japan, it's probable that you've seen statues of foxes at Shinto shrines. Foxes, or *kitsune,* are common in Japanese folklore and religion, and are often depicted as intelligent and spiritual beings who possess magical abilities. Some *kitsune* are good, and can bring tidings of good fortune, like omens of a bountiful rice crop. Many, however, are not. They can be mischievous, or even downright evil. They are polymorphs (shapeshifters) and will often take human form. They can also possess humans and force them to hallucinate and do unusual or unspeakable things (like kill, froth at the mouth, or run naked through the streets). Sometimes they even have the power to feed on the life or spirit of a human, like little furry vampires.

Where the Japanese people saw *kitsune* as part of a unifying force, bridging socioeconomic and cultural barriers to forge a national identity of inclusivity and patriotism, Edgar Salinger and the OSS saw opportunity. One of the most effective ways to demoralize the enemy is to prey on their superstitions, and Project Fantasia called for exactly that.

The initial plan called for balloons. Lots of balloons.

Beginning in late 1943, the OSS experimented with fox-shaped balloons covered in luminous paint that would be lofted on the end of fishing line. These glowinthedark foxes would pop up over the battlefield and terrify Japanese military observers, who would pass along the sinister omen to the rest of their comrades.

At the same time, sleeper agents in town would blow on whistles that simulated what the documents called a foxlike "cry of the damned." These same agents would walk through the streets acting as though they were possessed by evil fox-spirits. There's no indication in the record how (or when) the agents would be infiltrated into Japanese cities—or if they were already there (a very interesting component of the story that remains unclear). Nonetheless, the combination of balloons, whistles, and people pretending to be possessed would really tie the operation together.

Yet something was missing. Wouldn't a more direct approach make more sense? Why go to the trouble of designing and manufacturing foxshaped balloons when you can just use the real thing?

Real foxes. Sprayed with glowinthedark paint. Set loose on the beaches of Japan. What could go wrong?

According to the final plans for Project Fantasia, the operation would consist of several phases. First, pamphlets would be distributed to the Japanese population, warning them of the coming doom. Some of these could be airdropped, while others were intended to be passed along by the same sleeper agents we talked about before (who would still be charged with tooting their fox whistles and acting possessed). This time, however, the OSS planners decided to add a special touch to the musician agents. Apparently, someone at OSS contacted a chemist at one of the top American government contractors—who was already doing secret war work—and asked him if he could help the operation. The idea was for the chemist to create "fox odors" that the agents could smear on their bodies to make it more convincing that they were possessed. These came in both powder *and* paste form, presumably to offer the undercover agent. It's the little things that count. We all need to feel as though we have control of our options before we go behind enemy lines, pretend we are possessed by animal spirits (while slathered with stinky animal smell), and play our fox whistles in tune.

With the difficult parts of the operation taken care of, all that remained was procuring the foxes and covering them with phosphorescent paint for some obligatory field testing. This was about the time that the OSS decided it needed to brief General Douglas MacArthur, the commander of all Allied forces in the Pacific, on Project Fantasia. It was, after all, his operation that Fantasia was supporting. Mac-Arthur had always had a deep appreciation of the utility of psychological operations (he understood their power as a force multiplier), and he was certainly willing to listen to any idea that might make his war against the Japanese go a little easier.

It didn't take long for MacArthur to notice a glaring weakness in the plan: Perhaps the key word in the phrase "islandhopping campaign" is "island." Unless the foxes were going to be parachuted onto the islands (and, as we saw from Chapter Two, animals typically make poor parachutists), they would have to swim ashore like the rest of the troops. It was one thing for 1940s technology to master glowinthedark paint; it was another thing to ask engineers to invent *waterproof* glowinthedark paint. The terrifying fox ghosts would just be normal foxes by the time they got to dry land.

But OSS wasn't deterred. Or they were incredibly stubborn. Or maybe both.

To prove MacArthur wrong, OSS set up a controlled test. They took a couple of painted foxes and dumped them into the Chesapeake Bay. That would show him.

Or not. When the foxes reached shore, most of the paint was gone—but not all! There's no record of the reaction of the OSS personnel on the beach, yet we can imagine that after all of this they were holding on to whatever positive news they could. If there was still *some* paint left, the foxes might still glow enough to be scary.

Alas, no. Within minutes, the foxes had licked off the remaining paint.

We (and they) probably should have seen this coming from a mile away. Foxes are in the same family as dogs, and, while not as obsessive as cats in terms of grooming standards, anyone who has spent time with a dog can testify to the fact that they can spend twenty minutes licking an imaginary speck of God knows what off their paw. The paint didn't stand a chance.

But one minor setback wasn't going to stand in the way of a vaguely promising idea for which countless hours of research and funds had already been committed. In all seriousness, ignoring for a second how silly and offensive this plan was, these were patriotic American scientists trying to figure out ways to save lives. So they tried another test. This time with less water. And more New Yorkers.

For test number two, the OSS collected thirty foxes, painted them appropriately, and let them loose in Central Park during a busy weekend evening. And as you might expect, this scared the bejesus out of the unsuspecting residents of the Big Apple. Meaning, the test … actually worked. As one newspaper described, no one expected to see dozens of foxes racing at them "painted with a radiant chemical which glowed in the dark." The article continued, "Horrified citizens, shocked by sudden sight of the leaping ghostlike animals, fled from the dark recesses of the park with the 'screaming jeemies.'"

I don't know what a "screaming jeemie" is, but if New Yorkers, who are used to seeing sewer rats the size of small children on an average Tuesday afternoon, were terrified by these phosphorescent foxes, then OSS had a winner on their hands. They'd just have to work out how to keep the foxes dry somehow.

With testing complete, OSS planners were ready to scale up from the laboratory to the battlefield. Thirty foxes was plenty for Central Park, but they would need hundreds for an Allied invasion of the Japanese main islands. Fortunately, Australia and China had sufficient animals to meet the operation's needs, and the fox roundup began in earnest. Soon the OSS would have all of the animals they needed to implement their mischievous plan. But, as you might have noticed, I haven't been all that specific when it comes to dates, months, or years for this project. I wanted you to keep reading, and not stop the minute you realized that all this planning and testing was taking place just weeks before the equivalent of 25,000 tons of TNT was dropped on Hiroshima and Nagasaki.

Project Fantasia never fully got the chance to get off the ground due to the success of the atomic bombs in bringing about the end of the war. We will never know if glowing foxes could have been the deciding factor in the Pacific War. Although, given the whole plan was based on a wholly deluded (and racist) impression of the Japanese as superstitious, primitive and gullible, I know which way I would bet on it.

AND THEN WHAT?

Psychological Operations have continued to be a mainstay of intelligence and military missions worldwide. Just about every country tries to use PsyOps as a force multiplier, whether in peace or war, regardless of whether they are squaring off against another major power or against an asymmetrical threat. But while the nuts and bolts of PsyOps haven't changed all that much over the years, the delivery system for putting (mental) lead on the (psychological) target has indeed gone through an extraordinarily significant transition. After all, who needs to airdrop leaflets when you can reach tens (or hundreds) of millions of people through social media?

You've heard this all before. I'm not paving any new roads

to enlightenment here. We are surrounded by social media and all its ramifications. It's hard to ignore the impact of Twitter, Facebook, et al. Especially considering what might one day go down in history as *the* most effective use of PsyOps in human history: the 2016 US presidential election.

And before you start to mentally compose that letter of complaint to me, or this book's publisher, or to whomever, take a deep breath. I am not making any kind of political statement here. This is objective fact, not partisan politics. Russian intelligence convinced a huge chunk of the American population that a local DC pizza joint had a child sexslave ring in its basement. A man actually walked in there with a highpowered rifle with the intent of shooting up the place and saving the kids. This wasn't a mentally deranged person—he was lucid enough to realize his mistake when the workers there showed him that the restaurant did not even *have* a basement. He was just a guy who fell victim to an extremely wellfunded and efficient program of Russian psychological operations. And he wasn't alone. We are way too close to these events to know the complete extent of the damage, but it's clear from what we *do* know that hundreds of thousands (if not millions) of Americans of all political stripes were duped by Russian propaganda and madeup news stories, all intended to divide us, all propagated and fueled by social media.

As an American, I say: Damn you, Russians. We will return the favor one day.

But as an intelligence historian, I have to say: What. A. Thing. Of. Beauty.

5

BLUE PEACOCK

You might have heard of some of the code names given to secret military operations to disguise their real purposes. It wouldn't make much sense to name a military mission Operation We Are About to Invade Mexico, or Project Secret Stealth Aircraft.

No. Usually they are something obscure. And sometimes, something that sounds very cool.

Operation Wrath of God was the Israeli response to the massacre of Israeli Olympians at Munich in 1972. Operation Dynamo was the frantic plan to rescue hundreds of thousands of British troops from the beaches of Dunkirk in World War II. Operation Rolling Thunder was the American bombing campaign over Vietnam in 1967–68. Operation Urgent Fury was the US mission to invade Grenada in 1983.

Then you have Operation Iraqi Freedom, which is neither cool-sounding nor obscuring. But let's chalk that one up as an anomaly.

One of the most effective uses of a coding structure to hide the true nature of secret military projects was the British "Rainbow codes" system. In use from the end of World War

II until the late 1950s, Rainbow codes allowed the British to clearly identify secret projects without revealing too much information about what they actually were. Here's how it worked: Each Rainbow code name was created by taking (1) a random selection from a list of colors (black, blue, brown, green, indigo, jade, orange, pink, purple, red, violet, and yellow) and then (2) a word (a noun) taken from a list of prechosen possibilities (arrow, knight, prince, badger, orchid, and so on). For example, Black Maria was the code name for a fighter aircraft Identification Friend or Foe (IFF) interrogator—this tells you who are the good guys and bad guys in a dogfight, particularly useful when you don't have visual contact with the other aircraft. Blue Duck was an antisubmarine missile, while Blue Lagoon was an infrared airtoair detector. Blue Steel was an air-launched nuclear missile, and Green Cheese was a nuclear antiship missile. Other names of interest (at least for comic relief) are Indigo Hammer, Purple Passion, Purple Possum, Violet Mist, Yellow Duckling, Green Wizard, and, by far the Britishest of the British names, Orange Pippin (a fire control radar for antiaircraft, in case you really wanted to know).

Then there was Blue Peacock. One of the strangest ideas in a book of extremely strange ideas.

But before we talk about Blue Peacock, we need to take a brief detour to discuss the West's Cold War era grand strategy for fighting World War III. It was fairly straightforward: Nuke the hell out of the Soviet Union and her allies, then pray some of us survive the whole thing and can rebuild civilization out of the ashes and nuclear fallout.

Okay, maybe it wasn't quite that simple. The master plan

for the North Atlantic Treaty Organization (NATO) at the onset of the Cold War wasn't just a single word: nukes! But it really might as well have been. NATO had no intention of slugging out a conventional war with the Soviets in central Europe. That was a losing proposition. The Red Army, which had just about singlehandedly defeated the Nazi war machine in World War II, was powerful—and enormous.

Or at least we thought so at the time. Intelligence on the size and capabilities of the Soviet armed forces in the 1940s and '50s was spotty (at best) or nonexistent (more likely). We had very little real information to work with. So the worst-case scenario was accepted as inalienable fact.

It turns out we dramatically overestimated the strength of our communist adversaries. Many of their divisions existed only on paper, and our assessment of their strength did not take into account all of the problems they faced in some of the peripheral but essential aspects of warfare, such as maintenance, logistics, transportation, quality control (of soldiers and equipment), and command and control. The Soviets were *far* weaker than anyone thought.

But that doesn't matter. No, really. It doesn't. All that matters is that the Allied war planners of the 1950s thought the Soviets were unbeatable in a conventional war. Consider this: The West assumed that the Soviet army had 175 active divisions by the mid1950s. This comes out to 5.5 million men under arms, 35,000 tanks, and up to 19,000 aircraft. And that's just the Soviets. Non-Soviet Warsaw Pact forces (Poland, Czechoslovakia, East Germany, Albania, and so on) added another 60 divisions amounting to 800,000 troops and almost 3,000 more aircraft.

Compare that with NATO forces in Europe at that time.

In 1949, the year of NATO's creation, Western nations could draw upon only a handful of deployed divisions—three and a half US, two and a half British, and fewer than six French. Belgium and the Netherlands contributed about six between them. And even these numbers are misleading. Most of the troops were mainly focused on occupation duties inside West Germany, and they were not properly outfitted or trained for combat operations against a concentrated Soviet invasion.

After the Korean War broke out, things got a little better for NATO, as military planners and politicians began to finally reconsider the rapid demobilization they undertook after the end of World War II. During the early 1950s, NATO forces in central Europe grew to twenty divisions, and by 1955 NATO had available twenty-five active divisions *and* twenty-five reserve divisions in Europe.

But big deal, right? Despite this increase in manpower, the Warsaw Pact was still believed to have (at least) a ten-toone numerical superiority in readytofight divisions, and had a quantifiable advantage in aircraft, tanks, artillery, and mortars. It's no wonder the West saw nuclear weapons as its only chance to equal the playing field—to find *some* way to compensate for NATO's weakness in conventional forces. It was nukes or nothing.

The nuclear arsenal of the Cold War came in all shapes and sizes. It was a melting pot of mass destruction.

There were strategic weapons—the city-busters that detonated with a force equivalent to millions of tons of TNT. These could be launched from the ground or from submarines at sea, or they could be dropped from aircraft over the target, making up the three legs of the "nuclear triad." This wasn't *quite* developed in the mid1950s, as both missile and submarine technology were not yet ready for prime time, but both sides could still certainly wallop the other with untold destruction.

Then there were the tactical nukes, sometimes called "battlefield" nuclear weapons. There were tactical nukes for fighter aircraft, artillery shells, surfacetoair missiles, bunker-busters, antisubmarine weapons, and even the manportable Davy Crockett Weapon System, a watermelonsized tactical nuclear warhead that could be set up anywhere and lobbed against enemy forces by a threeman team. (Its main drawback was that it was very inaccurate, which meant it was likely that the blast radius of the nuclear detonation could be larger than the range of the weapon. This was bad news if you were a member of the Davy Crockett team.)

And then there were atomic demolition munitions (ADMs), more colloquially known as nuclear land mines. The intended use of ADMs was to destroy key terrain features (bridges, dams, tunnels, mountain passes, irrigation and hydroelectric systems, industrial plants, factories, oil refineries, canals, railway junctions), preventing them from being used by the enemy—whether through actual physical destruction, or just by blanketing the entire area with radiological contamination. You could also use an ADM to redirect enemy forces, either away from important strategic areas, or *toward* your own forces waiting in ambush. Not a bad tool to have in your shed.

ADMs had important strategic utility, but they also bore significant complications. First, unlike other tactical nuclear weapons, which would be dropped, launched, lobbed, or shot out of a cannon on command, ADMs had to be prepositioned in strategic areas *before* the war began, or at least long before the enemy arrived. This meant nuclear land mines would sit in the ground for months at a time, near important (but mostly civilian) infrastructure like bridges, tunnels, and so on. In Western democracies, it wasn't all that easy to convince your population to just deal with a nuclear weapon buried in their backyard—one that was intended to blow them, their home, and their neighborhood to kingdom come if World War III broke out. The politics of ADMs would be one of the greatest challenges to their existence.

But not the only one. There was also a daunting technical challenge.

Central Europe gets very cold in the winter. Really, really cold. And that could be a problem for nuclear land mines. They would be buried underground, where the cold would seep inside the device. The mine's electronics, and the conventional explosives used as a trigger to set off the nuclear reaction, needed to stay within a specific temperature range in order to work. If the ADMs got too cold, the Soviets might roll right through your bestlaid plans. Scientists and engineers in the West brainstormed ways to keep the internal components of ADMs at the correct temperature. Ideas were thrown around, some good, some ... not so good.

But it was the British that came up with what was *by far* the most idiosyncratic solution to the cold problem.

Blue Peacock.

The British War Office called for a nuclear land mine late in 1954, and work on Blue Peacock started that year at the Armament Research and Development Establishment in Kent—the same place where Britain's nuclear program had been set up in 1947. By mid1955, the concept for the ordnance was complete. The mine would be encased in a steel cylinder, about six feet in diameter, and weighing in at a whopping eight tons. The bomb itself would use the same design as the first British nuke, the Blue Danube (first tested in 1952 under another cool code name, Operation Hurricane). The specs called for a yield of 10 kilotons, which is slightly less, but in the same ballpark, as the Little Boy bomb dropped on Hiroshima. If detonated near the surface, Blue Peacock would produce a crater about 375 feet in diameter, but if it was buried 35 feet below the surface, that number would grow to 640 feet. That's a pretty big hole in the ground.

If it looked as though a Soviet invasion of Western Europe was imminent, the British would move the Blue Peacocks to strategic areas. They could be either deployed on the ground (near, say, a railroad crossing, or a dam), buried underground, or submerged in a river or lake. The weapon could be detonated two ways. There was an automatic timer, with a fixed duration of eight days, that could be activated by a soldier if he and his unit needed to get the hell out before the Red Army showed up. Or for a more controlled detonation, a threemile wire could be strung from the mine to a command post in the rear of the battlefield. When the Soviets came charging in, you could ruin their day in the most spectacular way.

But what if you set the timer, left the area, and then the Soviets came in and found the mine before it had detonated? Couldn't they just disarm it before it went off?

The British planned for that contingency. They made the mine tamperproof. The hull of the Blue Peacock was pressurized, so that if anyone tried to get inside after it had been activated, it would kick off a tensecond timer. It also had tilt switches, so if the Soviets tried to move it, the jostling would set off the same tensecond timer.

Ten seconds isn't a lot of time. I don't care how fast you run, or even if you are in a speedy vehicle. If you trigger that timer, you are in deep trouble.

The only thing that remained was to figure out how to get around that pesky cold issue. It wouldn't do much good to build all of these mines—not to mention base your broader war strategy on their effectiveness—and then have them fail because it got too chilly in the German winter.

One idea called for wrapping the electronics and other coldvulnerable components in fiberglass pillows. A relatively sensible idea. And kind of cozy, if you think about it. But if *that* was the only idea, this story wouldn't have made it into this book. Oh no. The far more interesting plan involved live chickens.

British researchers noticed that the mine was spacious enough to hold fully grown chickens. This was more than just an entertaining observation (like, "Hey, I bet your head could fit inside that box")—it could be a solution to the problem. Their body heat could keep the components warm enough to ensure that they would work if called upon. Throw a chicken or two into the mine, toss in some chicken feed, and seal it up. The chicken feed actually served two purposes. The first is the obvious: It let you keep the "live" in your "live chickens." But secondly, it keeps your chickens from getting hungry and pecking away at the electronics and essential components of an *armed nuclear weapon*.

At this point, you might be asking "What makes chickens such a good heat source?" I didn't know why either (for some reason, my history PhD program entirely skipped the physiology of chickens), so I looked it up. Fortunately, science has the answer.

According to the University of Kentucky's College of Agriculture, Food and Environment, chickens are something called "homeothermic." This means that they produce and dissipate heat into their surroundings to maintain a constant body temperature. If the chicken's body temperature is warmer than the air temperature of wherever it might be, the chicken will lose body heat—and consequentially, the air around the chicken will get warmer. This in itself is not something magical for just chickens. Most birds and mammals, including humans, are homeothermic. However, an adult chicken in its normal state walks around with a body temperature of between 105 and 107 degrees Fahrenheit. Stuck in a steel container in the middle of a central European winter, that means a lot of dissipating. Moreover, a chicken's body temperature can drop to as low as 73 degrees before it freezes to death. So there's plenty of heat to go around.

Maybe the most amazing thing about the Blue Peacock program is that it wasn't scrapped because of the chicken idea. No, that was considered completely reasonable by the British planners.

It was all the other stuff wrong with the project.

The British ended up building two Blue Peacock prototypes, but problems persisted. The thing was just way too big and way too heavy. It was a pain to move around, and secret testing was nearly impossible because of the size of the steel container. This was considered even more problematic when smaller and lighter warheads (such as the Red Beard) started to come online. There was also the fallout problem, which was twofold. Early warheads, like the Blue Danube used in Blue Peacock, were very "dirty" relative to modern weapons. That is to say, they released a ton of radiation. Combine this with a surface (or subsurface) detonation, which hurls tons of irradiated dirt and debris into the air, and the Blue Peacock design was operationally untenable, with or without the chickens.

But it was ultimately political obstacles that doomed this program. In February 1958, the British Ministry of Defence's Weapons Policy Committee decided to end work on the Blue Peacock design. The mission requirement to pre-position the weapon at or near the eventual detonation site was a non-starter for most European civilian populations. And why would they agree to this? It's not like it was really going to protect their homes, neighborhoods, and nations against the Soviet threat.

No. It was specifically designed to blow those things to pieces, and to leave behind a radioactive wasteland for generations to come. I'd have protested too.

Of course, there were no protesters. The Blue Peacock program, like most other nuclear weapons programs, was known only to those with the highest security clearances. The project was classified from the 1950s all the way until 2004, when on April 1 the British National Archives declassified the Blue Peacock documents.

Yes, they declassified the program on April Fools' Day.

Apparently, this wasn't the British government's idea of a hilarious lark. When the BBC asked if the entire chicken-heatednuclearbomb thing was an elaborate prank, the National Archives replied, "The Civil Service does not do jokes."

Quite.

AND THEN WHAT?

The end of Blue Peacock didn't mean the end of the atomic demolition munition as a concept. In fact, the US military is known to have produced at least six different variants of the ADM. Just not ones that needed livestock to keep them warm. The two longestserving models, which were part of the American arsenal from the 1960s through the 1980s, were the Medium Atomic Demolition Munition (MADM), and the Special Atomic Demolition Munition (SADM). The MADM was the larger of the two—it weighed about 400 pounds (compare that to the 16,000pound weight of the Blue Peacock).

By the 1980s, at the height of Cold War tensions, there were more than six hundred total atomic demolition mines in the US arsenal, a mixture of MADMs and SADMs. Nearly four hundred of these were staged in central Europe (West Germany and Italy), twentyone in the Pacific at bases in South Korea and Guam, and the remainder (a little over two hundred) in the United States. There were also specifically trained soldiers in the US military to maintain, operate, and, if the call went out, employ these weapons on the battlefield. The US Army mustered about 750 ADM specialists in the 1980s, while the Navy and Marine Corps added another 200 or so. The US government also made it a point to train engineers and special operators from allied nations in the use of American ADMs. Belgium, Britain, Greece, Italy, Turkey, West Germany, and the Dutch all sent soldiers to learn the ins and outs of the nuclear land mine.

Fortunately for everyone, atomic demolition munitions were never used in combat. By the end of the 1980s, with the collapse of communist governments throughout Eastern Europe, the United States decided to remove all ADMs from service.

PART II

ASTONISHING OPERATIONS

6

OPERATION FOXLEY

Many of us in the historian world hold a special place in our hearts for the legendary comedy show *Monty Python*. Which is partly because the Pythons, perhaps more than anyone else, use history so expertly for comedic effect.

If you ask me, the single greatest example of this comes during an episode of *Monty Python's Flying Circus*. Wryly titled, "The North Minehead Bye-Election," the episode is set (according to its caption) after World War II in "A Small Boarding House in Minehead, Somerset." It begins with the boarding house's landlady greeting two new guests (Mr. and Mrs. Johnson), and proceeding to take them around the house, introducing them to the other boarders.

One of the guests is a Mr. Hilter. Dickie Hilter.

Along with Dickie are his friends, Ron Vibbentrop, Heimlich Bimmler, and (phoning in) Norman McGoering.

Hilter is planning to run for local government, in the North Minehead bye-election, as the Nationalist Bocialist candidate. His plan is to annex Poland.

Hilarity ensues.

But, WHY is this so funny? Hitler was arguably the worst

human to ever walk the earth, responsible for the deaths of millions of people. Should we be laughing at anything that involves the most hated man in history?

And, of course, Hitler died in 1945. It doesn't make much sense for him to be at an English boarding house in post-war Somerset.

I think part of the humor stems from the fact that Hitler was a monster, and it is therefore cathartic to see him in such ridiculous circumstances. Hitler's suicide prevented his victims from getting the justice they so desperately deserved. He should have been captured and made to pay for his crimes against humanity. He should have been forced to face his victims, to look them in the eyes, to be judged. His victims were cheated, and maybe the chance to laugh at his fictionalized misfortune can bring a modicum of relief to our collective souls.

Or maybe it's not that deep. Maybe it's just fun to see him look stupid.

In any case, things would have likely been much easier for everyone if Hitler had been killed or captured, rather than allowed to commit suicide. Of course, it's not for lack of trying. The Germans themselves plotted to kill Hitler more than two dozen times prior to the start of the war in 1939, and another dozen or so assassination schemes were planned or attempted during the war.

But why didn't one of the Allied countries step in and launch an operation to kill Hitler before he had the chance to kill himself?

They did!

Well, at least they thought about it.

The "operation" part in Operation Foxley is a bit of a misnomer. Foxley wasn't a single operation. But if you really want to stretch the definition of the word, it was an operation that evolved multiple times, with multiple options, until it finally settled on a specific plan of action. It was the brainchild of the Special Operations Executive (SOE), founded in 1940 by Winston Churchill to "take action by way of subversion and sabotage against the enemy overseas," or as Churchill would state much more succinctly, "set Europe ablaze." They got very good at this.

The object of the operation was, "The elimination of HITLER and any high-ranking Nazis or members of the Führer's entourage who may be present at the attempt."

An early idea called for an attack on the Führerzug (Hitler's train), to try to derail and destroy it while he was on board. But the concept was deemed too risky. Hitler's schedule was unpredictable, and because of security concerns the timing and route of the train was not revealed until the very last minute. SOE saboteurs would have to be always at the ready, and even then, would have to be extremely lucky to be in the right place at the right time to catch the train in motion.

But what if the SOE could get someone *on* the train? Either one of their own agents (unlikely), or someone they recruited from the train staff? That person wouldn't need to get directly next to Hitler to do the job; he or she just needed to get close to Hitler's food or drink supply. The SOE had developed poisons for all sorts of occasions, and had one perfect for this party. It was known as "I." It was tasteless and odorless, and could be dropped into most any liquid without signs of contamination (except for wine or tea without milk). "I" was chosen as the most suitable poison because,

Its effect is not immediate like that of "R" or "F". In fact, taken in sufficiently small doses its symptoms may not appear before 6 or 7 days. Under such circumstances there is no antidote … The delayed action of this medium is its chief advantage since it affords the best chance of the intended victim [Hitler] taking the necessary lethal quantity before suspicion has been aroused.

And Hitler apparently drank a lot. Not booze (he was a teetotaler), but according to reports he was "extremely fond of apple juice," and is a "tea addict." And, fortunately, he always drinks his tea with milk.

The Führer wouldn't know what hit him. And when he did, it would be too late.

That is, if you could get someone close enough to pull off the poisoning. Which was near impossible, mainly due to the fact that the security on Hitler's train (and around it when it was in station) was extremely high.

Which makes sense, since, you know, people kept trying to kill him.

So no to the poisoning plot. What else can we try?

The answer came soon after the invasion of Normandy by Allied forces. During the ensuing battles, one of Hitler's former person guards was taken prisoner. As he was interrogated, he provided the Allies with tantalizing information about Hitler's habits while he spent his time at his mountainside residence, the Berghof. Located near the market town of Berchtesgaden in Bavaria, and within a broader retreat area known as Obersalzberg, the Berghof was Hitler's happy place. He spent more time there than any other location during the war. It was deep inside German-controlled territory. It was secure. When Hitler was there he relaxed. He dropped his guard. He became vulnerable.

And it wasn't difficult to know when Hitler was in residence. When he was there, there was a huge "swastika flag which is flown on such occasions from the flagpole at the car park in front of the Berghof." Essentially, a great big sign saying, Hitler is here. Come and kill him.

Here's where things get interesting. The prisoner's tantalizing information? It was that Hitler took a walk nearly every day at precisely 10 a.m. to a nearby teahouse.

And he did the walk alone. Always.

According to SOE intelligence documents, Hitler strolls in a fairly leisurely manner. The walk takes 15 to 20 mins. at normal pace. There is an SS guard at each end and an SS patrol (one man) patrolling the route. Hitler cannot bear to feel himself watched, and if he sees an SS man following him about, he shouts at him "if you are frightened, go and guard yourself." In consequence guards have been instructed to keep him in sight but to remain unobserved themselves.

What this meant, in layman's terms, is that Hitler could be assassinated, and there was next to nothing the SS could do about it.

You just needed to get someone close, or at least close enough to use a high-powered rifle with a telescopic scope. And by "someone," you really needed a well-trained marksman who could blend into the Bavarian countryside and pass himself off as a German soldier (specifically a Gebirgsjäger, the German mountain troops who made up the majority of German forces in the area). The SOE documents specified the weapons and equipment this commando would bring along: "Mauser sniper's rifle, telescopic sight (carried in pocket), explosive bullets in magazine, wire-cutters (for making hole in wire fence), H.E. [High Explosive] grenades carried in haversac [sic] for close protection and assistance in making get-away."

There are two items on this list that stand out: 1) Explosive bullets; the British had no intention to leave anything up to chance – Hitler was not going to luckily survive a gunshot. And 2) the grenades; this was not going to be a suicide mission. SOE men were far too valuable to sacrifice in such a way. If the agent is killed in the process of completing the operation, that happens in war. But he is going to go down fighting. And maybe he can take some Nazis with him.

Any good operation has a contingency plan, and Foxley was no exception. There were actually multiple contingencies. If the sniper couldn't take the shot, or if Hitler somehow survived the assassination attempt, the British could still take him out on his return trip to the Berghof. Hitler always walked to the teahouse, but always returned home via car. A second team, armed with a PIAT gun or bazooka, could blast Hitler's car to smithereens. This team wouldn't get into position until Hitler arrived at the teahouse, "after observing the sniper's failure" to bring him down, which would help them to avoid detection. The benefit of this plan was thought to be surprise: after the first, failed attempt on Hitler's life, "the guards would hardly expect a second attack to be made."

An additional contingency plan was contemplated in case Hitler couldn't be successfully targeted, or as a special bonus even if the plan went off without a hitch. Endearingly called "Little Foxleys," these contingencies centered on the chance to take out other high-ranking members of the Nazi government. Since this was where Hitler spent most of his time, so did a who's who of Nazi leadership, including Martin Bormann (head of the Nazi Party Chancellery, and Hitler's private secretary), Heinrich Himmler (the main architect of the Holocaust), Hermann Göring (the successor designate to Hitler), Joachim von Ribbentrop (Reich Minister for Foreign Affairs), Albert Speer (Reich Minister for Armaments and War Production), Otto Dietrich (Reich Press Chief of the Nazi Party), Julius Schaub (SS officer and one of Hitler's personal adjutants), Alwin Albrecht (also a personal adjutant to Hitler), and Eva Braun (according to the SOE documents, Hitler's "secretary").

This could have been quite the haul for the Allies. The death of any of these personalities would be a huge blow to Hitler and the Nazi Party command structure. Hitler and one of them? Or failing to kill Hitler, several of his closest advisors and his "secretary"? How can you say no?

Of course, they did say no. Operation Foxley, after months of planning and after considerable resources were used to collect intelligence on the target, was cancelled. Hitler was allowed to live, at least until he took his own life, and the life of his secretary-turned-bride Eva Braun, on April 30, 1945.

But why? This plan seemed to have a chance of success. It was meticulously planned, researched, and analyzed. Why would the British pass up the opportunity to kill Adolf F***ing Hitler?

It depends on who you ask. Some historians who are more willing to dabble in the counterfactual maintain that Operation Foxley wouldn't have worked, regardless of the reason it was ultimately cancelled. Hitler's last visit to Berghof ended on July 14, 1944, just about the time the British were learning of his long walks in the woods. He never returned.

And even if he had, it's unlikely he would have been going anywhere alone. Just six days later, on July 20th, another assassination attempt was carried out, this time by members of the German Resistance led by Graf Claus von Stauffenberg. The attempt, sometimes known as Operation Valkyrie, led to dramatically increased security surrounding Hitler.

But since you've made it this far in the book, you know I don't care about any of that. The British had no idea Hitler would never again set foot in Berghof. Or that his security was ratcheted up after von Stauffenberg tried to kill him.

The British cancelled Operation Foxley for their own reasons, which we can only speculate about. And some are more compelling than others.

There are those who argue the plan was scrapped because of the rapid success of the Allied armies following D-Day. This overtook the need for an assassination attempt on Hitler's life, as the war was coming to a close regardless. The SOE could be pulled off the proposed mission, and their considerable talents for creating mischief could be applied elsewhere. This makes some sense. The SOE's time and talent shouldn't be wasted on unnecessary operations tangential to the ultimate winning of the war (no matter how tempting they might be).

But not as much sense as another explanation. There were those who were worried that, had Hitler been assassinated, he would have become a martyr to the cause. Maybe not with all Germans, but enough to propagate the myth that Germany might have won the war if Hitler had survived. The last thing the Allies wanted was to give the Germans an excuse to believe that "We lost because Hitler was killed." This could leave them angry and unrepentant, and could easily have led to a repeat of what happened after World War I, when Hitler and the rising Nazi Party were able to harness the bitterness caused by the German loss to blame minorities and scapegoats—eventually leading to both World War II and the Holocaust.

This is a cogent, logical, emotionally resonant, and convincing argument for why Operation Foxley was cancelled. It would absolutely make the most sense of *all* the reasons to scrap Foxley, if it wasn't for this, the most compelling of the bunch:

Hitler was a godawful military strategist. The worst. Putrid, abysmal, dreadful, appalling, horrendous—there might not be a good word in English for how bad he was. He was schrecklich, fürchterlich, entsetzlich, scheußlich. He micromanaged every aspect of the German war machine, insisting on total control of the war. And did I mention he was bad at it?

And so, for the Allies, he was the strategic gift that keeps on giving. Need someone to snatch defeat from the jaws of victory? You can count on Adolf for that. It would be idiotic to remove someone like that from his position of ineptitude.

You might get stuck with someone who knows what they are doing. Like Albert Speer, or Admiral Karl Doenitz, or generals Erich von Manstein, Helmuth Weidling, and Erwin Rommel. You could get someone with more strategic sense than Hitler, like Himmler, or Goering, or Josef Göebbels, or your uncle Bert, or my 12-year-old niece (who would have never committed so many forces to the siege of Stalingrad).

So, instead, you let Hitler run Germany into the ground.

Until, of course, he decides to take care of things himself.

AND THEN WHAT?

When Hitler's body was discovered in his underground bunker in Berlin (along with the body of his once "secretary," now new bride, Eva Braun), German soldiers brought it upstairs, wrapped it in a Nazi flag, doused it in gasoline, and lit it on fire. His body wasn't completely destroyed, but close enough. The Soviet Red Army was closing in, and the soldiers needed to get out the area as quickly as they could. Hitler's body was unceremoniously dumped in an artillery shell crater and hastily covered with lose dirt. The Soviets found the body, and for the next several decades Hitler's remains were moved from one undisclosed location in the Soviet Union to another. Finally, in the 1970s, KGB director Yuri Andropov ordered the body destroyed and the ashes sent to a far-off location only known by a very select few—where apparently, they still reside today.

OPERATION NORTHWOODS

I almost didn't include this story.

Not because it isn't historically important. It is.

And not because the story is so well known that it would be seen as tiresome, stale, or boring. It isn't.

It's because Operation Northwoods has been (and will probably continue to be) a lightning rod for conspiracy theorists. This story is just as appealing to the mild-mannered "second shooter on the grassy knoll" kind of conspiracy theorist as it is to the tinfoilhatwearing "the lizard people are going to drain our blood" kind of wacko. It's an equal opportunity offender: It can bring out a natural, innate distrust of government in just about anyone.

As much as we might like to, it's hard to blame conspiracy theorists for latching on to this story. I certainly don't. Because in the end, Operation Northwoods may be one of the most shameful plans in the history of the US military. But maybe, just maybe, we can learn something from it.

On April 17, 1961, more than fourteen hundred Cuban exiles forming the Brigada de Asalto 2506 landed on the beaches of Cuba at Playa Girón in the Bahía de Cochinos—the Bay of Pigs. Their mission was to overthrow the regime of Fidel Castro, Cuba's increasingly communist leader, who had himself overthrown the regime of American ally Fulgencio Batista just over two years before. A communist leader just ninety miles from Key West was a rather painful thorn in the side of the newly inaugurated President John F. Kennedy, and getting rid of him was considered a high national security priority, as it had been for Kennedy's predecessor, Dwight Eisenhower. The invasion was backed by the US government and the CIA.

We can argue why the Bay of Pigs invasion failed until we are blue in the face (and many people still do). For many in the Cuban exile community, the mission failed because JFK refused to give American naval and air support, elements called for in the original plan developed by the Eisenhower administration.

Maybe this is true. The problem here is that we begin to descend into the realm of the counterfactual, the "if onlys" and "what ifs"—things that we are doing our damnedest to avoid. Look, I've met a lot of the Cubans who took part in the invasion, many of whom have permanently settled in or around Miami—my hometown. They are impressive men, and I wouldn't put anything past them. If they say they could have kicked out Castro with US air and naval support, who am I to argue?

... but I still will.

Because things are much more complicated from an intel-ligence perspective. Despite the lack of air and naval support, and despite the intensity and desire of the Cuban exile forces, it would have been immeasurably difficult to overcome one of the most problematic aspects of the entire invasion: Castro not only knew they were coming, he knew when and where they were coming. A combination of pisspoor information security (or in today's parlance, InfoSec) with the ability of Cuban intelligence to infiltrate the Miami exile community meant that the "secret" mission to free Cuba of Castro was anything but.

It's not like this was a huge surprise for the CIA or the US military. The Cuban intelligence service was very good, and some in the exile community had loose lips. In this environment, it was nearly impossible to conduct effective counterintelligence and keep the invasion secret. Most telling of all, the Soviets had *literally broadcast their knowledge of the mission four days before it happened.* On April 13, Radio Moscow released an Englishlanguage newscast in which they "predicted" an invasion of Cuba by CIAtrained exiles within the week. It seems they were trying to warn us against carrying out the invasion, a type of deterrence through propaganda, a "Hey, we know you are coming, so perhaps now's not a good time for your secret operation." Clearly, it didn't work.

The blowback from the failed mission was significant on multiple levels. More than a hundred members of the 2506 Brigade were killed in combat, along with four American volunteer pilots from the Alabama Air National Guard (who were contracted by the CIA). Hundreds more in Cuba would be executed in the days and weeks following the invasion, as Castro eliminated anyone suspected of abetting the exiles. More than twelve hundred of the brigade would be captured by the Cuban government, and some of those members were subsequently executed.

The Kennedy administration was embarrassed by the failed

mission. The US government looked inept in failing to maintain order even in its own backyard. In the zerosum game of the Cold War, where victory for one of the superpowers was defeat for the other, this was a huge win for the Soviets. Not to mention that the invasion pushed Castro even more firmly into the Soviet sphere of influence. And as far as the strength of the regime was concerned, the Bay of Pigs invasion did the exact opposite of what was intended. It made Castro's regime more powerful than ever before. The operation was a great political victory for the Cubans at home and abroad. Castro was a hero in the eyes of his people for defeating the Yanqui invasion, and was able to consolidate his power. The fiasco also elevated the Castro government to a newfound global status, transforming communist Cuba from an aggrieved little country to an equal in the eyes of the world. In fact, Argentinian physician turned Cuban revolutionary leader Ernesto "Che" Guevara actually *thanked* the United States for the failed invasion.

The CIA bore the brunt of the blame for the failed mission. President Kennedy fired CIA director Allen Dulles, along with Deputy Director Charles Cabell and Deputy Director for Plans Richard M. Bissell—the three men who made up the core of the Agency's leadership, particularly in the realm of covert action. Kennedy also removed (at least temporarily) major paramilitary operations from the purview of the CIA. For more than a decade, the CIA had been the agency with primary responsibility for paramilitary covert action, but now it was benched.

Into the void leapt the US military.

In June 1961, about two months after Bay of Pigs, President Kennedy approved National Security Action Memoranda 55,

56, and 57, which codified the shift in paramilitary responsibility from the CIA to the Pentagon. Nothing else really changed—the US government was still looking for ways to oust Castro from power, just through a different government agency. By fall, Assistant Secretary of Defense for Special Operations, Brigadier General Edward Lansdale, a legendary intelligence officer (or infamous; or both, depending on your perspective), was asked to brainstorm ideas to get rid of Fidel.

He didn't disappoint. In February 1962, Lansdale provided a document titled "Possible Actions to Provoke, Harrass [*sic*], or Disrupt Cuba." Some of the ideas are pretty good, some are quite silly, and some are downright abhorrent. Here is a smattering of the plans contained within:

Operation Free Ride
In an attempt to create "unrest and dissension" among the Cuban people, American pilots would airdrop hundreds of valid oneway airline tickets for flights from Cuba to Mexico City, Caracas, or a number of other USfriendly countries. Whether people used them or not probably didn't matter all that much. The idea was to get the Cuban security services worried about a mass exodus, paid for by the US taxpayer.

Operation Defector
Using the vague premise of "intelligence means" (whatever that is) with the promise of equally vague "rewards," Operation Defector was intended to induce Cuban soldiers (or even entire units) to defect along with their equipment. Not only would this reduce Cuban military readiness, but it would create "havoc" within Cuban security and intelligence agencies as they scrambled to prevent military desertions.

Operation BreakUp and Operation FullUp

Two plans that were intended to reduce Cuban confidence in the equipment of their Soviet benefactors. Operation BreakUp would "clandestinely introduce corrosive materials" to Soviet-supplied aircraft, vehicles, and ships, to cause accidents, increase supply and maintenance problems, and "seriously" affect combat capability and readiness. Operation FullUp called for an introduction of a "known biological agent" into jet fuel storage, which would multiply until it "consumes all the space inside the tank." The Cubans would believe that the fuel was contaminated when it arrived, and since it was supplied to them by the Soviet Bloc …

Operation Dirty Trick and Operation CoverUp

As astronaut John Glenn prepared to become the first American to orbit the Earth, the US military (mainly the Navy) was gearing up to support the operation. This meant dozens of ships—to monitor the launch, to take in scientific data from the mission, to preposition themselves in case of emergency, and even if there wasn't an emergency, to recover Glenn and his space capsule upon reentry. Operation CoverUp would use this naval buildup to try to convince (it doesn't say how) the Cubans that it was actually a smokescreen for something else. I'm not being cagey when I write "for something else," because the document itself says that "it should not be revealed as to what the cover is." I suppose the obvious conclusion would be cover for an invasion force, but they apparently wanted to keep the Cubans guessing … or they didn't have a plan beyond that, and they wanted us to think they were being *extra* sneaky.

Operation Dirty Trick took things a step further.

Remember, at this point the United States had *barely* put two men into space. Alan Shepard's mission was *just* high enough to be considered a spaceflight, and Gus Grissom's was similar—and then we lost Grissom's capsule to the bottom of the ocean, and almost lost Grissom too. So we didn't have a superb track record on sending people into space and recovering them safely back on Earth. There was a fairly decent chance that John Glenn's mission would be a disaster (and it almost was—his flight was shortened due to a mechanical malfunction). If things didn't go well, we were ready to blame it on the Cubans. The objective of Dirty Trick was to manufacture "irrevocable" evidence that, should Glenn's flight fail, we could show that Cuban "electronic interference" was the cause. Contingency planning at its worst.

Operation Good Times

The objective of this plan was to "disillusion the Cuban population" with fake pictures of Fidel Castro—such as a fat Castro standing in a room in his house with "two beauties" (one on each arm). The house would be "lavishly furnished," and the dining room table would have an enormous spread of "delectable" Cuban food.* The airdropped photos would be supplemented by an "appropriately Cuban" caption—something like "My ration is different"—all in the spirit of putting "even a Commie Dictator in the proper perspective" with the underfed and underprivileged Cuban masses.

All of the above operational ideas were relatively hohum if you think about it. More devious than diabolical. But one item on Lansdale's list took things to an entirely new

---

*That's somewhat redundant, as *all* Cuban food is "delectable."

level—and more important, set the stage for what would become the infamous plan mentioned in this chapter's title.

Operation Bingo was designed to overthrow the Castro regime "in a matter of hours," using the full force and might of the US military. The concept was what many today would refer to as a "false flag" operation—that is, an operation that would appear to be conducted by the enemy military, but would in fact be perpetrated by our own forces. The term "false flag" comes from the days when pirates stalked the high seas. If a pirate ship wanted to sneak up on and attack another ship, it raised the national flag of the victim ship to pretend to be its ally. A clever ruse that left the victim ship nearly defenseless against the pirate onslaught as they realized far too late that their friend was in reality a mangy scallywag buccaneer.

In this case, the victim was the US naval base at Guantánamo, which would be "attacked" by a simulated force of "Cuban" soldiers (in reality, it would be noisemakers, gunshot simulators, and the like). Once the president had been "informed" of the Cuban treachery, he would order a counterattack, targeting Cuban airfields and strategic communication lines with American combat aircraft. Airborne troops (prepositioned, because somehow that wouldn't be suspicious) would drop into multiple areas to secure Cuban airfields, road and rail terminals, and other important strategic infrastructure. A naval fleet force (again, inconspicuously "standing by on alert") would begin to bring in more troops and resupplies for the soldiers and Marines already on the ground. Taken together, this show of military strength would "overwhelm the Cuban military and cause its defeat."

The generals who made up the US Joint Chiefs of Staff

took this concept and ran with it (while dismissing most of the rest of Lansdale's ideas as insufficiently suitable for the purpose of expelling Castro from power—so basically, not crazy enough). In a perfect world, Cuba could be goaded or provoked into attacking the United States. In this ideal scenario, Castro would make it unnecessary for the United States to concoct an unseemly plan to convince our friends and enemies that *we* were the victim. Castro would do the dirty work for us.

Fidel Castro is a lot of things to a lot of different people. A revolutionary hero or a brutal dictator. A courageous and enlightened thinker or a murderous thug. A nationalist fighting for Cuban independence or a communist stooge of the Soviet Union. Take your pick. There's no wrong answer. Castro was all of these. But there's one thing we know Castro wasn't: stupid. He wasn't about to give the United States a perfectly valid excuse to invade his country.

This meant that the Joint Chiefs had to stack the deck, and that made the ideas behind Bingo very interesting. They needed to make it appear as though the Cubans had attacked legitimate and vital American interests. At least they needed the rest of the world to agree to suspend their disbelief so that the United States could claim victimhood and retain a modicum of plausible deniability that it wasn't really the US military behind the attacks.

In March 1962, the Joint Chiefs sent a memorandum to Secretary of Defense Robert McNamara as a "preliminary submission suitable for planning purposes." The memo was titled "Justification for US Military Intervention in Cuba," and it laid the foundation for the plan that would later be presented to President Kennedy. This plan would become known as Operation Northwoods.

After a litany of caveats—the courses of action listed in the document were "only for planning purposes"; the document should be considered a "point of departure"; it would be more desirable to use "legitimate provocation" as the basis for American intervention in Cuba—Northwoods jumps right into its laundry list of ways to pretend the United States had been wronged by Castro and the Cubans. It's a long list, so I'm only including the particularly interesting ones here.

One of these ideas should sound familiar: a simulated attack on Guantánamo. Lansdale's original plan had moxie, but it was short on details. Northwoods provided an eleven-point checklist of operational ideas regarding the faux assault on Gitmo. First, using clandestine radio, the plan called for starting rumors of a pending attack by Cuban military forces on the American base, followed closely by an actual assault on the base by Cuban exiles (the document calls them "friendly" Cubans) dressed in Cuban military uniforms. US forces would capture some of these "friendly" Cubans attempting to sabotage key Gitmo facilities, while other "friendlies" would start riots near the base main gate—the Cuban people autonomously rising up to demonstrate against the American occupiers. This is the point at which the mission went kinetic (or in layman's terms, when we would start to blow stuff up). The next step called for setting fires inside the base that would blow up ammunition stores, and burn aircraft parked on the airfield. Concurrently, the "friendly" Cubans would launch mortar shells into Gitmo, causing "some damage to installations," and saboteurs would set fire to an American ship in the harbor, or even sink one near the harbor entrance (this could happen along with the requisite funerals for "mockvictims" of the attack). These sabotage operations would occur simultaneously with a fake ground assault on Gitmo. After "capturing" the assault teams in the vicinity of Gitmo, and "capturing" the militia group that "storm[ed] the base," the United States would have the necessary pretense to respond with "large scale" military operations to oust the Castro regime. Problem solved.

But if you—President Kennedy—don't like *that* idea, don't worry, sir. There are many, many others. A more detailed proposal for the sinkaship idea was also on the docket in case you want to go in that direction. Northwoods opined that a new "Remember the *Maine*" incident in Guantánamo Bay could be an impetus for a full-scale invasion. If you still retain your SpanishAmerican War history (and who doesn't, right?), you'll recall that the catalyst for the war was the mysterious explosion of the battleship USS *Maine* in Havana harbor. While we know now (and probably then, too) that the ship most likely blew up because of an accident, the US government used the incident to instigate a war against Spain. If it worked once, why not again? A nice little touch at the end of the plan really ties it all together: "The US could follow up with an air/sea rescue operation covered by US fighters to 'evacuate' remaining members of the nonexistent crew. Casualty lists in US newspapers would cause a helpful wave of national indignation." A *helpful wave of national indignation.* Malevolence can be so poetic sometimes.

As someone born in Washington, DC, who was raised in Miami, and now lives back in Washington, item number four on the Northwoods plan is especially irritating to me. It begins, "We could develop a Communist Cuban terror campaign in the Miami area, in other Florida cities and even in Washington." The terror campaign (and it's extraordinary to me that they even use the words "terror campaign" here with seemingly no thought as to how wrong that is) would be primarily targeted at Cuban exiles in Miami or refugees seeking asylum in the United States. "We could sink a boat-load of Cubans enroute to Florida (real or simulated)." Let that fester a bit. Real *or* simulated. Had enough? Too bad, there's more. It continues, "We could foster *attempts on lives* of Cuban refugees" in the United States "*even to the extent of wounding* in instances to be widely publicized" (emphasis mine). So how do we carry out this terrorism? By "exploding a few plastic bombs" in specific locations around the Miami area. My parents were dating each other as undergraduates at the University of Miami around this time. I don't need to have seen *Back to the Future* as many times as I have to understand how problematic this could have been for me. It's not like the US military has a sterling historical record of limiting collateral damage.

On March 16, 1962, President Kennedy met with his top national security advisers to discuss Northwoods. All of the top brass were there: Attorney General Robert Kennedy, Chairman of the Joint Chiefs of Staff General Lyman L. Lemnitzer, National Security Adviser McGeorge Bundy, Military Representative to the President General Maxwell Taylor, Deputy Under Secretary of State for Political Affairs U. Alexis Johnson, Deputy Secretary of Defense Roswell Gilpatric, CIA director John McCone, and finally, General Lansdale. Future CIA director Richard Helms and CIA legend and covert action specialist William Harvey were asked to wait outside. Lemnitzer briefed the president on the basics of the plan, explaining that the United States now had an operation that could create "plausible pretexts to use force."

The president said no.

According to the documentary record of the meeting, President Kennedy "said bluntly that we were not discussing the use of US military force." *Bluntly*. That's about as close to a "hell no" as you are going to get in a transcript of an official White House meeting. Kennedy wanted nothing to do with Northwoods.

Historians have their own theories as to why President Kennedy so quickly dismissed the ideas contained in Operation Northwoods. Perhaps he was showing his true grit, standing up to the generals when they dumped this abhorrent plan in his lap. Perhaps he was afraid of yet another public relations (and political) disaster so soon after the Bay of Pigs fiasco. The official document states that Kennedy told the assembled group that the United States couldn't spare the four Army divisions the plan required, for fear that they would be needed in Berlin in case of a Soviet provocation. None of this really matters to me. My key takeaway from the story of Operation Northwoods is this: The system worked. A little over 240 years ago some very wise men decided to give a civilian, the president, control over the military. I'd like to think it was to prevent something like Operation Northwoods from happening. If so, nicely done, gents.

AND THEN WHAT?

The debate over how to justify an invasion of Cuba was made moot after the resolution of the Cuban Missile Crisis in October 1962. As part of the diplomatic agreement between the United States and the Soviet Union that ended the standoff (in which the Cubans were essentially a bystander), the United States agreed to a noninvasion pledge of Cuba if the Soviets would agree to remove their intermediate and longrange ballistic missiles. This effectively ended any talk of regime change through military action (covert action, on the other hand …).

Yet the underlying issues that surround Operation Northwoods continue to this day. How much should civilian politicians defer to military leaders on national security policy? In our hyperpartisan country, it can be comforting to think that an institution—the US military—is somehow above the fray. We sometimes act as though soldiers aren't people (with biases, political leanings, prejudices, and personal motivations), and afford them a veneration that assumes an apolitical mindset that is, frankly, completely unattainable for most everyone. Don't get me wrong, I greatly admire and respect the dedication and service these soldiers, sailors, Marines, and airmen have given to our country. I used to be one of them. Their training, selfsacrifice, experience, and patriotism likely mean they have fewer stupid ideas than the rest of us.

But they still can have stupid ideas.

8

FELIX AND HIS RIFLE

According to Fabian Escalante, the former chief of Cuba's counterintelligence branch, the US government (read: the CIA) tried to assassinate Fidel Castro 638 times.

If 638 seems like an impossibly outsized number, that's because it probably is. This is likely grossly inflated. But in Escalante's defense, who can really keep up? The CIA tried to kill Castro a lot. So much so that Fidel reportedly quipped, "If surviving assassination attempts were an Olympic event, I would win the gold medal."

The US government was obsessed with El Comandante. Perhaps "terrified" is the appropriate word. This is partly due to Cuba's proximity to the United States, partly due to Castro's leftist politics and coziness with the Soviet Union, and partly due to American politics and the need to win Florida, with all its Cuban exile voters.

For our purposes here, the reasons don't particularly matter—nor does the exact number of times we tried to take Fidel out. What matters is that the Americans wanted Castro gone, and tried just about every means to get the job done. Bombs, bullets, chemical weapons, biological weapons, femmes fatales, poisons, exploding seashells, cigars laced with drugs, exploding cigars, hair removers, gangsters, and hallucinogenics. You name it, we tried it.

Or at least we thought about trying it.

Some of these schemes never made it past the idea phase. Some were developed further and perhaps even tested. Some became executed operations.

Of course, none of them worked.

Unless the final plan, attempt number 639, was a secret operation called "Project Wait for Castro to Get Really, Really Old, Smoke a Lot of Cigars, and Eventually Die of Natural Causes"—in that case, Mission Accomplished!

But caught up in all of the crazy ideas, and lost in the shuffle of the myriad of overcomplicated plans, seemingly stolen from the pages of a James Bond novel, is one of the most extraordinarily simple concepts for eliminating Castro.

One man. One rifle. One bullet.

Felix Rodriguez was just a teenager when he lost his country. In fact, he wasn't even there to see it happen. Fidel took Cuba while Felix was abroad, attending high school in Pennsburg, Pennsylvania. In the 1950s, uppermiddleclass Cuban families could send their kids to school in the United States, so when Felix's uncle offered him the chance to go study in the United States, he chose to attend the Perkiomen boarding school, just north of Philadelphia. With a diploma from this prestigious institution, he would have the opportunity to attend a good college and get a wellpaying job in the United States. His future was bright.

But Felix wasn't going to just sit back and let Castro and

the communists destroy what generations of his family had built. He was ready to fight.

Against his parents' wishes, he joined a group forming in the Dominican Republic—the AntiCommunist Legion of the Caribbean. His father didn't want him to go, saying, "You're going to get yourself killed. We're not going to sign your death warrant. We won't have that on our conscience." Felix was only seventeen, not old enough to legally sign up, so he forged his father's signature (right in front of him, just to prove a point) and set off to kill communists.

He'd have to wait a while. While the AntiCommunist Legion did in fact invade Cuba in 1959, Felix wasn't with them. His commander in the unit was also the father of his close friend Roberto and a friend of his parents. As Felix and his buddy jumped on the helicopter taking off for Cuba, his commander told him to get off, saying only one of them could go—in case the mission was a disaster, the commander couldn't stand to lose both his son *and* the boy he thought of as a son. Felix was younger and had less military experience than Roberto, so it was an easy decision. And for Felix, a fortunate one. The mission was an unmitigated disaster. Castro knew they were coming, and all the soldiers were either killed or captured. Roberto was captured and spent the next twentyeight years in Cuban custody.

After this fiasco, Felix returned to the United States to finish school, and then settled in Miami, the city his family— like so many other Cuban exile families—now called home. It wasn't long before he began to hear rumblings and rumors about a US government-backed force of Cuban exiles forming to take another run at the Castro regime. This, as we know, would become the illfated Bay of Pigs invasion in

April 1961. The men who made up the 2506 Assault Brigade were determined to bring freedom back to their home island at whatever cost, and Felix wanted in.

He was eventually assigned to what was known as a "Grey Team," organized to infiltrate into Cuba on the eve of the invasion to coordinate sabotage and guerrilla operations, in much the same way as the Office of Strategic Services or British Special Operations Executive worked with resistance forces during World War II. Sneak in, link up with resistance operatives/guerrillas, and support the broader invasion with sabotage and smallunit paramilitary attacks.

In the fall of 1960, the brigade was sent to Central America to train for the upcoming invasion. By the end of the year they had been fully immersed in Soviet and East European advanced weapons and equipment, a key skill for infiltration teams who would likely need to live and fight with whatever they could get their hands on. It was around this time, New Year's 1961, that Felix had an idea. It wasn't the most unique idea, but even if Felix wasn't the first to have this idea, apparently he was the first to vocalize it to the American trainers (read: CIA) who were running the camps. He told his "plan" to the acting camp commander, a man they knew as Larry (*not* his real name), and volunteered his services. *Send me in to kill Fidel, and I'll make all our problems go away.*

It's not clear, at least in my mind, if this was a real offer or just soldierly bravado. Of course, Felix claims he was dead serious … in his memoir written more than two decades after the event. What else would you expect him to say? "I was joking that I could singlehandedly end this thing with a single bullet, but then the silly Americans took me up on it?" Not likely.

But then again, maybe he *was* serious from the beginning. I've met the man on several occasions. He's dedicated and resolute. He's a force to be reckoned with. I wouldn't put it past him.

In the end it really didn't matter if he meant it. The CIA was ready to send him in. In January 1961, Felix and a friend were flown to Miami to link up with another Cuban, who would serve as the team's radio operator. In Miami, he also got his rifle, and it was love at first sight. "What a weapon it was," he writes, "a beautiful German boltaction rifle with a powerful telescopic sight, all neatly packed in a custommade padded carrying case." He wouldn't even need to sight the rifle (adjust it to ensure a straight shot), since it had already been zeroed for him. "Apparently the resistance had obtained a building in Havana facing a location that Castro frequented at the time, and they'd managed to presight the rifle."

Felix and his team were then sent to Homestead, Florida, a sleepy town just south of Miami, to await the boat that would take them to Cuba. They were put up in what Felix thought might be an old motel, with a pool where the team practiced paddling the rubber rafts they'd use to get from their mother ship to the Cuban shoreline. The obvious gravity of the situation aside, there's something about picturing these three Cuban men, full of machismo, sitting in a rubber dinghy in a swimming pool, paddling like they are invading the beaches of Normandy.

Once it was time for the mission, they drove down to the Keys to a predetermined location near the shore. As if in a spy movie, the team was instructed to blink their headlights. This would signal a small boat to come ashore, pick them up, and bring them to the ship that would carry them the ninety miles to Cuba.

Also straight out of the movies was their transport ship. This was no clunker steamer used for transporting questionable goods under the radar. No, this was a luxury yacht—apparently owned by John F. Kennedy's brotherinlaw and founding director of the Peace Corps, Sargent Shriver—with airconditioning, leather seats, and woodpaneled cabins. James Bond would have felt right at home. The captain was an American, likely a CIA contractor, but the crew was made up of toughlooking anticommunist Ukrainians with captured Soviet Bloc weapons. The yacht was scheduled to meet up with a Cuban boat at a secret location near Varadero Beach—a smart idea, since Felix knew the area well from his childhood. That boat would take them to members of the antiCastro resistance, who would drive the team to Havana, put them up in a safe house, and then, when the time was right, move them to the room from which they'd take out Fidel. Then they would try to escape. (Best of luck with that.)

But according to Felix, escape was the furthest thing from their minds. Sure, this might be more of that famous Cuban machismo, but Rodriguez was adamant: "The truth is that escape meant very little to us. We were young, committed, and idealistic enough to try anything." Suicide mission or not, it was worth it.

"Three times my friends and I tried to infiltrate Cuba with that damn rifle, and three times we failed."

I guess I just spoiled the ending: but unless you've been living under a rock for the last seventy years, you already know that Felix and his team didn't assassinate Castro in early 1961.

Why not? The plan was simple enough, the men were

trained and motivated, the location was scouted, the resistance was ready.

The answer: They couldn't even get onto the beach. What should have been the easiest part of the plan—Cuba is an *island*—was its downfall.

The first attempt failed because when the team made it to their rendezvous point near Cuba, they never saw a boat in their area. Back to the Keys, and more D-Day practice in the swimming pool.

A week later, they made a second try. This time they found a boat! But it was the wrong one. A huge ship, a hundred feet long. Way too big to be their contact. Strike two.

On trip number three they didn't even have the opportunity to find the wrong boat. The operation was canceled by the yacht captain halfway across the Florida Strait. Something about a hydraulic failure. But it was clear the order came from on high, because when they returned to the Keys, the CIA took away the (gorgeous, exquisite, magnificent) rifle and ammunition, and told the team they'd changed their minds about the mission.

Felix was not happy: "My colleagues and I couldn't understand why the Americanos were denying our initiative. After all, it was our war, and it was our lives. And if we were willing to risk getting killed, it was our business."

AND THEN WHAT?
Then the wheels fell off.

Newly inaugurated President Kennedy had other priorities besides Cuba, but his military and intelligence services pressed the issue. When he briefed Kennedy about the planned Bay of Pigs invasion, CIA Deputy Director of Plans

Richard Bissell (the guy in charge of the CIA's covert operations) told JFK, "You can't mañana this thing." Castro had to be dealt with.

The Bay of Pigs operation was, of course, a disaster, and needless to say, the United States wasn't going to try something like that again. In fact, a year and change later, as part of the agreement with the Soviets to end the Cuban Missile Crisis, the Kennedy administration made it official, promising that the United States would never invade Cuba to remove Fidel Castro.

But that pledge didn't preclude covert operations. Sure, we couldn't send in the Marines—or another army of Cuban exiles—but we could try every underhanded ploy under the Caribbean sun to kick Fidel out of power. And we would. Some were silly, some were stupid, some were downright ridiculous. None had much chance of working.

Most of the plans were developed and controlled from a unique facility in Miami. Known as JM/WAVE, the facility was a covert operations and intelligencecollecting CIA station located on the site of an old dirigible air station used during World War II. In the 1960s it was part of the South Campus of the University of Miami.

CIA stations are not supposed to be *inside* the United States. The National Security Act of 1947, which created the Agency, dictated that the CIA was only authorized to operate outside the country. So there are CIA stations in capital cities around the world, as you would expect. Some are big, some are small. All are on foreign soil. JM/WAVE was the sole exception.

And it was quite the exception. By the end of 1962, JM/WAVE grew to become the largest CIA station in the world other than the Agency's headquarters in Langley. It employed three to four hundred professional CIA officers, as well as an estimated fifteen thousand Cuban exiles (including Felix), all engaged in monitoring Cuba and dreaming up plans for its leader's demise. According to some accounts, the CIA was one of Miami's largest employers during this period (if not *the* largest), possibly accounting for a full third of the city's economy. CIA spooks needed to buy houses (both personal and safe houses), cars, cover companies, furniture, groceries, marinas, hunting camps (for training), merchant shipping, exileoperated publishing houses (for producing propaganda), and more. JM/WAVE had three or four people employed just to organize and manage real estate. They even operated a gaggle of boats and aircraft, so many that the CIA maritime fleet was the third largest in the Caribbean, after only the American and Cuban navies.

Maintaining cover was important. The sign on the building couldn't say "CIA Station." This was a clandestine facility. The main headquarters was fronted by a false corporation called "Zenith Technical Enterprises, Inc."

It was the worstkept secret in Miami. My father, a college student who worked at a department store, knew. So did everyone else. The only people who didn't know that everyone knew were the people who worked there. When a national magazine publicly outed JM/WAVE, the University of Miami denied knowledge of the operation (which convinced no one), and the station changed its name to the "Melmar Corporation." The CIA in Miami would also operate under the cover names "DoubleChek Corp.," "Gibraltar Steamship Corp.," and "Vanguard Service Corp."

The names changed, but nothing else did. The mission was

always the same: Get Fidel Castro out of Cuba, dead or alive … but preferably dead.

On May 23, 1967, the CIA's inspector general prepared a report for the director called "Report on Plots to Assassinate Fidel Castro." It was top secret, and would only be formally released to the public in 1999 (still heavily redacted). It details the CIA mission to oust Castro, through direct and indirect covert action, known as Operation Mongoose. We also know a good amount regarding the CIA's obsession with the Cuban leader through the 1975 report of the Church Committee (formally known as the "Select Committee to Study Governmental Operations with Respect to Intelligence Activities").

Each of the wide variety of ways the US government tried to kill or incapacitate Fidel could fill its own chapter in this book, so I will provide just some of the highlights here:

Castro gave frequent radio speeches to the Cuban people. He saw it as a way to spread the ideals of the revolution, and to keep his country united against the antiCastro exiles and their American benefactors. One CIA plan called for contaminating the air of the radio station with an aerosol spray that, when inhaled, would produce reactions similar to those of LSD. Fidel would breathe in the chemical. Live across the airwaves, he would go on a magical mystery tour. Cuba would then rise in revolt.

A similar plan involved Fidel's affinity for cigars. The CIA apparently laced a box of cigars with some sort of chemical that would produce a "temporary personality disorientation." The documents don't say how, but the idea was to get Castro to smoke one before giving a speech, and then "make a public spectacle of himself." Cuba would then rise in revolt.

Castro's nickname was "The Beard." It was a key element to his broader image as an intellectual, a revolutionary, and a man of the people. A modernday Samson. Why not try to make it fall out? This scheme involved thallium salts, a chemical found in many depilatory (hair removal) products, such as Nair. If the CIA could sprinkle these salts inside of Fidel's shoes (maybe when he put them outside his room overnight to get them shined), his beard would fall out, and with it his mystique and machismo. Cuba would then rise in revolt.

Fidel Castro was an avid reef and ocean diver, and so the CIA concocted several schemes to take advantage of this proclivity. (1) They tried to give him a wetsuit laced with fungus (or in some versions of the story, botulism toxin). (2) They tried to give him a snorkel system infected with tuberculosis. (3) They either planned to, or actually did, plant an explosiveladen seashell near where he liked to dive. According to the story, it was so amazingly beautiful that Castro was sure to pick it up. With its leader in pieces on the ocean floor, Cuba would then rise in revolt.

"Elimination by Illumination" was a plan that called for convincing Cubans that Fidel was the Antichrist. The CIA would spread the rumor that the Second Coming of Christ was imminent, and then (presumably when enough Cubans were convinced) an American submarine would surface just outside of view of the shore and launch what are called "starshells" (essentially fireworks). This would be the Sign. Here comes Jesus to kick Fidel square in the beard. And then? You guessed it. Cuba would then rise in revolt.

Two of my favorite CIA plots deserve special attention. One of them centered on the establishment of "a seaborne propaganda balloon launching facility for the infiltration of antiCastro, antiSoviet propaganda into Cuba." Sounds manageable, right? Take a boat, get upwind of Cuba, tie some notes to balloons, and let them go (and wait for Cuba to rise in revolt).

But according to the memorandum that outlined the plan, it would cost approximately *fifty thousand dollars* to establish a balloon launching capability. The CIA also thought it would take "a minimum of two months" to establish an operational capability. And that's just the startup costs. From there, it would cost $22,000 *per month* for the first sixmonth period to launch a total of a thousand balloons—without factoring in the cost of the propaganda itself. I once managed to inflate hundreds of balloons for a kid's birthday party in a single afternoon without CIA training. And unsurprisingly, no one paid me thousands of dollars.

Finally, there is the story of Marita Lorenz, Fidel Castro's on-again, off-again lover, and almost assassin. Lorenz was raised in Germany, but her father was a German cruise ship captain, which gave her a chance to see the wider world at an early age. At nineteen, she was aboard her father's ship in Havana Harbor when she met Fidel Castro. "I will never forget the first time I beheld that penetrating stare, that beautiful face, that wicked and seductive smile," she later recounted.

It seems Fidel also fell into lust at first sight. "I am Dr. Castro. Fidel. I am Cuba. I have come to visit your large ship," he said. I have invented a few conversations in this book, and you would be forgiven for assuming this is one of them. Is it not.

Before Marita knew it, she was pregnant with Fidel's baby. According to Lorenz's memoir, Castro was happy with the situation, but supposedly while he was away on a trip seven months into the pregnancy, Marita was drugged, and when she awoke the baby was gone. She had no idea if she had miscarried, if the baby was forcibly aborted, or if it had been successfully delivered.

Lorenz was (understandably) profoundly unhappy about what happened. She traveled to the United States, where the US government quickly recruited her to return to Cuba and take her revenge. She was given two botulism-laced pills to use against her lover.

But when she saw him again, Castro knew why she was there. He took his gun out of his holster, handed it to her, and said, "No one can kill me. No one. Ever."

Marita's love/lust for Fidel was rekindled. She dumped the poison pills and the two fell into bed together. When they were done, Castro left, and Lorenz returned to the United States.

There's a great joke about Castro's longevity. It goes like this:

In some kind of diplomatic exchange, Castro is presented with the gift of a Galápagos turtle. He's polite to the man, but he declines the turtle after learning that it might live for more than a hundred years. "That's the problem with pets," Castro says. "You get attached to them, and then they die on you."

But whatever happened to Felix Rodriguez, the wouldbe hero of this story?

He infiltrated Cuba with the rest of his 2506 Assault Brigade gray team members just prior to the Bay of Pigs invasion. When the day went bad, he made his way to the sanctuary of the Venezuelan embassy in Havana, where he remained for several months until he could escape back to the United States. Between the fall of 1961 and the summer of 1962 he continued to work from Miami with those opposing Castro, and personally managed to smuggle some ten tons of military equipment into Cuba for use by those resisting Fidel's rule.

For the next five years, Rodriguez worked for the US government and for exile groups working against the Cuban regime (work that often overlapped). But in 1967, he got a chance to do something every other Cuban exile could only dream of. The CIA asked him to train and lead a team of counterinsurgency soldiers in Bolivia. Their target: Argentinian physician and hero of the Cuban Revolution Ernesto "Che" Guevara.

And they caught him. Felix's orders from the CIA were to do all within his power to keep Che alive. The Agency wanted to take their time interrogating him. They wanted to see what intelligence he could provide about the Castros in Cuba, or other Latin American communist movements he might know about. But the Bolivians refused to let him live, and they had the authority in their own country. He had tried to overthrow their government, and they wanted him dead. Felix did get a chance to talk to him before Che's execution, and in the last known picture of Che alive, he is standing next to Felix Rodriguez.

9

PROJECT SEAL

On Friday, March 11, 2011, at 2:46 p.m. local time, a magnitude9 earthquake started fortyfive miles east of Tohoku, Japan. This was a monster. It struck along what is known as a subduction zone, where two of Earth's tectonic plates collide. In this case, one plate had spent the last few centuries sliding under the other. At some point, the plates stuck together, but they continued *trying* to move, building up tension over the years, decades, centuries, until one day—this particular Friday—all of that tension released, and the world shook.

And when I use the phrase "the world shook," it's not to be flowery or figurative. The six minutes of the Tohoku earthquake actually shifted the Earth on its axis of rotation, and *shortened the length of a day* by about a microsecond. Japan's main island, Honshu, moved eastward by eight feet, and about 250 miles of Honshu's northern coastline dropped by two feet. Tremors were felt as far away as Norway, North America, and Antarctica. The earthquake even produced an infrasonic (lower frequencies than humans can hear) rumble that was so loud it was detected by a satellite in space.

But the most amazing thing about this massively powerful

earthquake is how well Japan was prepared for it. Because earthquakes are such a common occurrence in Japan, the country has mandated a high standard for building codes, and developed a wellfunctioning early warning system. Residents of Tokyo received an entire minute of warning even before the seismic tremors hit the city. The public received text alerts, and highspeed trains, assembly lines, and other potentially vulnerable locations were battened down. As a result, very few Japanese citizens were injured or killed as a direct result of the earthquake.

Unless, of course, you consider a tsunami a "direct result" of an earthquake.

What quickly turned the triumph of decades of earthquake planning into a tragedy of historic proportions were the tsunami waves that began to arrive on the Japanese coast about an hour after the earthquake. Residents of the coastal cities had also been warned via text message of a tsunami risk, but a Japanese study later showed that many people underestimated the potential danger, having experienced tsunamis before and survived.

But this time, the tsunami waves reached as high as one hundred feet, and in some areas traveled as far as *six miles* inland. More than one million buildings were partially or completely destroyed. Twentyeight thousand people died or went missing, and almost half a million people were displaced. In Onagawa, Japan, a fourstory reinforcedconcrete, supposedly tsunamiresistant building was toppled like a toy.

When it all was over, and a full accounting of the damage was made (which included the meltdown of the Fukushima Daiichi Nuclear Power Plant), the Tohoku earthquake and tsunami would cost the Japanese $360 billion in economic damage, making it the costliest natural disaster in human history.

But it could have been much worse. As bad as it was, Japan's infrastructure was relatively prepared for a tsunami of this magnitude—or at least as prepared as it could be. Without this high level of preparation, Japan in 2011 could have easily been a repeat of the Indian Ocean tsunami of 2004, which killed 230,000 people, most of them in countries that had infrastructure far inferior to Japan's.

One can only imagine what this tsunami would have done to Japan if it had hit the islands several decades earlier, at a time when the country was predominantly made up of wooden buildings and houses, and when technology hadn't advanced far enough to provide citizens adequate advanced warning. Hundreds of thousands, or even millions, could have been killed. The Japanese economy could have been damaged beyond repair.

Today, this scenario sounds like a humanitarian tragedy of epic proportions.

In January 1944, it sounded like an opportunity to end a war.

They called it Project Seal.

The concept came from US Navy wing commander E. A. Gibson, who had been part of engineering surveys in the Pacific during the period from 1936 to 1942. While there, he noticed that blasting operations on submerged coral formations sometimes caused unusually large waves. This gave him an idea.

What if we could use explosives to create an artificial tsunami? We could harness the forces of nature. We could use the power of the sea to crush the Japanese. We could win the war.

(Little did Gibson know that slightly different forces of nature were being harnessed at that same time in laboratories in New Mexico. But I digress.)

In January 1944, Wing Commander Gibson had the chance to pitch his plan to Lieutenant General Sir Edward Puttick, chief of New Zealand's General Staff. Puttick thought the idea was just crazy enough to work, and so he instructed Gibson to put together a team to start preliminary testing. Not only that, but Puttick decided to put the proposal in front of American admiral William Halsey, commander of all Allied forces in the South Pacific ("COMSOPAC"). Halsey agreed: It was worth at least taking a closer look.

Initial testing was done in February at a site in New Caledonia under the direction of a joint US/New Zealand committee, which included some very senior military personnel and two professors from the Universities of California and Auckland. It's clear they thought they had something cooking.

And according to the final report compiled by Professor Thomas Leech (dean of the Faculty of Engineering at the University of Auckland and a member of the committee), the New Caledonia exploratory trials indicated that there *were* "reasonable prospects of developing techniques for favourable sites," at least reasonable enough to prompt the team to request additional resources for scaleup experiments. They sent the results of the New Caledonia trials and their request for additional testing to Admiral Halsey, who would have to give the final blessing, and hoped for the best.

To their relief, Halsey was impressed:

The results of these experiments, in my opinion, show that inundation in amphibious warfare had definite and far reaching possibilities as an offensive weapon. It would be very desirable to have further developments carried out to establish a practicable method and procedure which could be used in offensive warfare. I would be grateful if this development could be continued to completion by New Zealand officers. All practicable assistance of facilities and personnel in this Command will be at your disposal.

Two things worth pointing out: (1) "Inundation in amphibious warfare" is quite the euphemism for what is essentially drowning your enemy with an enormous wave, and (2) that last sentence is important, but don't read too much into it. It's not a blank check. The word "practicable" is key here. Halsey is telling them: You have a blank check ... but for a bank account that has limited funds. Don't get carried away.

Phase two of the Seal testing, which was still mostly relegated to smallscale experiments, began on June 6, 1944. This wasn't a date chosen in coordination with D-Day, or the fall of Rome to the Allies, both of which happened that same day. It was just a random Tuesday.

The site of the tests was an old fortress on the Whangaparaoa Peninsula in the Hauraki Gulf. Whangaparaoa was reasonably close to Auckland, so supplies and personnel were nearby, and it had existing buildings that had been previously used for New Zealand army units. Because it had been an army base, it was also favorably situated for security purposes. It wouldn't do the Allies any good if Japanese spies got an early look at what they were planning.

By the time they were done, the team at Whangaparaoa had conducted some thirtyseven hundred experiments with explosive charges of various types ranging from 0.06 pounds to 600 pounds in weight. The initial tests produced the conclusion: "Single charges were inefficient in regard to wave production."

This is hardly surprising. If they did, the undersea battles of World War II would have been causing tidal waves all over the place. Depth charges, torpedoes, and other weapons were used by the tens of thousands.

So why waste the time? Why not skip to more valuable experimentation, something that might shed light on the possibility of the weapon they were trying to design?

Science, that's why. Even when you think you already know the answer to a question, when you absolutely *know* how an experiment is going to turn out—you still do the experiment. You never *really* know until you empirically know.

And in fact they did find out something significant from these basic experiments. The critical depth of the charges mattered, and it mattered a lot.

Now you might be thinking (again), "Of course depth matters. No one would think you could just blast off a charge at any depth and get a tidal wave. This seems like common sense. Who would assume otherwise?"

Well, the British, for one.

They had conducted their own experiments on this subject earlier, but at a much greater critical depth. When it didn't produce a large wave, they closed up shop. Now the New Zealand/American team had shown that the British gave up prematurely. A shallow critical depth could produce much greater wave amplitudes.

And this discovery, when combined with part two of the experiment—multiple explosive charges—had the New Zealand/US crew excited. Multiple charges, spaced strategically and "suitably located to conform with geometrical patterns," were found to deliver "superior results." Bigger waves! And those "geometrical patterns" allowed them to push some of the wave effects in a particular direction (like at a target), further magnifying the force of the wave (at least a little).

So far so good. But it was now time for the next phase of the testing. No more baby explosives in controlled environments. The Project Seal scientists theorized that charges of TNT totaling 2,000 tons, divided into ten equal amounts and "suitably disposed," could produce wave amplitudes of the order of thirty to forty feet. It was time for a true, scaledup, operational experiment. This was scheduled to take place at Taronui Bay, North Auckland, between the Bay of Islands and Whangaroa (not to be confused with the team's phase one location, Whangaparaoa).

This was the moment of truth. The chance to make history. To control the magnificent forces of nature. To *command* the forces of nature. They knew the theory. They'd done the preliminary experimentation. The world was their oyster, and they were going to blow it to bits. Nothing could stand in their way.

Of course, that's not true. There were no happy endings for these poor scientists. For a number of reasons, Project Seal was canceled prior to the commencement of this testing. For one, the COMSOPAC, Admiral Bill Halsey, was no longer the COMSOPAC. In May 1944, he was promoted to commanding officer of the newly formed Third Fleet, which was great for Halsey, but a major problem for the experimental team. Once they lost their top cover, it was easy for others in senior leadership, who were less enamored with a pieinthesky project that was costing significant funds and diverting significant material and intellectual resources from the broader war effort, to put the kibosh on any further testing. Besides, the US Navy leadership—at least those at the highest levels— knew about something the Seal team members did not. Something that had a much better chance to end the war quickly. Remember when I mentioned those laboratories in New Mexico?

AND THEN WHAT?

Although Project Seal was scrapped, scientists on both sides of the Pacific kept the concept in the back of their minds as the atomic age came calling (across the Atlantic too—the British were now back in the tsunami game). On July 25, 1946, the United States tested an atomic bomb at Bikini Atoll in the Marshall Islands. Unlike other atomic bomb tests, this one was detonated underwater, allowing for a direct analysis of Seal team forecasts. As it turns out, even an atomic bomb didn't produce a tsunami, but the promise of potential future applications was enough to keep the idea floating around military circles in Washington, London, and Wellington well into the late 1950s, when some of the nuclear testing during Operation Hardtack I (in 1958) was specifically designed to see how much water could be displaced by a new generation of American weapons (thermonuclear weapons, also known as hydrogen bombs).

The answer: not enough. The "Umbrella" and "Wahoo" nuclear tests showed that detonations in both shallow and deep water (Umbrella, shallow; Wahoo, deep) do blast massive amounts of water into the air (you can find the videos online), yet neither test produced anything even remotely resembling a tsunami. The water went up. The water went down. Some nearby ships were affected (and it would have truly sucked to be on them). But no tidal waves.

But even *this* hasn't stopped some people from thinking a man-made tsunami is a possibility, even today. By now, we should know better. Clearly we don't.

In 2006, an Egyptian weekly reported that a combination of secret American and Israeli undersea nuclear testing in the Indian Ocean caused the earthquake that triggered the 2004 tsunami. Then, in 2015, an Israeli military tabloid published an article warning that Iran, if allowed to develop a nuclear weapons capability, could detonate a bomb in the Mediterranean and wipe out all of Israel with a massive tsunami.

Yes, both of these articles were from fringe publications, where conspiracy theories thrive and nonsense ideas are celebrated. The nuttier the better.

But what is the excuse, then, when in 2018, media around the world—traditional, respected, not-nutty media—went completely off the rails covering the "story" of Russian Federation president Vladimir Putin's announcement of an entirely new class of weapons—including stealthy, super-fast, nuclear submarine drones—designed to shatter the global balance of power?

Making matters worse, Russian military documents leaked in 2015 suggested that the new submarine drone could carry a nuclear warhead in the 50megaton range, which would equal the strength of the largest nuclear device ever detonated (the

Soviet Tsar Bomba test of 1961), thousands of times more powerful than the bombs dropped on Japan.

Within hours of the announcement, some "experts" were arguing that a nuclear weapon with a yield (power) in the range of 20 to 50 megatons, detonated near a seacoast, could *certainly* create enough energy to recreate the 2011 Japanese tsunami, and perhaps much more. Waves even as high as 330 feet are "possible," they argued.

"Experts" also pointed out that an underwater nuclear explosion near a seashore via super-stealthy Russian drone submarines could suck up tons of radioactive ocean debris and rain it down on the shore. So if you are walking along the beach after one of these goes off, *don't* pick up the glow-inthedark seashells.

Fortunately, several responsible journalists decided to interview scientists who might have a better idea about the physics of nuclear weapons. One of these scientists, a man who is actually a nuclear weapons physicist at Lawrence Livermore National Laboratory, was asked to weigh in. He answered that *maybe* you could cause a large wave, but he insists, "It would be a stupid waste of a perfectly good nuclear weapon."

As we now know, it takes a huge amount of energy to create a tsunami, and even the most powerful nuclear weapon is a drop in the bucket compared to the tsunami that hit Japan. The Tohoku tsunami released about 9.3 *million* megatons of energy, more than 150,000 times as much as the Tsar Bomba—or any of the modern nuclear weapons Russia's submarine drone could carry.

Okay, fine. But what about all that deadly radiation spewed into the air, beaches, and sunbathers of coastal cities?

Not such a big deal, apparently. Most of it would be trapped in the water droplets and would fall back into the ocean just a short distance from the detonation. Only a very small fraction would make it onto shore.

So don't eat the fish, but feel free to set up your deck chair and get back to work on that tan.

Finally, it's important that we take all of Vladimir Putin's pronouncements with a grain of salt. We don't know all that much about the testing that has gone into this new stealth submarine drone, nor do we know how well his laser guns are going to perform in real combat, but if the new nuclear-powered cruise missile is any indication, we have very little to worry about. Of course, it's possible that you might be reading this book by the eerie light of the afterglow of a nuclear holocaust. In that case, my bad. But in 2018 the Russians tested their cruise missiles, again and again. And they crashed, again and again. The most successful test, by far, lasted only two minutes, and the missile traveled a whopping twenty-two miles before it nosedived into the Russian countryside.

So don't leave your seaside paradise and move to Nebraska just yet. Enjoy the time while you can. In fifteen years it'll be underwater anyway.

10

OPERATION MONOPOLY

Tucked into the Northwest quadrant of Washington, DC, is the idyllic neighborhood of Glover Park. With tranquil parks, highly rated public schools, neighborhood gardens, quaint row houses, delicious restaurants, and one of the lowest crime rates in DC, it's not hard to see why this area's average home price is in the ballpark of $1 million.

And if you can cobble together all that money and move here one day, you'll have some interesting neighbors.

At 2650 Wisconsin Ave NW—just up the road from the official residence of the vice president of the United States—is the embassy of the Russian Federation. But that shouldn't really be a big deal, since embassies are mostly filled with policy wonks and paper pushers. Right?

In capital cities around the world, embassies are hotbeds of espionage. And there are concrete, logical reasons for this. Mostly it comes down to the fact that in many cases (depending on the nationality of the embassy and the city where the embassy is located), a solid chunk of embassy personnel are not employed by state departments or foreign ministries. They're employed by intelligence agencies. They might not *reveal* to you that they are, but don't be fooled when the "diplomat" you meet in a bar in DC tells you he is the "second deputy agricultural attaché" for the Krasnovian embassy. This guy is a spook.

This is what is referred to in the intelligence world as an "official cover." While your new friend's day job might legitimately include some light hedge pruning, in the evenings he is out scouting for potential recruits, assets who could provide *his* country with *your* country's secrets. The great thing about this is that if he's caught spying by your country's counterintelligence officers, he has diplomatic immunity (since his "official" posting is with the embassy), and the best you can do is to declare him persona non grata and kick him out of the country.

So reason number one for why embassies are so important for espionage is that they provide cover and protection for intelligence officers. Reason number two is more straightforward: Embassies are where really important conversations take place. Conversations about national policy, both in regard to the host country and, more broadly, toward the world in general. Conversations between ambassadors and heads of state, between policymakers and policy enactors. Conversations about military readiness, treaty obligations, alliances and partnerships, trade policy, immigration policy, economic policy, and so on and so forth.

It's a potential treasure trove of vital information. A smorgasbord of scintillating intelligence. A veritable plethora of tasty tidbits—on adversaries and friends alike.

That is, if you can get your hands on it.

The Soviets went first. It started in August 1945, even before the end of the Second World War, when the United States and the Soviet Union were still nominally allies. A delegation from the Young Pioneer organization of the Soviet Union (like the Boy Scouts, but for communists) presented American ambassador Averell Harriman with a handcarved wooden plaque of the Great Seal of the United States as a "gesture of friendship," to commemorate the wartime collaboration between the two nations. Harriman, the consummate diplomat, decided to hang the plaque on the wall of his study in Spaso House, the residence of the US ambassador in Moscow.

As well as really tying the room together, it also provided the Soviet Union with what might go down as the greatest signals intelligence (SIGINT) operation in history. Inside the Great Seal (which is now colloquially known as "The Thing") was a device known as a passive cavity resonator, a special type of bug that will only turn on when a specific frequency is beamed at it from an external transmitter. You know how in the movies, when the good guys are searching for bugs, they wave some kind of wand thing around the room to see if their gadget makes a beepbeep noise? Well, that's an effective technique, but only if you are looking for *active* listening devices—ones that are constantly sending out an electromagnetic signal for you to detect. A passive listening device, like The Thing, isn't sending out anything unless it has been turned on. So as long as the Soviets wait for the embassy security teams to sweep the ambassador's study before they fire it up, The Thing will remain undetectable.

Which it did for *seven* years.

From 1945 to 1952, the Soviets listened in to some of the most important diplomatic, political, military, technological, and economic conversations of the early Cold War. Think about all that happened during this period: Churchill's Iron Curtain speech, the Truman Doctrine, the Marshall Plan, the establishment of Israel, the Berlin Airlift, the formation of NATO, the formation of West Germany, the Alger Hiss trial, Mao's takeover of China, the testing of the first Soviet atomic bomb, the beginning of the Korean War, the conviction of Julius and Ethel Rosenberg for passing atomic secrets to the Soviets. There's more, but you get the point. Each of these monumental events was almost certainly discussed by top American officials in the ambassador's residence. And each one of those discussions was almost certainly captured for Soviet intelligence by The Thing.

I have to tip my cap to the Russians on this one. They took the Americans to the cleaners. Worse yet, it was only blind luck that led to the discovery of The Thing in 1952. A radio operator at the British embassy stumbled upon the signal at the exact time the Soviets had activated it. He didn't mean to, it just happened.

And fortunate for the Americans. Spaso House remains the official residence of the US ambassador to Russia, so The Thing could still be listening to the most secret of conversations even today if he hadn't.

Not that it ever really had to. The Soviets created numerous different ways to eavesdrop on embassy conversations. Some weren't discovered until far too late.

In 1964, American officials found forty different bugs hidden throughout the foundations of their Moscow embassy. Though they had long suspected the presence of bugs, they never found any until they started breaking down walls. No one knew how long they had been listening, but rust on the bugs suggested they probably weren't recent installations.

Then, in 1984, Americans discovered Soviet transmitters hidden inside typewriters in use by US diplomats since 1982. The transmitters picked up the sounds of documents typed by embassy staff and sent the information to antennas hidden in the embassy walls. Those signals were relayed to a listening post outside, and then Soviet analysts used the distinct sound of each keystroke to reconstruct the secret document.

When the United States decided to build a new embassy in Moscow in 1969, Soviet intelligence saw a unique opportunity to literally *build listening devices into the foundation of the embassy.* Soviet workers were able to emplace eavesdropping devices in pillars, beams, and floors of the building, all while it was under construction. These were fully uncovered by 1985—before any real damage had been done—but it was years before a consensus could be reached on what to do with the new embassy building, now sardonically nicknamed the "Great Transmitter." In 1988, President Reagan suggested demolishing the building and starting from scratch, but a year later the newly inaugurated Bush administration reconsidered, and a middle ground was reached. At a cost of $240 million, the US embassy in Moscow was taken apart piece by piece and rebuilt. The top two floors were replaced completely, with four new extremely secure floors, built by American workers, using materials shipped over from the United States. Crisis averted … at least as far as we know.

But surely America would have tried to settle the score? And they did … but not with quite as much success as their opponents. The plan was called Operation Monopoly, and it would take advantage of the new Soviet embassy, whose construction was near completion in the late 1970s. The compound site in Northwest DC's Mount Alto neighborhood was 350 feet above sea level, and had a clear line of sight to both the White House and the Capitol—useful for sightseeing, as well as electronic eavesdropping. During the Nixon administration, when the planning for the new location began, officials from the NSA, CIA, and the FBI all spoke out against the embassy's favorable geography. We don't know exactly why, but someone in the government overrode those objections.

So they moved on to Plan B. If the Soviets were going to get their ideal embassy location in DC, the Americans could at least take full advantage of their presence. In 1977, the FBI and the NSA began digging an underground tunnel to tap into the communications systems and the physical infrastructure—the rooms themselves—of the Soviet embassy. They used several houses in the area, secretly purchased by the FBI, as discreet observation posts, and one house as the starting point for the tunnel. To maintain cover, two FBI agents, pretending to be a young married couple, moved into the tunnel house to keep the neighbors (and the Russians) from getting suspicious.

That didn't really work: Most of the neighbors knew something was up. One of the FBI houses always had its shutters drawn, and no mail was ever delivered—yet neighbors watched people come and go through a rear entrance (almost as if they were on shifts …). Every so often, someone would see a telephoto lens sticking out of one of the windows that faced the embassy. Neighbors complained of poor TV reception (in the days before cable or satellite TV) and that from time to time their phones would mysteriously go dead for short stretches of time—like someone was messing around with the phone lines.

While the FBI was trying (unsuccessfully) to keep a low profile above ground, the NSA was running into its own subterranean issues. One problem was obvious: How do you get rid of all that dirt from digging the tunnel without anyone noticing? This was actually less of an issue than you might think. The embassy itself was still under construction at that time. There were trucks, and cranes, and girders, and pallets of building materials, and (of course) big piles of dirt. At night, once the construction workers had gone home and embassy security was less alert, the tunnel dirt could be secretly added to the existing piles from the embassy's construction.

A much bigger issue was that no one really knew where the tunnel would come up into the Soviet embassy. The NSA/FBI team had the plans for the building, but they had no idea what each room would be used for. As one FBI agent who worked on the operation said, "It might end up being a Xerox room or a storage room. What you want is a coffee room where people talk. Or a secure room where they think no one can hear them." It was a crapshoot, and all the US intelligence agencies could do was hope for the best.

And since you are this far into this book, you know "the best" is not what happened.

Interestingly, Monopoly's failure had nothing to do with the problems outlined above. Sure, the neighbors suspected something, and if it was that obvious to untrained civilians, Soviet counterintelligence probably could have figured it out as well. And it wasn't even the problems associated with digging the tunnel—which also included periodic flooding and glitchy eavesdropping equipment.

Notice I said failure—not cancellation.

It was a spy. One of the most wicked, corrupt scumbags

in the history of intelligence had tipped off the Soviets to the secret program. This sad excuse for a human betrayed his country and rendered useless an ambitious intelligence operation that cost the American taxpayers hundreds of millions of dollars. His name is Robert Hanssen. And when he wasn't working as an employee of the FBI, he was working as an asset for the KGB.

For most of his FBI career (which spanned from January 1976 until his arrest in 2001), Hanssen worked in the Bureau's Intelligence Division (later renamed the National Security Division). Because of his job, he had access to classified information relating to the foreign intelligence and counter-intelligence of not just the FBI, but just about every other US intelligence agency as well, most notably the NSA, CIA, and DIA. According to Count 1 of his indictment, Hanssen

did knowingly and unlawfully combine, confederate, and agree with other persons, both known and unknown to the Grand Jury, including officers of the KGB/SVR [SVR is the successor agency to the KGB], to knowingly and unlawfully communicate, deliver, and transmit to foreign governments, specifically the Union of Soviet Socialist Republics (USSR) and its successor, the Russian Federation, and to those foreign governments' representatives, officers, and agents, directly and indirectly, documents and information relating to the national defense of the United States, with intent and reason to believe that the same would be used to the injury of the United States and to the advantage of the USSR and its successor, the Russian Federation, such communication, delivery and transmission resulting in the identification by a foreign power.

It goes on forever. But it's Count 13 of the indictment that we should pay special attention to. On September 25, 1989, at a dead drop site in Canterbury Woods Park in Fairfax, Virginia, Hanssen transmitted to the Soviets "Documentary material containing details of a United States program of technical penetration of a particular Soviet establishment, which information was classified TOP SECRET/SCI [Sensitive Compartmented Information] and directly concerned communications intelligence."

This is our Operation Monopoly. Hanssen gave it up in 1989. The (now) Russian embassy didn't even open until 1994. We didn't know it, but the scheme was doomed from the beginning.

AND THEN WHAT?

To avoid the death penalty, Robert Hanssen pleaded guilty to fourteen counts of espionage and one count of conspiracy to commit espionage. He is currently serving fifteen consecutive life sentences at a federal "supermax" prison near Florence, Colorado (known as ADX Florence, or alternately as "the Alcatraz of the Rockies"). Joining Hanssen at ADX Florence are Zacarias Moussaoui, the socalled twentieth hijacker of 9/11, Faisal Shahzad, the perpetrator of the 2010 Times Square car bombing attempt, and Ramzi Yousef, mastermind of the 1993 World Trade Center bombing (and uncle to 9/11 mastermind Khalid Sheikh Mohammed). Don't forget the Unabomber, Ted Kaczynski. Timothy McVeigh, who carried out the 1995 Oklahoma City bombing, was housed at ADX before he was sentenced to death in 1997 and transferred to federal death row. McVeigh's coconspirator, Terry Nichols, is still there, serving 161 life sentences. One of the most recent arrivals is Dzhokhar Tsarnaev, the perpetrator of the Boston Marathon bombings.

Hanssen and the others are held in what is known as "administrative segregation." They are confined in a specifically designed singleperson cell for twentythree hours a day. For that last hour, they are brought out of their cells to shower and exercise. Then back in their cells for another twentythree hours. What a horrendous way to live.

And you thought this story wouldn't have a happy ending.

But what about the tunnel? Since we didn't know about Hanssen, we still finished it and put it to use. One of the questions that still remains is whether the Soviets/Russians were able to use the knowledge of the tunnel to their advantage. One thing they *could* have done is to pass disinformation along as though it were real intelligence. While there is no direct evidence of this, some analysts have argued that the possibility warrants serious consideration.

But did the tunnel provide the Americans any kind of useful intelligence? Probably not. According to John F. Lewis, the former assistant director of the FBI, Operation Monopoly was a bust.

In the 1990s, the FBI decided to seal the entrance to the tunnel—but not fill it in completely. When asked why they decided to seal it off at all, Lewis quipped, "Of course you'd want to seal it up. How would you like to be living in the house and suddenly the Russians walk in?"

When Russia's ambassador to the United States, Yuri Ushakov, was asked about the tunnel, he couldn't resist sticking it to the FBI: "If we find it, perhaps we can use it as a sauna."

Every so often, there is a story in the *Washington Post* or one of the local magazines about Operation Monopoly and the secret tunnel in Glover Park. The FBI has never fully acknowledged the locations of either the observation houses or the specific house that held the entrance to the tunnel. Maybe you could live in them one day and not even know it. There are a lot of people who *think* they know. At the International Spy Museum, we *think* we know. Maybe, maybe not.

11

OPERATION HOUSE PARTY

In 2003, a research team in the Department of Biochemistry at Oxford University published a study called, "The Genetic Legacy of the Mongols." This was a scholarly article, published in an academic journal, so you'll have to excuse the understated title. Despite its humble opening, the article made a bold argument: 16 million men living in the world today are direct descendants of Mongol conqueror Genghis Khan. That's about 0.5 per cent of the entire male population—or 1 in every 200 men *on the planet*. Even more stunningly, the study concludes that 8 per cent of all men living in the region spanning from the Pacific Ocean to the Caspian Sea—which covers most of Asia—are Genghis's great, great, great, great (and so on) grandsons. So 1 out of every 12 or 13 men living today, in much of the world's most populous continent, share some DNA with the famous Mongolian leader.

When I first read this study, I had a lot of simultaneous thoughts, the first of which was—what with all this fathering, how did he find time to do *anything* else?

Because Genghis Khan was a very busy man. Among his other achievements: building the largest contiguous land empire in history. An empire that his sons and grandsons and great-grandsons ruled for generations. They conquered areas in Asia, the Middle East, and Eastern Europe. They beat the Great Wall, crossed hundreds of miles of inhospitable desert, crossed mountain ranges of over twenty thousand feet, smashed the best forces the Arab and Eastern European world could throw at them, and did it without breaking a sweat.

You might be tempted, then, to assume Genghis's army always vastly outnumbered his enemies—that the Mongol hordes just swept across the steppes of Asia, overwhelming everyone and everything they encountered, through sheer size alone.

Don't give in to the temptation. If you do, I can promise you your friends will mercilessly mock you for your lack of knowledge of thirteenth-century Asian military history (that might just be my friends, but why take the chance?). The Mongol forces under Genghis Khan (and his offspring) were almost *always* outnumbered. And not just a little bit. Significantly outnumbered: often by five to one. For any lesser leader, this would be an insurmountable obstacle to victory.

Not Genghis. He didn't care about how many more men you had.

So why was he so successful? Well, it's a little bit of this, a little bit of that, and a whole lot of something I'll get to shortly. But first:

1. Exceptional communications—The Mongols used fast riders and a system of relay stations to pass messages from the battlefield to Genghis, and vice versa. This also allowed the Mongols to execute coordinated

attacks from multiple directions, including from the rear.

2. Adaptation—The Mongols were nomadic people, and didn't have much experience in attacking large walled cities or fortresses. Fortunately, they were quick learners. Under Genghis's guidance, they adapted technologies such as siege weapons from the Chinese, Persians, and Arabs. From these same cultures they also learned siege strategies, such as blockades to cut off supplies, rerouting streaming bodies of water to flood towns and supply points, and even nascent biological warfare—catapulting dead animals over the walls and into cities to spread disease.

3. Ridiculously good intelligence operations—Genghis Khan and his offspring developed intricate spy networks that spent weeks and months before an attack probing enemy defenses, collecting intelligence on enemy logistical support (and how to cut it off), and analyzing political, economic, social, and military strengths and weaknesses. They were particularly adept at what we today call "Geospatial Intelligence," or GEOINT. This meant collecting and analyzing intelligence about supply sources and escape routes, mapping roads, understanding local weather patterns, and understanding enemy topography. Cartography was a key component to Genghis Khan's success. Scholars made detailed maps of all of the areas already under Mongol control, and interrogators worked to produce detailed reports of unconquered lands from captured prisoners. This also meant using merchants

(most notably Venetian merchants) to provide to them strategic intelligence from far-off places that might one day fall into the crosshairs of the Mongol leader. According to sources, the Venetian merchant network allowed the Mongols to create detailed maps of all of Hungary, Poland, Silesia, and Bohemia, long before the Mongol horde got anywhere near Eastern Europe.

4. And last, but very much not least—the Mongols under the leadership of Genghis Khan were *masters* of deception. To hide their numerical inferiority, they employed multiple tactics, including building dozens (or more) fake campfires at night to trick the enemy into miscounting the Mongol forces, placing straw soldiers on spare horses to make the army look larger, sometimes putting children and old women on horses to do the same (since from a distance it was impossible to tell the heights of the "warriors"), and tying brooms and sticks to the tails of their horses so that they would kick up a disproportionate amount of dust—all so the army would appear to be many times the size it actually was. The Mongols also would send some of their men, dressed as civilians, into towns they were about to attack to breathlessly inform the townspeople about the "massive" horde of Genghis Khan's bloodthirsty soldiers. Reportedly, several towns along the Mongol advance surrendered without a fight, afraid to stand up to Genghis and his multitudes.

But if battle couldn't be avoided, Genghis and crew had

another, devastating, deception tactic up their sleeves. It was called a "feigned retreat." In the midst of battle, the Mongol army would turn around and move rapidly away from the fighting—as though they were retreating. The enemy would think it had won the day, and enemy commanders would order their men to pursue the Mongols and finish Genghis off for good. The enemy forces would break cohesion. They would naturally pursue at different speeds (fast runners vs slow, faster horses vs slower and so on), and this would cause their ranks to divide and spread out. Commanders would have a hard time reining in the bloodlust of their men, and many would disobey orders and get out ahead of the main body.

At which time, the Mongols would strike—turning their forces around to engage the now discombobulated and sprawling enemy army. They didn't stand a chance.

All of this made Genghis Khan history's pound-for-pound champion of deception. He held the belt, won the prize, received the accolades, and accomplished the fame and fortune that comes with being the best of the best.

He was undefeated and undisputed for hundreds of years.

… Until the Second World War, when British Intelligence decided to challenge him for the title.

People today refer to it in several ways: The "Twenty Committee." The "Double-Cross System." The "XX System" (which works for both—XX as in double-cross, and XX as in the Roman numeral for 20). But it doesn't really matter what you call it, its purpose was still the same: to catch enemy spies and use them to really (really) screw with the minds of the Germans. Disinformation and deception, on steroids.

How good were they at their jobs? Well, consider this: Each and every spy the Germans sent to the UK during the war gave themselves up, or were captured.

Every. Single. One.

Some of them were given the chance to stay out of prison by working for the British. They were "turned" and used against the Germans as double-agents.

Once turned, many of the German spies were used to send disinformation back to Germany. The British got the Germans to believe this false intelligence by mixing in real information, but usually too late, or sometimes too vague, to be useful. Because some of the information turned out to be real, the Germans assumed they had a solid source of intelligence. A great example of this is the Allied invasion of North Africa (Operation Torch). The British allowed the real intelligence about the operation to be leaked to the Germans—just too late for them to do anything about it. The Germans thought they had been given great information, but they were unlucky to have it take so long to get to them. The trap had been set.

This deception operation continued throughout the war, and had a number of significant successes, including deceiving the Germans about the accuracy and efficacy of their V-1 and V-2 missile systems. Although many of the V-1 (a cruise missile) and V-2 (a ballistic missile) salvos were missing their targets, sometimes substantially, the British-controlled German spies reported direct hits on key British strategic targets. So the Germans kept firing them. And the German missiles kept landing in the middle of empty fields. The V-1s even had radio transmitters that showed they were landing short of their intended targets, but they trusted their human intelligence assets so much, they ignored the contradictory technical data. Oops.

The "intelligence" passed along by the turned spies was so "good"—and the spies themselves became so trusted by the German government—that German intelligence stopped sending agents into the UK entirely. Since the ones who were already there were doing such a great job, why would you need any more?

The Twenty Committee, and its roster of double-agents, worked under the command of the London Controlling Section (LCS), which was in charge of all military deception operations during the war. In 1943, the LCS launched what many have called the most successful deception operation in history: Operation Bodyguard. The name of the operation was chosen because of something Winston Churchill had said to Stalin: "In wartime, truth is so precious that she should always be attended by a bodyguard of lies," and it was designed to fool the Germans into thinking the location for the invasion of Europe would *not* be the Normandy beaches. The Bodyguard operation was multifaceted—it had a lot of moving parts. But two of the most important were a deception scheme designed to make Hitler and the Germans think that General George Patton was leading the invasion with an army (the fictitious First US Army Group) staged across the English Channel from the French city of Calais. In fact, there was no army—Patton was in charge of nothing. He was a decoy.

The second important element were the double-agents. Throughout the planning of the operation, the Twenty Committee agents sent word back to Germany that the invasion of Europe would take place at the Pas de Calais. They also exaggerated the size of the Allied armies, which included reinforcing the Patton ruse across from Calais. One of the agents, Juan Pujol García (Codename: GARBO), sent hundreds of messages to the Germans between the beginning of 1944 and D-Day, all designed to deceive the Germans about the true plans of the Allies.

And it worked. Amazingly well.

Even after thousands upon thousands of Allied troops landed on the beaches of Normandy, Hitler insisted the main attack would still come at Calais. Twenty-one German Army divisions were held back at Calais for all of July and August (instead of being plowed into the vulnerable Allied beachhead in Normandy), because the German High Command believed deep in their hearts that the *real* invasion would come there. Some reports indicate that the Germans actually *reinforced* the Calais region, and there were more German troops there two months after D-Day than there were on June 6.

What else made this deception one of the best, if not *the* best? Even after it was clear the main invasion was at Normandy, and not Calais, the Germans *still* didn't believe they'd been duped. For his "service" to the Führer, Juan Pujol García was awarded the Iron Cross, which was normally given only to soldiers who showed heroism in combat, and required Hitler's personal authorization. Agent GARBO was also given an MBE by the king for his real service, making him likely the only person to be awarded such high-level decorations from *both* sides in World War II.

British deception in World War II was a work of art. It was a thing to behold, with unparalleled success on multiple fronts.

You might be tempted to think, then, that something so refined, so impactful, so ... perfect, would be continued after the war ended. It didn't cost a lot of money, and you weren't building anything if you didn't need to. It would just be a group of people brainstorming ideas to keep the British on top of the deception game. Why lose all of the institutional knowledge? Why forget all the hard-won lessons of the war? It would make complete sense to maintain this kind of unique capability.

Of course it would. And, of course, the British didn't do this.

Like everything else at the end of the war, the London Controller Section was reduced to a skeleton staff—and would have been eliminated entirely if it wasn't for some highly placed benefactors. As it was, by 1946, the LCS constituted a whopping three people, one from each of the military services.

And just like everything else at the end of the war, the LCS was hastily staffed up again once it became apparent the West would be engulfed in a Cold War with the Soviet Union. Once it was resurrected from the (near) dead, it took the LCS some time before they figured out how they could be useful. It was clear, however, that deception would need to fit into Britain's primary strategic philosophy of the Cold War—deterrence. Thus, the conversations at the LCS centered on this fundamental question: How can we use deception to deter the Soviets from launching an attack on the UK?

There was not one answer, but many. Exaggerate the strength of British weapons; exaggerate Britain's willingness to use them early in any war; leak false information about advances in aircraft design, anti-aircraft weapons, submarines;

the production of fissile material for atomic bomb development; the development of a death ray; the idea that Britain would disperse its army and industries throughout the Commonwealth in case of war; a plan to protect airbas—

Wait, wait, wait. Hold on a second! What did you say?!

A plan to protect airbases? Dispersal of industry? Submarines?

No. Not those. You know *exactly* what I'm getting at.

Oh, the death ray?

Yes. The death ray.

Well, since you insist …

The death ray concept, as crazy as it sounds, seemed to get serious consideration toward the end of the 1940s. The idea was straightforward: once the Soviets develop atomic weapons (which they are certainly going to within a short period of time), can we make them question their usefulness? Put another way, can we make the Soviets believe we have already developed a *better* weapon than the atomic bomb, one that makes their new toy obsolete?

The deception project was named HOUSE PARTY, which was also assumed by the committee that was tasked with developing all strategic deceptions against the USSR. The idea was this—disseminate the idea that during the British research into atomic weapons in World War II, scientists discovered a way to build a special weapon, a ray of some sort (what the ray was made of is not clear, but since lasers were not developed until the late-1950s, we can assume it was something akin to a radar beam) that could destroy a target up to a mile away. The Soviets would hear about this new weapon through strategic leaks from those officials in the know. They would also hear about this new weapon through lower-level, and unauthorized British personnel, who would themselves be deceived by the LCS. Thus, this was an operation that would actually depend on British citizens passing along classified information to the Soviets. It's just that the information would be pure hogwash.

The planners also decided they needed to build physical infrastructure to back up their deception plan—facilities, personnel, materials. Or at least draw up the plans for the infrastructure that would be required for the operation. Plans that could later be leaked.

But (you might ask), why in the world would the Soviets believe the British could develop a death ray, and one that could counteract their eventual nuclear arsenal? This seems fantastical, or less euphemistically, completely insane.

But, be careful. Thinking this way is understandable, but it is only because you have historical hindsight at your disposal. We *know* there is no magic death ray, in 1950 or 2019. We know that wasn't developed by the British, the Americans, the Soviets, or anyone else.

But they didn't. And the advance of science at the time must have felt breathtaking for those paying attention. Just a decade earlier, no one but a handful of scientists would have believed a single bomb could destroy an entire city. Just a decade earlier, no one but a handful of engineers would have believed an airplane could fly without a propeller. Or radar could detect incoming aircraft. Or computing machines could calculate numbers at speeds hundreds, or thousands, or even hundreds of thousands of times faster than people could. This was a time of great innovation. Of sky's-the-limit dreaming. Of believing that if you could conceive of it, you could make it. Just look at the science-fiction of the 1950s to get an idea of what so many people thought the very-near future would look like.

The death ray wasn't that farfetched, in this context.

So why, then, didn't we hear about this secret weapon? Why didn't the Soviets cower with fear at the scientific and technical prowess of the mighty British death ray? Why was this idea scrapped and sent to the dustheap of "almost was"?

It was primarily because the British discovered that deception operations against the Soviets would be far more difficult than deception operations against the Germans in World War II. For one thing, deception, at its heart, is a psychological operation: it's reliant on a deep understanding of one's target. You need to know how your adversary thinks, what makes them tick, what stimuli they will respond to. You need to know how to mess with their mind. And the British knew the Germans. They knew just about everything they could about their World War II enemies. There was a shared culture and a shared history. There were deep ties between the leadership, the military, the people. The British understood the German mind—and took full advantage.

The Soviets, however, in the words of Churchill, were a "riddle, wrapped in a mystery, inside an enigma." There was very little shared culture, history, or familial ties. Despite fighting on the same side in the war, the Soviets shared very little with their British and American allies. It is hard to deceive who you don't know.

Also, the Soviets were well aware of the British use of deception in World War II, and so they were already on guard against falling for it themselves. There would be a good chance they wouldn't bite.

Not that the British would know if they didn't, and that's

a major problem too. The British got immediate and up-to-date feedback on the effectiveness of their deception operations against the Germans from two sources: 1) signals intelligence, collected mainly from their mastery over the German Enigma coding system, and 2) the collection of British double-agents, who could pass along information, from the Germans, that would tell the British their programs were working. Neither of these could be counted on against the Soviets, who had far better communications security than the Germans, and exponentially better counterintelligence. The British did not have the upper hand in the early Cold War spy game, and this meant they would have no idea if their deception was working.

But even if it did work, and worked perfectly, there was no way of knowing if the death ray concept would succeed in deterring the Soviets. The Soviet Union had just walloped the vaunted German Army, they controlled almost all of Eastern Europe, and while the West was disarming and demobilizing after the war, the Soviets maintained much of their wartime power. Death ray or not, they might not have cared.

And then the worst-case scenario: what if they cared, and cared a lot, so much so that they initiated a crash-course research program to develop their *own* death ray? The British weren't entirely sure it couldn't be done. That's what made the deception so potentially effective. It was plausible. What if the deception goes bad, and all of a sudden you are dealing with a death ray gap? It was hard to imagine their American allies wouldn't have been seriously annoyed to find out that not only did the Russians have the atomic bomb, but now they could shoot down American bombs with their death ray—something they *never* would have thought of if it wasn't for the Brits' silly deception operation. Operation House Party was quietly shelved.

AND THEN WHAT?

And then … they had the same idea a couple of years later. In 1954, the Air Defence Committee Working Party of the Chiefs of Staffs Committee met to discuss a proposal by a Lieutenant Colonel S. E. Skey, called "Defence by Deception." The great thing about this proposal is that the document itself is readily available. Which means I can tell you about it using Skey's words.

After explaining that the purpose of the deception operation is to bring the Soviet's "capability of delivery [of nuclear weapons] continuously into doubt," he lays out his idea. Which should sound very familiar:

> The "Eldorado" of scientific fiction has always been some form of "Death Ray." It is probably true that such a conception would never be scientifically possible, but nevertheless it is a popularly held belief. It is suggested that here is a weapon, for example, though perhaps an over-imaginative one, which we might build up as the keystone for our long-term deception.

But, if it's not scientifically possible, then what would be the point?

> It would be necessary to enter wholeheartedly into research on whatever weapon should be chosen, whether with present scientific knowledge it was really imagined to be possible or not. Moreover, it would be highly desirable

that those actually working on the weapon should genuinely believe in its possibility. This would make the deception more convincing, while the research carried out might just conceivably lead to a useful development.

Okay, but how long do we need to keep this up?

Such work would continue over the years [years?!]. The fact that this research was going on would probably not elude the Soviet intelligence, but we could from time to time allow hints to leak out … The major difficulty in this deception would be its maintenance over an indefinite period.

No question, because the longer it goes, the more likely the deception will be revealed.

Clearly only a very small inner ring, at the top, operating the deception, would be aware that it even was a deception. Their work would necessitate the highest ability and a most careful choice of individuals would be necessary.

Got it. But what's the point?

If such a scheme could be effected, then for comparatively low cost, doubts could be continuously maintained in Soviet minds of their ability to deliver their atomic weapons on this country. Such doubts would force them to ever greater technical and economic strain in order to outflank our "weapon," thereby turning the tables on them. Ultimately this strain might become intolerable and lead them to a desire to live peaceably with the democratic world and to settle their differences by negotiation, but in any case atomic attack on the UK would have been warded off.

LTC Skey should be applauded for his imagination, if not his originality. But the idea that the death ray project might lead the Soviets "to a desire to live peaceably with the democratic world and to settle their differences by negotiation" might actually be the craziest thing in this chapter.

PART III

TRULY EXTRAORDINARY TECHNOLOGY

12

PROJECT HABAKKUK

What if you could develop a completely invincible ship? An aircraft carrier impervious to enemy weapons?

You would own the oceans. Nothing the enemy could throw at you would make a difference. You'd sit there and laugh at their feeble attempts to damage your fleet.

This is the dream of every admiral in every country's fleet. The unsinkable ship.

During World War II, the difference in capabilities between Allied land-based aircraft and carrierbased aircraft was significant. Because they needed to be lighter than their landbased counterparts to effectively take off and land on small (by today's standards) aircraft carriers, carrier-based planes had limited range, inferior armament, poorer survivability, and slower speeds. This would be fine if their main opponents were the carrier-based aircraft of their enemies. But they weren't. A major part of the Allied strategy was to use naval aircraft to support ground invasions of distant shores. Which meant that they would be going headtohead with betterarmed, better-armored, faster planes with superior range. Not a good way to win a war.

Then there was the problem of the submarine war in the Atlantic. German Uboats were slicing up Allied resupply convoys crossing the ocean between North America and Europe. When the convoys were close to land, they could count on air cover from nearby landbased aircraft. But in the middle of the Atlantic, it was carrierbased aircraft or nothing.

And that usually meant nothing. Not only were the carriers busy supporting ground actions (like the invasion of North Africa, or the war in the Pacific), but a fat, expensive, poorly maneuverable aircraft carrier would make the juiciest of juicy targets for German Uboats.

So what could be done? Build bigger and stronger aircraft carriers that could launch and retrieve better aircraft.

Sounds rather straightforward. But it was much more difficult in practice.

The most pressing problem was the paucity of steel and aluminum, which couldn't be produced at levels needed for full wartime industry. And what was available was needed for other purposes—like building tanks, bombers, fighters, trucks, destroyers, battleships, landing craft, helmets, rifles, pistols, bombs …

The rest of the war needed the steel and aluminum. Something else would have to do.

In stepped Geoffrey Pyke, an English inventor, journalist, and educator. He was one of the most creative minds of the twentieth century. I'll never do as good a job describing him as English author Henry Hemming did in *The Ingenious Mr. Pyke*:

Shortly before the end of the Second World War, he had collected an unlikely set of lives. Over the past two decades he had been described as everything from eccentric genius to war correspondent, jailbreaker, bestselling author, educationalist, speculator, mass-observer, advertising copywriter, political activist, military inventor and scientist, while for those in MI5, the British Security Service, Pyke was thought to be an undercover Soviet agent who had gone quiet in recent years. In each of these descriptions there was, it would later emerge, at least an element of truth.

His obituary called him "one of the most original if unrecognized figures of the present century." A contemporary proclaimed that Pyke was "one of the greatest … geniuses of his time." A scientist at the time said he "stood out among his fellows like the North Face of the Eiger in the foothills of the Alps." Another: "[He was] the sort of man who would have invented the wheel." Theoretical physicist Lancelot Law Whyte compared Pyke to Einstein, and said his "genius was more intangible, perhaps because he produced not one, but an endless sequence of ideas."

It's no surprise then that, despite having absolutely no military experience (or any other applicable qualifications), Pyke was made the Director of Programmes for the British Combined Operations office, working under the British military's Chief of Combined Operations, Lord Louis Mountbatten, who was one of the men most responsible for the British war effort. According to legend, Pyke walked into Mountbatten's office and told him, "You need me on your staff, because I am a man who thinks." Apparently, that's all it took.

In October 1942, Pyke submitted a plan to Mountbatten to solve the aircraft carrier problem. It was called Habakkuk, and it proposed the construction of cheap, enormous aircraft carriers, capable of launching and retrieving landbased aircraft from the middle of the ocean, thousands of miles from any nearby land base. Such a carrier would be two thousand feet long, three hundred feet wide, and would have walls forty feet thick. It could easily house two hundred Spitfire fighter planes inside its cavernous interior. It would weigh in at two million tons—putting USS *Ford* to shame.

It would also be made of ice.

Pyke's proposal called for using an iceberg, either naturally occurring or artificially made, as a mobile floating airfield. In his mind, ice was the perfect material. It was difficult to damage (as shown by the near invulnerability of icebergs to shellfire), and melted very slowly when properly insulated. And ice, as you'll know if you've ever pushed an ice cube down under the surface of a drink and watched it pop straight back up, doesn't sink.

Pyke's idea had people intrigued. In December 1942, British prime minister Winston Churchill ordered that research on what was now being called the "bergship" should begin with the highest priority. He insisted, however, that the first stage of the research should focus on trying to build the gigantic craft out of an already existing iceberg or ice floe. But this didn't last long. It became quickly evident that nothing natural would be sufficient for the cause. Most of the available ice structures either had too small a surface above the waterline, or they were too thin and brittle to survive the harsh weather and waves of the Atlantic (the thickness of the ice pack even at the *North Pole* was only about three and a half meters).

So they would have to build one. It would have to be

seaworthy enough to withstand nature, have a large enough deck to support air operations, and be able to propel itself and at a high-enough speed to prevent it from drifting in the wind. And, of course, it had to be hard to sink.

After two months of experimentation, it looked as though Geoffrey Pyke's big idea was dead on arrival. Mechanical stress tests had shown that ice was far too brittle to be used to build a combat-ready warship. As a structural material, it was too unreliable under pressure—it was tremendously difficult to predict its reaction to explosives or other modern weapons. Scientists were extremely frustrated by conflicting data. In several tests, it was determined that ice could handle about 22.5 kilograms of stress per square centimeter before rupturing. But then every so often, an ice beam would rupture at only 4.9 kg/cm^2.

The verdict was in: Ice wasn't safe as a construction material. It couldn't be trusted.

But as Pyke and the British military and civilian leadership digested this sad news, a discovery from the other side of the Atlantic rekindled the spirits of those hoping to build the bergship. Two chemists at Brooklyn Polytechnic, Hermann Mark and Peter Hohenstein, not incidentally Pyke's former professor and his assistant, announced that the inclusion of a small amount of wood pulp in ice dramatically improved its mechanical properties. Wood pulp is ground spruce or pine wood—essentially the raw material that makes up newspapers. Or papier-mâché. Mark and Hohenstein named their new discovery after the inventor of the bergship project: pykrete.

Pykrete was a game changer. A 15 percent mixture of wood pulp frozen into ice was exponentially superior to regular ice. You could hit a chunk of pykrete *with a hammer* and it wouldn't break. You could shoot it with a gun. Nothing. A bullet would penetrate the same distance into pykrete as it would into a cement block. A one-inch column of pykrete could support the weight of a car. And it takes *much longer* than normal ice to melt. Best of all, it still floats.

Speaking of shooting guns at pykrete, one of the best anecdotes of this story apparently occurred at the Quebec Conference in August 1943. All of the bigwigs of the western part of the alliance were there: FDR, Churchill, and all of their civilian and military leadership (Stalin was invited, but could not attend). During one of the meetings, Lord Mount-batten pulled out a chunk of ice and a block of pykrete to show the British and American admirals and generals the potential of the new material. He drew a pistol and blasted the block of normal ice. It did what you'd expect, shattering into hundreds of pieces. Then he shot the pykrete. Not only didn't it shatter, but the bullet just bounced off the material and almost hit American admiral Ernest King, Chief of Naval Operations.

The demonstration was ill-advised, foolish, and almost deadly. But it worked. Roosevelt, Churchill, and the military brass were convinced, and ordered Mountbatten to give Pyke the blessing to begin producing and testing large amounts of pykrete in secret. Pyke had already set up shop in the rear of a refrigerated meat locker in London, hidden behind a row of frozen dead animals. British commandos disguised as butcher's assistants guarded the experiments, and when Mountbatten visited to check on progress, he too had to disguise himself (as a lowly civilian) to maintain operational security.

At the same time, the Engineering Division of the British National Physical Laboratory worked on strength tests, and the Road Research Laboratory of the Department of Scientific and Industrial Research investigated pykrete's explosive resistance. All of this was done under the general direction of the Department of Scientific Research of the British Admiralty. And all of the testing was successful.

With laboratory (and meat locker) experimentation and production completed, and with the requisite signoff from the British and American leadership, it was time to scale up the project. But where, oh where, could they perform the scaled testing? You needed something far enough away from the war to keep the experiments safe from German guns (and spies), remote and spacious enough to give you the room to conduct large experiments without giving away the secret (the Thames River wouldn't do), and cold enough to do the yearround testing on your bergship (so Miami was out of the question).

Jasper National Park in Alberta is the largest national park in the Canadian Rockies, spanning more than fortythree hundred square miles. Even in its warmest month (July), the temperature rarely reaches 21 degrees Celsius. It's big, it's cold, it's remote. It's perfect.

Two lakes, Patricia Lake and Lake Louise, were used for testing, the Patricia Lake tests focused on the problems that might be encountered during the construction of the bergship, and on making scientific observations regarding the behavior of pykrete in the middle of summer (which might sound obvious—it melts—but it was important to know the thermal properties of ice at very specific levels). To do this, the team constructed a "small" prototype bergship—sixty feet long, thirty feet wide, and weighing a thousand tons. Apparently the secrecy of the project was so great that most of the workers (largely conscientious objectors who refused to fight in the war) had no clue what they were working on.

The really fun stuff happened at Lake Louise. It was the job of the Louise team to determine the strength of the ice itself. This meant blasting it with artillery and bombs, and trying to blow holes in the sides with torpedoes. According to legend, when Lord Mountbatten visited the site, he decided to test things for himself. He pulled out a shotgun (somehow he always seemed to have some kind of firearm lying around) and tried to take a chunk out of the side of the pykrete block. To his smug amusement, the stunt didn't make a dent.

But Mountbatten wouldn't be smiling for long. The testing at Lake Louise exposed the project to an unfortunate truth: To make the bergship impervious to bombs and torpedoes, the hull would have to be at least *thirty-five feet thick*. For comparison, the belt armor on an *Iowa*class battleship of World War II was 12.1 *inches* thick. This would mean a need for the manufacture of 1.7 million tons of pykrete, just for a single ship. According to a report written just following the end of the war, to produce this much pykrete would have required a manufacturing plant covering a hundred acres of land—more than seventy-five football fields, or about the size of Vatican City. As a result, a single full-sized bergship would cost more to produce (in money, labor, machinery, and other resources) than an entire fleet of conventional aircraft carriers.

And yet if Habakkuk was the only possible way to win the war, then no amount of money or resources was too much. Right?

It wasn't, and that's what really led to the project's demise in early 1944.

Since 1942—when Pyke, Churchill, Mountbatten, and crew were fretting over the Uboat threat in the Atlantic—the Allies had also been hard at work on three key developments. First was the construction of escort carriers and escort warships (usually destroyers) to keep submarine attacks at bay. The second, related to the first, but slightly different, was the dedicated antisubmarine warfare mission of the Allies in the Atlantic. Germany built 1,156 submarines during the war, and 784 (68 percent) were destroyed. Of the forty thousand or so German submariners, almost thirty thousand were killed, an attrition rate of nearly 75 percent. Finally, a dedicated code-breaking effort in Poland, Britain, and the United States had finally cracked the German Enigma machine. This allowed resupply convoys to avoid areas in which German Uboat wolf packs stalked their prey.

Across the board, things had dramatically changed for the better. The range of combat aircraft had increased so much due to the introduction of new fuel tanks that it had become possible to provide air cover for most of the Atlantic with just land-based aircraft. This was particularly true once Portugal gave the Allies permission to use its airfields in the Azores archipelago in the midAtlantic. The Pacific was covered also, as the Allied island-hopping campaign kept creeping closer to the Japanese main islands. It seemed increasingly likely that an invasion of Japan could be successfully conducted without the use of massive floating iceberg air bases.

But, unlike many of the plans recounted here, Habakkuk was actually a pretty good idea all told. Its key elements worked, it offered tangible tactical value, and it wasn't disturbingly inhumane. It just wasn't feasible, or, in the end, necessary.

AND THEN WHAT?

The infrastructure for the Patricia Lake tests was abandoned and allowed to sink to the bottom of the ninety-eightfoot-deep lake. In the 1970s, the remains of the experiment were rediscovered by some vacationing scuba divers, to the delight of the Archeology Department at the University of Calgary. In 1988, the Underwater Archeological Society of Alberta marked the test site find with an underwater monument. But if you want to commemorate the ambitious project that almost was without getting wet, you can visit a plaque on the shoreline of the lake, which was put up in 1989 by the National Research Council and the National Parks branch of Canada.

13

TAGBOARD

Kelly Johnson could *see* the air.

Or at least that's how Hall Hibbard, Johnson's boss at the Lockheed Corporation, explained the genius of one of the greatest (if not *the* greatest) aircraft designers in history.

Over more than five decades at Lockheed, Johnson designed (or significantly contributed to the design of) as many as forty groundbreaking civilian and military aircraft. These included the P38 Lightning (the first production aircraft to exceed 400 mph), the Lockheed Constellation (which redefined civilian air travel), the F80 Shooting Star (the US military's first operational jet fighter), the F104 Starfighter (the first fighter to exceed Mach 2, or two times the speed of sound), the C130 Hercules (which is still in operation today—the longest-serving military aircraft in history), the U2 (which is *also* still in operation today), and the A12/SR71 (the first production aircraft to exceed Mach 3).

From the age of twelve, Johnson knew he wanted to design airplanes. In 1933, he got his chance when he joined Lockheed—and immediately announced to his new bosses that the design of their new aircraft, the Model 10 Electra airliner, was going to create dangerous instability in flight. This guy had confidence.

To their credit, the higher-ups at Lockheed didn't send Johnson packing, but instead insisted he put his money where his mouth was: Okay, kid, you think you see a problem. Fix it.

And Johnson did. He redesigned the tail to include a double vertical configuration (resembling an H) that not only resolved the instability issue, but would also become one of the signatures of the company's aircraft for decades to come.

From there, nothing could hold him back. By 1938, Johnson had become Lockheed's chief research engineer. In 1952, he was appointed chief engineer of the company's Burbank, California, plant; in 1956, vice president of research and development; in 1958, vice president for advanced development projects; in 1964, a member of Lockheed's board of directors; and in 1969, senior vice president. He was offered the position of president three times. He turned down each one. All he wanted to do was design airplanes.

In 1955, Johnson and his team created the world's first dedicated spy plane, the U2, just *nine months* after receiving an official contract. It came in on time, and under budget. He followed it up with his second spy plane, the A12/SR—to me, the most gorgeous aircraft ever envisioned.

Then, in 1962, Johnson had an idea. The trickiest part of spy planes was keeping the pilot alive and out of enemy hands. Also, the frailty of the human body limited aircraft performance. You could design only up to the point at which you'd kill the pilot. And, of course, if the aircraft gets shot down, the pilot could be captured, interrogated, paraded in front of the world as a propaganda coup for our enemies. This is exactly what happened in 1960 to American U2 pilot Francis Gary Powers. It was a black eye for the United States, and a propaganda windfall for the Soviets.

But what if we could develop a spy plane without a pilot?

Of course, this is not such a big deal today. Drones are ubiquitous. They're everywhere. They're a core part of military strategies across the globe (and also probably driving you crazy in your local park).

This also wasn't the first time anyone had thought of building an unpiloted vehicle. "Drones" of some sort or another have been around since as early as World War I, when unmanned aircraft were used as crude aerial ramming missiles.

Kelly Johnson's idea, however, was to build the first UAV in history *specifically designed* for intelligence collection. It would eventually be called the D21, and the CIA and US Air Force project to develop it became known as Tagboard.

It would be the most classified project of Johnson's storied career.

The concept behind Tagboard was … well, simple is the wrong word. The drone would be launched off the back of an A12, which would already be traveling at about two times the speed of sound, if not faster. The unmanned vehicle would then fly for up to three thousand miles on its own, at speeds of three and a half times the speed of sound and altitudes of between eightyseven thousand and ninety-five thousand feet. So high and so fast that no air defense at the time stood a chance to shoot it down. It would carry a camera for aerial reconnaissance, but unlike the U2 or A12/SR71, the drone was not designed to bring the film back to base for processing and developing. Instead, once all of the mission's required pictures were taken, the aircraft would eject the film canister, which would be slowed by a parachute until it was plucked out of the air by a specifically modified C130 Hercules. This might sound a little crazy, but it's exactly how the film from the first three American spy satellites was collected. The Corona, Gambit, and Hexagon (the first US spy satellites—and the last to use physical film) all dropped their photographic payload through the atmosphere to be grabbed by waiting aircraft. This process actually *almost* always worked. On one or two occasions, the C130 missed the precious intelligence cargo and it landed in the ocean. But like any good mission, there were contingency plans put in place. In case of a water landing, special flotation devices were attached to the film canister. It would theoretically float on top of the water until it could be successfully recovered. Theoretically.

There was one major difference between the film retrieval process of the early satellites and the D21 drone: Once the drone had ejected its film, the D21 was designed to self-destruct, leaving no evidence of the new American spy technology. The trip would be one-way.

The D21 would be propelled to these extraordinary speeds by what is known as a "ramjet" engine. A ramjet is a special kind of propulsion system that uses the engine's forward motion to bring air into it. The engine compresses that air, combusts it, and then shoots it out the back (as thrust) at a ridiculously high speed. They don't even work at low speeds, and are most efficient at around 2,300 mph (Mach 3).

Kelly Johnson and Lockheed had been playing around with ramjet engines since the 1940s. The experimental aircraft

X7, which operated between 1951 and 1960, used a ramjet engine to reach speeds of Mach 4.3 and altitudes of nearly a hundred thousand feet. The X7 would eventually evolve into the AQM60 Kingfisher system, used as targets to test early American antiballistic missile surfacetoair (SAM) systems. Unfortunately, the Kingfisher was *too* good. It was too fast to shoot down. Eventually the program was canceled, mainly because it made the military look so inept.

One of the trade-offs of all this speed is endurance. Ramjets (at least those built in the 1960s) could only operate for about thirty minutes at a time, so despite their incredible speed, they had a very short range. Johnson, however, didn't care about this problem. The D21 was going to be brought to the edge of the surveillance area by another plane, then set free to fly its mission. It didn't need to go all that far.

Johnson and his team produced a full-scale mockup of the D21 in only six weeks, and then began conducting tests at an area known as Groom Lake (you might have heard of it called by a different name—Area 51). The experiments centered on testing the aircraft's ability to avoid radar detection (these were called RCS tests, for "radar cross section"). The drone had the smallest RCS of anything Lockheed had ever designed. It also underwent wind tunnel testing to make sure the drone could, you know, fly. In March 1963, the CIA and the US Air Force jointly contracted Lockheed to commence development of the aircraft.

The specially modified A12 from which the D21 would be launched was rechristened the M21—the "M" stood for "mother" or "mother ship," and the "D" in D21 stood for "daughter." The A12 only had one seat (the Air Force's SR71 had two), but the modifications that turned the A12 into the

M21 included the addition of a second seat, for the drone's launch control officer. Lockheed eventually built two M21s and thirtyeight D21 drones.

Flight testing began in late 1964. At first, the idea was to see if the M21 could even fly at high speeds with a drone riding piggyback. Satisfied that the awkward configuration would fly, they then moved on to launch testing in the spring of 1966. This was the scary part.

In Kelly Johnson's record of the M21/D21 testing, he admitted that the separation was "the most dangerous maneuver we have ever been involved [with on] any airplane I have ever worked on."

I'm sure the pilots felt great about that.

In fact, during the first actual separation flight, the drone was released from the mother ship and then hung in the air for a couple of seconds before it finally sped off. Yikes.

The second launch went a *little* smoother. On April 27, 1966, the D21 separated from the mother ship and blasted off to Mach 3.3 and an altitude of ninety thousand feet. Brilliant, right? Well, no. After fourteen hundred miles the D21 crashed due to a hydraulic pump failure.

But that's why things get tested. To iron out the kinks. To fix the bugs. To work out the problems we run into on test flights, and to try to predict (and prevent) other issues before they happen.

So on to the next one. The good news is that test number three had absolutely *no* hydraulic problems (fixed!). The aircraft was able to successfully complete the experimental mission's entire 1,840-mile flight distance. It even was able to execute multiple preprogrammed turns.

The bad news was that an electronics failure prevented the

camera system from releasing the film. It doesn't do anyone any good if the drone flies straight, fast, and true, but then doesn't do the one thing it was designed for in the first place: collect aerial intelligence. To be fair, the drone did *collect* the intelligence, but it blew up before it was able to pass it on.

The fourth and final launch from the back of an M21 was a heartbreaking disaster, so I'll stop the sarcastic asides in deference to a brave pilot who gave the ultimate sacrifice for the security of his country. The July 30 test would be slightly different from the others. In the first three tests, the D21 was detached from the mother ship while the M21 was in a slight dive (0.9g—nothing dramatic, but enough to play it safe and provide a better launch angle). The problem was, in real-world missions the crew might not have the opportunity to go into a dive to launch the drone. They might need to stay at altitude to avoid enemy fighters or SAMs. Johnson needed to know if the D21 could successfully separate at level flight.

The answer, tragically, was no, it couldn't. For the first few seconds after launch, it looked as though everything was going according to plan. The D21 was in the process of clearing the back of the mother ship, until it got caught in the shock wave coming off the M21 (remember, both of these aircraft were traveling at more than two times the speed of sound). The drone lost its aerodynamics, rolled 45 degrees, and smashed back into the rear part of the mother ship's fuselage, nearly shearing it in two.

The two men in the M21 were Lockheed test pilot Bill Park and Launch Control Officer (LCO) Ray Torick. As a test pilot, Park had been through aircraft emergencies before (in 1964, an A12's flight controls locked up on him and he had to eject from the plane at an altitude of only two hundred feet), so despite flying at Mach 2 in a plane which is now in two pieces, amazingly, extraordinarily, unbelievably, he didn't panic. Park and Torick remained totally cool. Park and Torick rode their disintegrating airplane as it tumbled out of the sky. When it finally descended to an altitude safe for them to bail out, they ejected over the Pacific Ocean. Park survived, but Torick drowned.

There are several theories as to why Ray Torick did not live to fly another day. One is that he panicked and opened his suit's visor too quickly, allowing the suit to fill with water. I'm not convinced. Ray Torick was a test pilot—and as we've seen, he didn't panic easily. Plus, those suits are extremely buoyant, and unless the suit's body is damaged, it's hard to believe enough water could flow into the helmet to drown someone. Another theory is just that: Shrapnel from either the crash or Torick's ejection damaged the suit. When he hit the Pacific, water came in through the shrapnel holes, and even someone as fit as a test pilot wouldn't be able to overcome the weight of the suit and the ocean. Finally, it's altogether possible that Torick was injured from the crash or the ejection (pilot injuries from ejections are sadly all too common). Although the flight suits are buoyant, if he was severely injured he might not have been able to stay afloat.

Or it could have been a combination of any of these. Unfortunately, we will never know.

The death of Ray Torick was the end of the Tagboard program. It had proven far too dangerous to launch a drone off the back of an aircraft in supersonic flight.

But that wasn't the end of the D21. You couldn't safely launch a drone off the *top* of an airplane, but what if we dropped it from the *bottom* of one? But this wouldn't be another modified A12. Instead, the new D21 program, which was eventually given the code name Senior Bowl, would drop drones using a US Air Force B52 Stratofortress bomber as a mother ship. This, of course, had one major advantage: gravity.

Yet there were still issues to deal with. For one, the B52 is slow. Really slow. And a ramjet needs to be going very fast before its engine can do its thing. The solution was to attach a rocket booster to the drone, which would kick in once the B52 released its cargo. The booster would propel the drone to supersonic speeds, at which point it would detach and the ramjet would take over. Not a bad idea. Maybe it could work …

… but then you'd be reading a different book.

The first time Johnson, Lockheed, and the Air Force tried to launch a D21B (new name, but other than the down versus up launching, same thing), a stripped nut on the B52's wing pylon gave out during the flight and the drone *fell off the plane* before it had reached its launch point. The next series of launches was less embarrassing for Johnson and crew, but most of them were just as unsuccessful. An engine failure here, an electrical problem there, an internal navigation system going kaput. Problems on top of problems. But every so often things would go right. Maybe not all at the same time. Maybe not as perfectly right as the team would have liked. But enough to give it a shot in a real-world scenario.

That's right: This one actually saw action.

Four operation missions were conducted under Senior Bowl in 1969, 1970, and 1971. All of them were flown over the People's Republic of China, and each targeted the Chinese nuclear weapons test facility at Lop Nur, deep inside the Xinjiang Uygar region in the northwestern frontier of China. This was *way* inside China. The region is three times the size of France, and is so remote and isolated it is considered the country's "Wild West." The Chinese detonated their first atomic bomb there in 1964 and their first hydrogen bomb in 1967. It was an important intelligence target for the United States, and the perfect field test for the D21B.

Here's how the four Senior Bowl missions played out:

1. November 9, 1969—A B52H flying out of Anderson Air Force Base in Guam brought the D21B to the edge of the launch point (without it falling off the plane). After a successful drop, the drone flew in the direction of the Lop Nur test facility. So far, so good. The RCS testing really paid off, as the Chinese had no idea what was happening, and they never detected the drone as it began its flight over their airspace. It continued on over Lop Nur ... and then continued on. And on. And on. It was programmed to make a Uturn and head back to the open ocean, but the first operational D21B failed to execute its turn and continued flying until it ran out of fuel and crashed somewhere in the eastern part of the Soviet Union (needless to say, not a great place to lose super-secret technology).

2. February 21, 1970—The mission began as the first: a successful drop, then the drone flew in the right direction (this might not seem like a big deal, but let's give them all the credit we can), no Chinese detection, *and* it actually made the 180degree turn

back to the film drop point. And then it dropped its film, just as it was designed to.

But the parachute didn't deploy correctly, and the film canister hit the Pacific Ocean at terminal velocity. Yes, the canister was equipped with flotation devices in the unlikely event of a water landing, but it wasn't designed for meteoric speeds of descent. The canister, and the Chinese nuclear secrets it contained, were lost to the ocean depths.

3. March 4, 1971—This was as close to a perfect mission as we had. Up until the very end, at least. It started off great: good drop, good direction, no detection, pictures taken, turn made, canister detached, parachute opened!

But the C130 tasked with snatching the descending canister out of the air missed its mark, and the canister splashed down into the Pacific.

But! Since its parachute deployed, the canister landed gently in the water. It had flotation devices for this exact contingency. Everything was still good to go. A US Navy destroyer serving as a recovery ship was already on station and moving in to grab the precious cargo. Absolutely *nothing* could go wrong now … unless the Navy ship runs over the canister.

4. March 20, 1971—The fourth and final mission of the D21 ended in a whimper, much like the program itself. For some reason unknown to the operation's planners, the drone went down over China during its photographic run to Lop Nur.

It took them four months after the final mission to make

a decision, but in July 1971 the CIA formally terminated the Tagboard/Senior Bowl program. The failure of the project to yield results was a major factor, but ultimately it was only one of several reasons for the decision to kill Tagboard. Perhaps a more significant reason was the growing secret— and then later, open—attempt by the Nixon administration to establish a relationship with China. The D21B flights were seen as an unacceptable risk to the possibility of rapprochement between the People's Republic and the United States. And this was especially true at a time when newer and more capable reconnaissance satellites could pick up the slack.

Kelly Johnson was unhappy about the end of his drone project, but he was smart enough to understand the big picture. Still, the news stung a bit: "It was a sad occasion for us all. We will probably see the day when we will greatly rue the decision taken to scrap the program."

AND THEN WHAT?

The remaining D21Bs were secretly shipped out of Lockheed's test facility at Groom Lake and retired to the US Air Force "boneyard" at Davis-Monthan Air Force Base near Tucson, Arizona. In 1977, a civilian journalist just happened upon them accidentally and forced their public acknowledgment. Without this bit of happenstance, we might never have heard about this extraordinary program.

The wreckage of the drone that went down somewhere in the eastern Soviet Union was recovered by the Soviet military. They attempted to reverse-engineer the technology and make their own drone (they called it the Raven, or Voron in Russian), but they saved themselves the eventual anguish and never built the thing. It turns out that the D21B had self-destructed over Siberia. We only found out when in 1986 a KGB officer slyly gave a piece of the drone to the CIA.

The wreckage of the drone from the fourth mission, the one that went down inside China, was apparently recovered by local authorities and then closely studied by the Chinese military. It later wound up at the China Aviation Museum near Beijing, where it was finally put on display in 2010.

Lockheed test pilot Bill Park continued to fly advanced experimental aircraft into the late 1970s. At one point he even landed a U2 reconnaissance plane on an aircraft carrier (which is insanely difficult). But during a test flight of the first Have Blue prototype (the aircraft that evolved into the F117 stealth fighter of Operation Desert Storm fame) in 1978, Park was on approach and beginning to land. At the very moment the landing gear touched the ground, the aircraft unexpectedly pitched up. Park kicked the throttle up and climbed out to circle for another attempt, but the plane had smacked the ground fairly hard and Park's landing gear were no longer operable. After trying in vain to get the landing gear to work, he was forced to climb again and wait until his fuel ran out (if you are going to crash a plane, it's better not to do so with it full of explosive jet fuel). Then he ejected from the plane. He survived the ejection, but suffered a concussion during the violent lurch from the aircraft. He was knocked unconscious (luckily his parachute was designed to automatically deploy), and his limp body smashed against the desert floor. He broke his leg and cracked a vertebra. When the rescue teams arrived, his heart had stopped beating. He was successfully resuscitated, but forced off of flight status. He stayed with Lockheed until his retirement in 1989, finishing his career as director of flying operations at the company's top-secret Skunk Works (for decades led by none other than Kelly Johnson). In 1995, Park was one of five test pilots inducted into the Aerospace Walk of Honor.

It is possible—some might say likely—that the failure of the Tagboard program led to the delay of any full-scale deployment of unmanned systems by the CIA. Of course this is counterfactual, and we have no idea if the D21 had any real impact. But it's hard to imagine how this project could have had a *positive* influence on anyone thinking about increasing the CIA's investment in drone technology. Finally, during the war in Bosnia in the early 1990s, CIA director James Woolsey sponsored the UAV that would eventually be known as the Predator, and reinvigorated the CIA's love affair with drones—twenty years after the cancellation of Tagboard. You don't need more than a quick glance at the front page of the newspaper on any given day to see where that ended up.

14

THE X-20 AND THE MOL

In the fifteenth and sixteenth centuries, prolific inventor Leonardo da Vinci hoped to develop a human-powered flying machine (he also dabbled in painting, architecture, poetry … and apparently mastered karate and the katana too). For research, Leonardo studied birds in flight. He was particularly interested in how birds like the albatross could fly hundreds of miles while only minimally flapping their wings. He sketched the birds, added annotations about their patterns of flight, and carefully studied their aerodynamics.

He didn't know it at the time (although he might have suspected), but Leonardo was on to something. Without being able to define it, or to know the physical principles behind the phenomenon, he was the first to document what would later be called the "dynamic soaring" flight maneuver.

Here's how it works (in a really basic sense): The albatross (and other birds) are able to harness energy by flying through the boundary layer between slower-moving and faster-moving air—difference in wind speed is called wind shear. Traveling in and out of different wind speeds in certain patterns has the potential to provide extra energy. Thus birds, if they are crafty enough, can soar indefinitely, as long as they bounce from shear to shear, picking up energy.

In the 1950s, the US Air Force began development of a top-secret space vehicle that would ride a big rocket into space, and then would come back to Earth under a controlled descent. Fairly straightforward, right? Kind of. Here's the difference: Before it came back down, the space plane would use its wings and its speed to bounce around the world along the upper atmosphere. Boing, boing, boing. Down and up, down and up, until its loss of energy and speed required it to begin reentry procedures. Once inside the Earth's atmosphere, the space plane would glide down to the surface and land.

Now you know why I was telling you about birds (I hope). Same basic concept, isn't it? But instead of wind shear, it's the upper atmosphere. And instead of albatrosses, it's spacecraft. The similarities were so apparent to the developers of the space plane that they decided to name it in homage to the physical principles it exemplified: dynamic soaring. Unfortunately, the obvious portmanteau—and the one they chose—is the … Dyna-Soar.

Setting aside its silly name, the Dyna-Soar didn't just materialize out of very thin, outer-atmospheric air. It is the culmination of a long line of experimental aircraft developed during the Cold War to push the boundaries of human flight. Its immediate predecessor was the North American Aviation X15, which was developed in the mid-1950s. After being dropped from the bottom of a B52 bomber, the X15 rocket plane could reach a maximum speed of Mach 6.7 (4,520 mph) and a maximum altitude of more than sixtyfive miles. It flew so high that the pilots had to wear full-pressure flight suits, similar to what NASA's astronauts would later wear. It flew so high that its wings and rudders were basically useless. It depended on small "reaction thrusters" to maneuver. By 1955, the US Air Force was trying to determine the next step in aircraft evolution. Engineers had been toying with multiple concepts, each designed to address a specific mission need. One was for a rocketpowered bomber, another was for a high-speed, high-altitude reconnaissance plane, and one was called HYWARDS, which stood for "Hypersonic Weapons Research and Development System." Eventually, the Air Force amalgamated these ideas into a single request for a vehicle that might have the capability to do everything, but in *space*. In 1957, they asked for design concepts for their new program, "System 464L." The Boeing Company eventually won the contract, and in 1959 the S464L was rechristened the Dyna-Soar.

The plan was to roll out Dyna-Soar in three stages. Dyna-Soar I would be used for proofofconcept research to test velocity, range, and the ability to use rocket boosters to drive the space plane to altitude. Dyna-Soar II would be focused on the reconnaissance mission. Once the plane reached altitude, the pilot would monitor the operation of several pieces of intelligencegathering hardware, including a high-resolution camera, a side-looking radar, and electronics intelligence sensors. It could spy on ground targets with ease, but could also take a close look at enemy satellites in space. Finally, Dyna-Soar III would be the complete package. It could easily carry out intel missions, but could also be equipped with a nuclear weapons delivery system that could reach anywhere on the globe in a matter of minutes, from any direction, with limited radar visibility, and with little warning of an attack. Flying in space gave you those capabilities. Unlike an ICBM or an SLBM, the Dyna-Soar could be recalled during the mission if the geopolitical calculus changed after launch.

Seven pilots were originally chosen for the program. One of the new pilots was asked to come up with the emergency launch abort procedure, in case one of the rockets used to blast the Dyna-Soar to altitude decided to blow up on the launch pad. The way things were set up, the pilot would be only a hundred feet above the ground while waiting for launch, with the space plane's nose facing straight up in the air. Ejecting from this low height—and since the plane was vertical, ejecting *sideways*—was an insane and almost certainly deadly task. So the pilot had some figuring out to do.

He decided to test things out in another aircraft, a Douglas Skylancer, which could somewhat mimic the conditions on the launch pad—with some imaginative flying. He flew two hundred feet off the ground at almost 600 mph, and then pulled straight up and screamed to eight thousand feet. He flipped the plane around, got it upright, and then softly landed the aircraft. It was a crazy maneuver, and this written description doesn't do it justice. But it proved a point—if the rocket began to explode beneath the Dyna-Soar, the pilot could just kick the plane's engine in gear and blast off as fast as he could. The acceleration of the plane would allow the pilot to escape the fireball below and reach an altitude at which he could roll it over, turn it around, and find a good place to park.

The pilot who discovered this maneuver ended up leaving the program. It's not because he did anything wrong, or that he didn't like the work he was doing, or even that he didn't think the Dyna-Soar was a cool plane.

He just got a better job offer. His name was Neil Armstrong.

The remaining six pilots (I suppose I should be calling them astronauts) assigned to the program were introduced to the public on September 19, 1962. Five of the six were US Air Force pilots, and the remaining one was with NASA and had participated in the X15 program. These were some of the best of the best.

But storm clouds were forming over the project. The problem was that no one seemed to be able to identify the role Dyna-Soar was supposed to play. During the Kennedy administration, Secretary of Defense Robert McNamara questioned the logic of spending hundreds of millions of dollars on a program whose mission parameters could be achieved by other platforms. America's new satellites could take care of the global reconnaissance mission, while spy aircraft such as the U2 and SR71 could pick up any slack left over. ICBMs and SLBMs could maintain strategic deterrence. And NASA's Mercury program was well on its way to answering many of the questions of thermodynamics and human spaceflight that Dyna-Soar was tasked to answer. For a numbers guy like McNamara, it didn't make a lot of sense for the Air Force to spend that much taxpayer money for a space plane just because it was pretty cool.

It's hard to dispute the logic, but it was still disappointing for all involved in the project when, in mid-1962, the Department of Defense renamed the Dyna-Soar the X20. The experimental Xplane designation meant that innovation for the sake of science and knowledge would continue, but the Dyna-Soar would never become a full-scale production vehicle.

And then, despite having spent close to $3 billion in today's dollars ($400 million at the time), in December

1963 McNamara formally dropped the hammer on the X20 project. It had no military mission, and was too expensive to serve only as a research system. It had to go. Its budget was needed elsewhere.

On the same day the Department of Defense announced the cancellation of the X20 program, December 10, 1963, they announced a new initiative for the development of what was called the Manned Orbiting Laboratory (MOL). In a press release, DoD explained their new shiny object: "The MOL program, which will consist of an orbiting pressurized cylinder approximately the size of a small house trailer, will increase the Defense Department effort to determine military usefulness of man in space."

The MOL appropriated the remaining funding set aside for the X20. It would be a huge technological step forward for American ambitions in space. The space station would allow astronauts to conduct observations and experiments for up to a month at a time, before the crew would enter a modified Gemini capsule for their return trip to Earth. At that point, the longest trip in space had been the Soviet Union's Vostok 5, which stayed in space for four days, twentythree hours, and change in June 1963. The design of the MOL system also "permit[ted] rendezvous in space between the orbiting laboratory and a second Gemini capsule, so that relief crews could replace original crews in the laboratory."

A little less than two years later, once the preliminary conversations about budget, logistics, testing, and so on were complete, President Lyndon Johnson announced to the public he had ordered the DoD to "immediately proceed with the development of a Manned Orbiting Laboratory." According to LBJ:

This program will bring us new knowledge about what man is able to do in space. It will enable us to relate that ability to the defense of America. It will develop technology and equipment which will help advance manned and unmanned space flights. And it will make it possible to perform their new and rewarding experiments with that technology and equipment ... We believe the heavens belong to the people of every country ... and we will continue to hold out to all nations, including the Soviet Union, the hand of cooperation in the exciting years of space exploration which lie ahead for all of us.

What a beautiful sentiment. Unfortunately, it was solely for public consumption. In reality, the MOL program was designed to include capabilities for a highly secret set of experiments and collecting vital intelligence from space. The project was called Dorian, and it called for the United States to use the MOL as a manned reconnaissance space station, to gather both imagery intelligence (IMINT—photography) and signals intelligence (SIGINT—in the most basic sense, intercepting communications and other electronic signals).

MOL would require a special (and somewhat unprecedented) partnership among three government entities: the Air Force, NASA, and the National Reconnaissance Office (NRO). It was nominally an Air Force program, and they would provide the manpower for the space station, but the Air Force needed NASA's help to safely bring their airmen to and from the MOL. To do so, the Air Force secured the use of the aforementioned NASA space capsules developed for the Gemini program. These were modified with a hatch on the bottom of the capsule, to allow the MOL crew members to travel through a passageway to the laboratory section of the station—the orbiting "pressurized cylinder approximately the size of a small house trailer." Once their mission was complete (perhaps a month later), the crew would return to the Gemini capsule (with their film and signals intelligence) for the return trip home.

The NRO provided the reconnaissance equipment—the whole reason for MOL's existence—and the rigid security guidelines for the program. The latter already existed for military space projects, so no one needed to reinvent the wheel. It would be as secret as you can get.

Now, it was one thing to have a broad outline of a technology and a general sense of potential mission goals and parameters. It was another to know specifics of what you would like to accomplish. That took some thinking. The Department of Defense set up a working group to brainstorm ideas and identify proposed MOL experiments. Starting with four hundred proposed experiments submitted by various defense and industrial agencies, the working group categorized them into technical areas—optics, infrared, radar, communications, and so on—to figure out the best way to consolidate these ideas into a coherent mission objective. After a first cut, they trimmed the list down to fifty-nine. A second, and final, series of eliminations pared it down to twelve primary (and eighteen secondary) MOL experiments. As well as more predictable ones to do with the collection and analyzing of data, they included "the performance of extravehicular operations peculiar to future military operations" (could people perform actions appropriate to future military operations ... while floating around in space?); evaluating "the astronaut's ability to control the Remote Maneuvering Unit (RMU)" (jetpacks); and investigating "those effects of weightlessness which can potentially compromise mission success". This last one was a pretty big deal. Humans had been to space at this point, but the missions were measured in hours. No one knew how the body would react to a mission longer than five days, let alone one that lasted a month. There was also arguably the most interesting experiment: "To evaluate man's ability to carry out a negation and damage assessment function." This doesn't tell us much, but it's all about checking out other countries' satellites, to see if they are hostile, and if they are, to "negate" them. The document stated that to "incapacitate or physically destroy the satellite as required … it is presently anticipated that negation missiles would use nonnuclear warheads." Which is good. I guess.

Sounds like a solid plan to me. Who could possibly object to a program that has the potential not only to provide insanely highresolution imagery intelligence, but could also give us valuable insight into the abilities of humans to operate in space for an extended period? The US government had already poured significant resources into the project and, as we have seen, thousands of man-hours of plotting and planning future mission parameters. What organization would be so bold as to take on NASA, the NRO, *and* the Department of Defense?

The Central Intelligence Agency. That's who.

The CIA had been responsible for America's first two satellite programs, Corona and Gambit, and was now angling for a new and highly advanced third generation of reconnaissance satellite known as Hexagon. MOL and Hexagon were both extremely expensive, and thus direct rivals for limited funding appropriations. They had similar purposes—spy on the other side—but significantly different capabilities. The Hexagon was designed to capture photos with a resolution of less than two feet. But it could also photograph huge tracts of land in a single pass—thousands of square miles at a time, during a single mission (some of the specifics of its resolution capabilities are still classified). The Hexagon was *big,* and carried sixty *miles* of high-resolution photographic film. The CIA couldn't wait to get it into service.

The MOL, on the other hand, focused on small areas using extremely high resolution—as small as twelve inches. A very narrow scope, but still. Twelve inches. From space.

I suppose it's unkind to blame CIA parochialism and bureaucratic infighting for the end of the MOL program. Unkind, but not unfair. In early 1969, President Richard Nixon decided to cancel the CIA's Hexagon program, citing cost considerations and redundancy concerns (with, of course, the MOL). This sent CIA director Richard Helms into a flurry of action, all aimed at reversing the decision. There could be only one—and it should be Hexagon, not MOL.

Helms and the Agency had anticipated having to fight for their program, and so more than a year earlier they began to prime the proverbial pump. On March 5, 1968, the CIA sent a statement to the DoD expressing the Agency's views. It read, in part, "Mr. Helms, Director of Central Intelligence, has reservations as to the value of better (than one foot) resolution photography for national intelligence purposes. He recognizes that photography with resolutions better than that obtainable by the Gambit3 system would be helpful but does not believe studies conducted to date show that the value of this increased resolution justified the expenditures associated with the MOL Program." To translate the government-speak: It's too expensive and we don't need it. But we *do* need something better than what we have.

The CIA argued that no important Agency estimates of Soviet or Chinese military elements (posture, weapons capabilities, size and composition of forces) would be changed significantly by the heightened resolution of MOL photography. While it would be really cool to have ground resolutions to twelve inches (I'm paraphrasing), it's far too expensive for the mission requirements. Our toy is better than their toy.

And it worked. In June 1969, Nixon changed his mind. He reinstated the Hexagon program and scrapped the MOL. The CIA had won. The United States would launch twenty Hexagons between 1971 and 1986, bringing back key intelligence that according to some analysts helped prevent World War III. With Hexagon-provided intelligence, American intelligence analysts were able to conclusively count numbers of Soviet and Warsaw Pact troops, tanks, aircraft, and ballistic missiles to make sure Moscow wasn't violating arms control treaties.

AND THEN WHAT?

The Soviets had their own version of the MOL, known as Almaz, which actually went into space in the mid1970s. It was less a pure reconnaissance platform (like MOL would have been) and more a battle station in space. Almaz was equipped with a 23millimeter rapid-fire cannon mounted on the outside of the station. The cannon would be aimed by rotating the entire station. Why have a cannon on a space station? Remember when we talked about "negation"?

Finally, the scientists, engineers, and bureaucrats who

worked on MOL were obviously very disappointed with the program's cancellation. But what about those men who had been chosen to fly the missions? They were clearly unhappy, but most didn't give up their dream of going into space. Seven of the seventeen MOL crew members were accepted into NASA's astronaut program. Richard Truly piloted the Space Shuttle *Enterprise,* became the commander of the Naval Space Command as a vice admiral, and then became the administrator of NASA from 1989 to 1992. Robert Crippen piloted or commanded multiple Space Shuttle missions (including piloting the very first one), and from 1992 to 1995 served as the director of the Kennedy Space Center. James Abrahamson reached the rank of lieutenant general (three stars) in the US Air Force, and was appointed the director of the Strategic Defense Initiative (SDI, or "Star Wars") under President Reagan. Robert Herres became a fourstar Air Force general, and rose to become the vice chairman of the Joint Chiefs of Staff.

One MOL crew member, Air Force major Robert H. Lawrence Jr., stands out among these greats. He was the first African-American to be chosen as an astronaut by either NASA or the military. When asked about the significance of his selection, Lawrence was a stoic test pilot through and through: "This is nothing dramatic. It's just a normal progression. I've been very fortunate."

Sadly, he never made it into space. On December 8, 1967, Lawrence was in the backseat of an F104D fighter aircraft while the pilot was practicing a special landing approach called a "flare" (later used during the Space Shuttle program). The pilot misjudged the approach and smacked into the runway, collapsing the landing gear and bouncing the aircraft two thousand feet down the runway, where it hit the ground again. Both Lawrence and the pilot were able to eject, but Lawrence was killed when his parachute failed to deploy. Because of the secrecy surrounding the MOL program, the American public had to wait years to learn of this trailblazing American hero. Finally, in September 1997, in tribute to his outstanding accomplishments as an American space pioneer, the crew of the Space Shuttle *Atlantis* carried his MOL mission patch into orbit. On December 8, 1997, the thirtieth anniversary of his death, Lawrence's name was engraved in the Astronauts Memorial Foundation's Space Mirror at Kennedy Space Center Visitor Complex, which honors astronauts who made the ultimate sacrifice.

15

BRILLIANT PEBBLES

When I was seven years old, my mother and father let me stay up *way* past my bedtime to watch a madefortelevision movie about the aftermath of a nuclear attack on America, called *The Day After*. If you've seen it, you can probably imagine the psychological damage this did to my developing brain, which usually found stimulation through GI Joe cartoons and Bugs Bunny. In fact (whether you want to call this "damage" or not), *The Day After* is the reason for who I am today. It was the catalyst for my interest in (some would say obsession with) nuclear weapons, their history, and the intelligence work surrounding their development, deployment, delivery systems, and global impact.

And I didn't know this at the time, but this movie left a lasting impact on many Americans, from multiple generations. One hundred million viewers tuned in to the broadcast, which is still the record for a TV movie: something like 62 percent of Americans watching TV that evening were watching *The Day After*.

Even President Ronald Reagan was captured in this cultural zeitgeist. Reagan watched the movie several days before its release, and felt strongly affected by the images on the screen. In his diary that evening, he wrote that the movie was "very effective and left me greatly depressed." He even insinuated that the film had changed his perspective on nuclear policy and nuclear war. The Ronald Reagan presidency continues to be politically polarizing, but it's clear to me as a historian that Reagan truly despised nuclear weapons, and especially the threat they posed to the security of the United States. Part of my belief comes from what happened during his negotiations with Soviet leader Mikhail Gorbachev. Ronny and Gorby agreed in principle to dismantle both countries' nuclear weapons arsenals at the Reykjavík Summit meeting in 1986. It didn't happen (obviously). But at least they tried.

When both men realized they might be willing to dismantle the entirety of their nuclear programs, they jumped at the chance. But Gorbachev insisted that Reagan give up research on America's Strategic Defense Initiative (SDI, or Star Wars as it was dubbed by the media). Why would the United States need a missile defense if the Soviet Union had no nuclear weapons? Gorbachev had a point, but Reagan was unswayed. Why would the Soviets care about SDI research if neither side had a weapons program?

We were *that* close. Yet neither man was willing to cede.

Both sides went back to their corners, and the Cold War continued (for a couple more years, at least).

People love to criticise Reagan for Star Wars—which ended up as a trillion-dollar quagmire—but it's clear to me that Reagan truly believed that ballistic missile defence could finally release America from the perpetual, soul-crushing threat of Armageddon. And after Reykjavík, the Reagan administration continued to dump billions of taxpayer

dollars into programs that were so ridiculous we *still* don't
have the technological knowhow *today* to make them work.
Not even close.

Except for one.

It was ambitious, extraordinarily complicated, and obnox-
iously expensive.

They called it Brilliant Pebbles, and it was the best chance
we had.

This chapter is all about the acronyms of Armageddon.
ICBM, MAD, MIRV, SLBM, BMD, SBI, ABM, BaMBI,
NORAD, GPALS, ERINT, HOE, KKV, ERIS, HEDI,
DEW, ALL, THAAD, GMD, MIRACL, LACE, CHEC-
MATE, SBKKV, BPI, SSPK …, and SDI.

I'll try my best to not overwhelm you with them, but it
won't be easy.

The US Army began thinking about missile defense all
the way back in World War II. As the German V2 ballistic missiles started to land in England, the Army scrambled
to figure out a way to stop this terrifying new technology.
They quickly realized it was extremely hard to do. They failed
again and again. Fortunately, the missiles had very little military value outside of scaring English civilians. At that point,
their inaccuracy, coupled with their relatively small explosive
payload, prevented them from having a significant strategic
impact on the war. So the Allies kept their heads down and
rode out the barrage until V2 launch sites could be captured
one by one. One day I hope we will figure this thing out,
they'd say to themselves. One day.

Seventy-plus years later, and we are still hoping. If a ballistic missile came for us this minute, we'd likely resemble our

ancestors in the cold streets of 1940s London: Get your heads down and pray for the best. Maybe we can ride this thing out.

The ballistic missile problem hasn't been solved, but as I'll explain, it's not for lack of trying. Scientists and engineers are still figuring out how to unravel this obscenely complex technological issue. Correction—this is *multiple* complex technological *issues,* each one as daunting as the next.

First, how do we detect a missile launch as quickly as possible? This is far easier today, due to advances in intelligence technology like multispectral and hyperspectral remote imaging from satellites and other platforms. But it's still not perfect.

Second, how can we best track the trajectory of the missile? The sooner we know where it is going, the better. Modern satellites help here too, but aren't without limitations.

Third, how do we differentiate between real ballistic missiles and decoys warheads that are used to confuse our defensive systems? A smart adversary would launch a combination of real nukes and decoys, with the hope that we would expend our limited resources against the fake nukes while the real ones slip through. Or worse yet, our systems, if automated, might freeze up because their computer brains get overwhelmed by the devious deception.

Fourth, how do we hit a ballistic missile, traveling *really, really* fast, with whatever we are using as an interceptor?

And fifth, how do we ensure the destruction of the target missile?

All difficult questions. None with an easy solution. Scientists and engineers rolled up their sleeves and got to work.

One of the easiest ways to deal with several of these problems, scientists thought, was to eliminate the need for pinpoint accuracy with our interceptor. How do we do this? Well, by using nuclear weapons, of course. Fight fire with fire. The bad guys send nuclear-armed bombers or missiles our way, we shoot them down with nukes of our own. Everything in the blast radius goes up in smoke.

This was the concept behind America's first series of surfacetoair (SAM) anti-ballistic missile systems. Building upon the Nike Hercules SAM, which was developed to shoot down enemy bomber formations with a nucleartipped warhead, the Nike Zeus, NikeX, Sentinel, and Safeguard programs were all designed to intercept a *limited* Soviet strategic missile attack with overwhelming force. The problem with all of these systems, however, was that they didn't stand a chance against a dedicated, allout Soviet strike. They could be overwhelmed by the use of radar decoys mixed with hundreds, if not thousands, of real warheads. When multiple independently targetable reentry vehicles (MIRVs—a single booster rocket carrying multiple warheads) were developed in the mid1960s, things got even worse. It was harder and harder to keep the defense in the game. The offense had all the advantages.

And, of course, Nike/Sentinel/Safeguard all called for the United States to actually explode nuclear weapons over its *own territory*. Talk about killing the patient to cure the disease.

Project Defender tried to rectify this. Started in 1958, under the Eisenhower administration, Defender brought together the nation's top scientific minds to brainstorm ways to keep the country safe from Soviet ICBMs. One proposal that came out of Project Defender was called the Ballistic Missile Boost Intercepts project—that's right, BaMBI (you can't say they didn't have a bit of a warped sense of humor). BaMBI was ambitious. It called for spacebased, rocketpowered projectiles to smash into rising enemy missiles, using kinetic energy to accomplish what was known as a "boost phase intercept"— kill the enemy ICBM in its initial boost phase before it had a chance to deploy its MIRVs. In case the kinetic weapon missed (which was … likely), BaMBI also would include a sixtyfoot rotating wire net laced with deadly steel pellets to thwack the enemy missile on the way by. Components of BaMBI were tested, but the program looked as though it would cost a ridiculous amount of money (in the tens of billions), and so it was canceled in 1963.

This is a good time to take a brief step back and refresh ourselves on the topic of kinetic energy, because we are going to need it later. Kinetic energy is the energy of motion. An object in motion has kinetic energy. We know from our physics classes that kinetic energy is calculated by taking half the mass of an object and multiplying it by the velocity of that object squared ($0.5m \times v^2$). This means that even though that five-ton truck is going only 10 mph, when it hits us it's going to leave a mark. Conversely, if a piece of metal the size of a grain of rice is traveling at an extraordinary velocity, it's also going to do some serious damage. This is one of the reasons why space is such a dangerous place. Objects in orbit can reach speeds of 22,000 mph. Space debris smaller than half an inch could penetrate the shields of the International Space Station's crew modules, causing extensive damage or even killing people. Something the size of an orange could shatter a satellite or spacecraft into pieces.

We will get back to kinetic energy weapons shortly. But first we should discuss what are known as directed energy weapons (DEW), because this was the sexy scientific concept du jour of the 1960s, and continued to be the "next big thing" all the way through the early 1980s. The development of what would become the most popular DEW began in the mid-1950s, and was based on an invention by a physicist named Gordon Gould. While Gould was working on his doctorate in optical and microwave spectroscopy at Columbia University in New York, he had an idea that he later said came to him in a flash one night in 1957. He subsequently wrote his revelation down in his research notebook, and made some rough calculations on the feasibility of his new invention, something he was calling "Light Amplification by Stimulated Emission of Radiation."

Gould knew he was on to something big, and scrambled to develop a working prototype. He dropped out of Columbia and joined Technical Research Group, a private research firm, hoping they would fund his project. They did, using a grant from the Pentagon's newly formed Advanced Research Projects Agency (ARPA—now called DARPA, with the "D" for "Defense"). ARPA loved the idea of the laser, but didn't like Gould all that much. You see, Gould had briefly worked for the Manhattan Project during World War II on the separation of uranium isotopes, but was dropped from the program because of his past ties to the Communist Political Association. Although others in the Manhattan Project also had communist flirtations in their pasts, they were considered integral to the program (like the project's scientific director, Robert Oppenheimer). Gould was just another scientist, so out he went. When ARPA began considering potential military applications for the laser, they deemed it vital to national security and classified it. Gould, because of his past, could not obtain a security clearance and was shut out of working on his own project.

But Edward Teller wasn't. He had his security clearance, a firm desire to develop a defense against Soviet nuclear weapons, and an infatuation with the possibilities of the laser. Teller was also a veteran of the Manhattan Project, and is widely considered to be the man most responsible for the development of the American thermonuclear (hydrogen) bomb, or the "Super," first tested in 1952. He also helped found the Lawrence Livermore National Laboratory (LLNL) outside San Francisco in 1952. He had the necessary street cred to push the project forward. In the late 1960s, the "O Group" at LLNL began working on Project Excalibur, the development of a new kind of laser—the Xray laser. An Xray laser would be exponentially more powerful than any laser that had come before. It could potentially use beams of concentrated Xrays to destroy enemy missiles *from space*. And unlike kinetic systems or groundbased missiles, the laser would fire its ordnance at the speed of light. Pretty cool, if you can make it work.

And that's the trick, because the O Group's Xray laser would require a thermonuclear explosion to produce enough high-intensity Xrays (which would be directed onto special rods) to zap America into nuclear invulnerability. It was ambitious. It was expensive. It was on the fringes of scientific understanding. And yes, it was a little crazy.

But Ronald Reagan loved the idea.

Reagan first met Teller in 1967, shortly after he had been elected governor of California. Teller gave him a tour of LLNL, and (some historians have argued) put the first bug in Reagan's ear about certain innovations and their potential for ballistic missile defense. When Reagan was elected president,

Teller (along with three of Reagan's close friends) visited the White House with the intention of selling the Xray laser as the solution to the Soviet threat.

It worked. LLNL was given the goahead (and the bankroll) to begin major testing of the concept.

But there was an issue with testing. And one that, it turned out, was practically unsolvable. How do you develop sensors that can record quickly and accurately what happened between the time of the firing of the laser and the destruction of the sensors by the expanding nuclear fireball a split second later? You could have the best sensors in the world, but if they were going to be vaporized by a nuclear blast before they could give you a solid reading on the effectiveness of the Xray laser, then what was the point?

(There wasn't one.)

This didn't seem to matter all that much to Teller, who after an underground nuclear experiment at the Nevada Test Site in December 1983 declared that the Xray laser was "now entering the engineering phase," implying that basic research was complete.

(It wasn't even close.)

In early 1984, Livermore physicists began to design a refinement of Excalibur known as "Super Excalibur" that could theoretically destroy even more Soviet missiles. It would be much more powerful than its Excalibur (super more, apparently), and would fire thousands of individual beams to knock out thousands of enemy missiles. This was a lofty claim, since Super Excalibur hadn't even had any underground testing, nor had the original Excalibur shown much in the way of results. But as we've seen, testing didn't seem to matter all that much to Teller and his team.

Teller was excited about the possibilities of Super Excalibur. He told the White House the technology could be deployable "in as little time as three years." (Not a chance.) In March 1985, the first underground test of Super Excalibur, code-named Cottage, was a failure, so much so that Congress launched an investigation. (Finally.)

Despite this, after later visiting President Reagan at the White House, Teller secured an extra $100 million to accelerate Xray laser research. Reagan was that committed to making this work.

It wasn't a complete free-for-all, however. The Strategic Defense Initiative Organization (SDIO), set up by the Reagan administration in 1984 to study multiple proposals for ballistic missile defense, sponsored a study of various concepts that were being tossed around. It was conducted by the American Physical Society (APS), which brought together some of the top scientific minds in the United States, including a Nobel laureate. They completed their report and released a redacted version to the public in early 1987.

The report took the measure of all of the systems then under development, including the science and technology behind DEW. It concluded that *not a single one* of the systems then under study or development was even remotely close to deployment. It found major gaps in the scientific and engineering understanding of many issues associated with the development of DEW technologies. It noted that every single system under consideration had to improve its energy output by *at least* one hundred times to be effective—in some cases, as much as a million times. Excalibur, despite Teller's claims to the contrary, was not even in the ballpark of the "engineering phase." As for Super Excalibur? The report correctly assessed that there was *zero* experimental support for any claims made by Teller and his peers at LLNL. DEW—"super" or not—was decades away from being ready for use. Furthermore, it would likely be another decade before we even fully understood which programs were feasible and which were junk science.

SDIO could see the writing on the wall. Directed energy weapons, whether Teller's Xray laser or other programs such as the US Air Force's chemical laser (MIRACL—Mid-Infrared Advanced Chemical Laser), a neutral particle beam accelerator, or hypervelocity railguns (the CHECMATE program—Compact High Energy Capacitator Module Advanced Technology Experiment), were not yet ready for prime time.

So what's next? Well, SDIO decided to take a step back before trying to take a leap forward. It was time to once again embrace kinetic energy weapons.

You'll never guess who was ready to step in and provide concepts for the new systems. Despite having already spent hundreds of millions of taxpayers' dollars on preposterously specious projects that, one by one, failed miserably, Lawrence Livermore National Laboratory was given the goahead to develop a concept they called "Brilliant Pebbles." It was the brainchild of a LLNL physicist by the name of Lowell Wood, who was a protégé of none other than Edward Teller.

Instead of building a couple of big, bulky, and insanely costly weapons, Brilliant Pebbles called for the creation of swarms of small, cheap rockets. Each weapon would be about three feet long and weigh about a hundred pounds, each with a silicon chip that would act as a "brain." It would also include an innovative, stateoftheart wideangle optical sensor that would help it to track the exhaust plumes of enemy missiles. What made this idea great was that the innate control package—the brain and the eyes—eliminated much of the need for outside guidance from other satellites or ground control stations. Each rocket could work nearly autonomously.

Unlike many of the past kinetic energy weapon proposals, Brilliant Pebbles wouldn't be Earth-based. Hundreds, if not thousands, of "Pebbles" would be launched into orbit around the Earth at more or less regular intervals. A set of deployed Brilliant Pebble interceptors, referred to as a "constellation," would be made up of several staggered rings orbiting about 250 miles above the planet, with a number of Brilliant Pebbles in each ring. The interceptors would be housed in protective containers, or "life-jackets," which would help with support functions like communications and general protection in a dangerous space environment, as well as housing solar panels for power. If an enemy attack was detected, the interceptors would pop out of the life-jackets, use their eyes and brain to select their targets, and launch themselves into the paths of the enemy ballistic missiles. They wouldn't even need any explosives to destroy their targets. In their "resting" state (when they were just circulating in their orbits), the interceptor would be traveling at about five miles *per second*. As a comparison, a highvelocity rifle round travels about half a mile per second. That is some serious kinetic energy.

Perhaps the greatest advantage of the Brilliant Pebbles concept was its cost. According to Lowell Wood, the expected cost for a single BP could be as little as $100,000 (once mass production techniques were developed, and assuming computer technology continued to advance at its current rate). Now, that might seem like a lot of money for a watermelon-sized piece of nonexploding spacemetal—particularly considering that the United States could need up to one hundred thousand Pebbles in orbit to fully protect itself from a full-scale Soviet strategic attack—but if you do the math, it really only amounts to $10 billion.

Again, that's a lot for most of us. But it's a drop in the bucket for the US government. And it's a drop in the ocean compared to the price tags of some of the other programs that truly deserved the derisive nickname "Star Wars."

So what happened to it? Why don't we have an orbiting horde of swarming micro-missiles waiting to pounce on any national security threat?

Well, for one thing, the Cold War ended. But Brilliant Pebbles didn't die quite that easily. Although the threat of full-scale war had diminished to almost nothing, the worry was that Soviet missile technology might be sold off as the former Soviet Union liquidated its assets in search of cold hard cash. As a response, the administration of President George H. W. Bush authorized research into a system known as GPALS, or Global Protection Against Limited Strikes.

GPALS would consist of multiple components. One was a new mobile ground-based missile, 750 of which would be deployed along with six ground-based radars (known as terminal phase ground-based radar trackers, or GBRTs). Brilliant Pebbles would constitute the spacebased element of GPALS, but the Bush administration called for the addition of approximately sixty loworbit satellites known as Brilliant Eyes, which would provide the Pebbles with enhanced targeting and tracking information. It was intended to be a fully integrated system, covering all aspects of a nuclear launch—the boost phase, the midcourse phase, and finally the terminal phase. Brilliant Eyes and Brilliant Pebbles would have responsibility for the first two, while the groundbased system would take care of the terminal phase—essentially anything that got through the space-based system.

It might have worked. Maybe.

But it was still prohibitively expensive, and difficult to justify in an increasingly disarming world, where American defense budgets were getting slashed, and regional and asymmetric threats were taking the place of global and great-power conflict. The Clinton administration decided to nix the space-based element of GPALS (Brilliant Eyes and Brilliant Pebbles), and instead invest America's nowlimited defense resources on ground-based systems. Although the George W. Bush administration was more enthusiastic about the broader concept of ballistic missile defense, it agreed with the precedent established by Clinton. The threat was no longer a barrage of Soviet or Chinese MIRVed thermonuclear missiles flying a ballistic trajectory over the Arctic. It was a single missile, launched by a regional power or a rogue state. Iran, Iraq, and North Korea replaced the big bad Russians as America's immediate defense priority—and our technology evolved, tailored to these new threats.

AND THEN WHAT?

Some historians of science and technology credit a physicist by the name of Theodore Maiman with the invention of the first laser. Maiman worked for the Hughes Aircraft Corporation in California, and in May 1960 he made the shocking announcement of a working laser. And there's no question this is true, but as we know, there is more to the story. Gordon

Gould had the idea for the laser in 1956, and even had his notebook notarized as proof. Because of his political leanings, Gould was kept away from its practical development, but it's altogether possible that he would have built a working laser before Maiman if he had been given the chance. In any case, after filing multiple lawsuits trying to get at least some credit for the invention, in 1987 he was finally awarded a patent on the "optical pumping" aspect of lasers, based in part on the designs he sketched out in that notebook three decades earlier. This might not sound like much, but optical pumping devices are used in 80 percent of the industrial, commercial, and medical applications of lasers.

And now he owned the patent.

Scientists and engineers have continued to try to perfect a system for intercepting enemy ballistic missiles. They have yet to be successful, despite now having more than seventy years of practice. But maybe we've been thinking the wrong way about this thing all along.

At the end of the Obama administration, the Pentagon wrote a report titled "Declaratory Policy, Concept of Operations, and Employment Guidelines for LeftofLaunch Capability." While this might sound like a bunch of DoD-mumbo-jumbo, it does offer potentially tantalizing hints of what could be on the missile-defense horizon. "Leftof-Launch" means taking out the missile before it has been sent our way. But not with a kinetic attack. Or an Xray laser. Or a railgun, or anything else we've discussed in this chapter.

No. Those would constitute a "use of force" under the United Nations Charter. And that's what makes this long sentence in the report so interesting:

Although left-of-launch actions that would constitute a use of force likely would require the President's approval as an exercise of the inherent right of national or collective selfdefense, *certain actions* would not necessarily constitute a use of force under the U.N. Charter, such as gathering intelligence or *developing capabilities that could be used in response* to an imminent attack [emphasis mine].

Certain actions. Developing capabilities. In other words, cyber.

The most cost-effective approach to disable your enemy's missile—and perhaps the most effective approach—is to develop digital weapons that can scramble launch controls, infect guidance systems, turn off targeting computers, corrupt command and control operations, or muck up parts of the missile's supply chain.

Create cyber chaos.

Edward Teller would probably approve. But only if you called it Super Cyber, or something.

THE SUN GUN

I probably shouldn't be admitting this (considering where I work), but here it goes anyway: I have a hard time keeping track of the plotlines of all the James Bond movies. Over more than fifty years there have been twenty-six Bond movies, depending on how you count (this question has actually been argued in a court of law). In each one, a suave British secret agent faces diabolical odds and an over-the-top villain. For some reason or another, at some point he will jump out of a perfectly good airplane with a martini in one hand and a ridiculously named blonde in the other. The world is saved. How can anyone keep up?

But despite all the fun poked in the direction of the villains' lairs, vehicles, nonsensical plots to take over the world, and overcomplicated methods for dispatching James Bond, sometimes the plots come strangely close to things *that actually happened*. *Die Another Day* (2002) has a pretty good bad guy in the form of Toby Stephens as Tan-Sun Moon/Gustav Graves, but the orbital mirror satellite "Icarus" is a legitimately scary superweapon. Icarus is a new, benevolent technology designed to help the world feed itself—it would focus solar energy to provide constant sunshine for crop development. But that's just a ruse. In reality, Icarus is a deadly weapon that can harness the extraordinary power of the sun. Moon/Graves could melt London. Vaporize Washington. Incinerate Moscow. Hold the world hostage for an obscene amount of money. Have the world cower at his feet. Ultimate power. Unstoppable power. Unlimited power.

Ultimately, what he decides to do is zap the minefield in the Demilitarized Zone between North and South Korea to make way for a land invasion of South Korea, which I found a tad anti-climactic.

Of course, I don't know what they used for their inspiration, but they might have looked back at history for a guide. Because as evil as Graves was, he'll never hold a candle to the most villainous group in human history: Nazis.

If you read any of the numerous biographies (or obituaries) of Hermann Oberth, they tend to paint a picture of the German physicist and engineer as one of the great minds of the twentieth century. Along with American Robert Goddard and Russian Konstantin Tsiolkovsky, Oberth is considered a pioneer in the fields of rocketry, astronautics, and astrophysics. After serving in the Austro-Hungarian army in World War I, Oberth turned to a career in the study of mathematics and physics. He tried to get his PhD in rocketry in 1922 yet, although he had studied with several notable scientists, his theory on rocket science (and his dissertation) was rejected. Oberth was ahead of his time.

However, Oberth knew he was on to something, even if his fellow scientists did not. He published his theories in a pamphlet titled "By Rocketry into Planetary Space." It's

usually referred to as a "pamphlet," but that is a bit misleading. This wasn't *Common Sense*. It was a 429-page tome that
mathematically proved a rocket's ability to leave Earth's orbit
by achieving what is known as its "escape velocity." Not only
that, but it introduced important concepts concerning how
rockets behave in a vacuum, which were key to understanding how they would operate for longer-distance space travel.

When these theories were finally published as a book in
1929, Oberth finally got the widespread belated recognition
he deserved, crowning him as an expert in the rocketry and
astronautics communities. With this success, he inspired
many young dreamers to reach for the stars. One of these
dreamers was a young man—he just eighteen—named
Wernher von Braun. You've maybe heard of him. He joined
Oberth as his assistant during early rocket tests. In return,
Oberth mentored the budding von Braun, setting the stage
for a lifetime of collaboration.

Skip ahead to 1940. Oberth had bounced around in the
intermediate years (Romania, Austria, Germany, the United
States), but during the second year of World War II he settled
back in Germany and became a German citizen. In 1941, he
deployed to the infamous Peenemünde rocket facility in
Germany and began working again with Wernher von Braun,
this time as *his* assistant. Together they developed the feared
German V2, the world's first ballistic missile.

All of this information is found in most of the Hermann
Oberth bios/obits. It's pretty standard stuff. Failed Doctorate.
Author. Rocket Guy. Von Braun. Nazi. The V2. But what's
wild is that by far the most interesting idea Oberth ever had is
absent from almost every one of these biographies. It's not in
his NASA biography. Not in his writeup for the International

Space Hall of Fame. Nor can you find any mention of it in his *New York Times* obituary. It's not even included in his Wikipedia page.

It's the sun gun. Nearly the very same one Moon/Graves employs in *Die Another Day*. Harnessing the energy of the most powerful object in the solar system to help the Nazis win the war. Thankfully, the German scientific machine never made this work. Or it would have been Hermann Oberth's ultimate legacy.

Near the Elbe River and a German town called Madgeburg sat one of the Nazis' most important weapons research centers. The Hillersleben Proving Grounds were used by the Germans to test-fire big artillery guns and howitzers. And when I say big, I mean big—massive railway guns that could launch a projectile miles into the distance. This was a huge enterprise. When the US Army took control of the facility late in the war, they were in awe of the scale of operation. There was no equivalent facility in the United States. It was, as one ordnance officer put it, "a maintenance company's dream."

But Hillersleben had a purpose beyond the testing, upkeep, and maintenance of conventional (albeit really large) artillery weapons. Tucked into a corner of the facility was a group of more than a hundred scientists and engineers working on all kinds of devious and dastardly experimental weapons systems. Things like a 600-millimeter-diameter (about twenty-four inches) mortar that could launch 2,000-pound projectiles up to three and a half miles, and parts of the sinister V3 super-cannon, which could blast a massive projectile one hundred miles—five times the distance from France to England across the Strait of Dover.

Meanwhile, some of these scientists and engineers were working on a different kind of project, one that cannot be lumped in with all the other "conventional" experiments. It was called the *Sonnengewehr,* and it was based on a design concept originally described by Hermann Oberth in his 1929 book *Ways to Spaceflight.** Oberth called for a space station[†] that would orbit about 625 miles above the Earth (for comparison, the International Space Station orbits at about 220 miles up). *Ways to Spaceflight* is full of detail on the project: It would be sent into space and constructed in prefabricated sections that would be linked together like a Lego set once settled in orbit; it would spin on its axis to produce artificial gravity within the station; it would be used for scientific and astronomical observations, meteorological observations, search-and-rescue operations, and telegraph relays. Oberth, clearly understanding that his concept would be undeniably alluring to the German military and national security community (even before Hitler came to power), also suggested that his space station could be used for the collection of military intelligence.

But one detail stood out among the others—at least as far as the Nazi scientists and engineers were concerned. Oberth's space station design included the specs for a hundredmeter-wide[‡] concave mirror, which would be used to redirect sunlight into a specific, concentrated point on Earth. Amazingly, Oberth thought his space mirror concept would only cost around three million marks—about $200

---

* *Wege zur Raumschiffahrt.*
† Called *Raumstations.*
‡ Three hundred and twentyeight feet. The whole world is on the metric system. C'mon, America.

million today—and would take only fifteen years to build. Oberth was not an economist, nor was he a construction manager, so who knows if these numbers are anything but wishful thinking.

But he did know space. And rockets. And he understood better than most anyone what might be possible with just a little elbow grease and a candoattitude.

And slave labor.

Hermann Oberth's original idea for the space mirror/sun gun was completely peaceful. He wanted to help the world, to provide the people of Earth with sunshine on demand, anywhere and everywhere on the globe. You need extra sunlight to help you out of famine? Zap. Instant sun. You need to instantly dry out a flooded marshland or city? Zap. The uses were virtually limitless. It could change the world for the better.

Yet Oberth wasn't completely naïve to the possible ramifications of his concept. He understood the inherent truth of what is known as "dual use" technologies, those that can be used for both civilian and military purposes, like nuclear power. He saw the writing on the wall: "My space mirror is like the hand mirrors that schoolboys use to flash circles of sunlight on the ceiling of the classroom. A sudden beam flashed on the teacher's face may bring unpleasant reactions."

And so they tried to build it. The German scientists and engineers at Hillersleben decided to soup up Oberth's original concept. It would be the Oberth *Sonnengewehr* on steroids. Nazi scientists wanted to build a mirror of at least *one square mile* in area, or about eleven times the size of the US Capitol building. Some German documents claimed the mirror might have to be as large as three and a half square miles in area, or a little more than two and a half times the size of Central Park.

Inside the station itself, Nazi scientists envisioned an environment in which electricity would be provided by solar power, but not what we would think of as "solar power" today. There wouldn't be photovoltaic cells hanging from the sides of the station. Instead, heat from the sun would warm water to drive a steam generator, much in the same way a coal or nuclear power plant works here on Earth. The Germans decided to nix Oberth's idea of centrifugal force to provide artificial gravity. The German astronauts would wear magnetic shoes instead.

Oxygen production would be an issue for the German crew. No matter how large the space station might be, you couldn't provide enough bottled oxygen for the entirety of the mission. You'd have to manufacture it yourself. The solution: greenhouses filled with hydroponic gardens of thousands of pumpkin plants. The massive leaves of the pumpkin plant suck up huge quantities of carbon dioxide, and pump back out plenty of life-sustaining oxygen.

When the Fatherland decided it was time to use their new toy, the German leadership would send a message to the station's crew through encoded radio or wireless telegraph. On command, the crew would use the station's rocket thrusters to maneuver the mirror into attack position. Once ready, the reflective surface and its special concave curvature would collect the sun's energy and blast a single ray to a particular focal point on the Earth's surface. The massive size of the mirror and the extraordinary power of the sun would converge to create a beam that could theoretically boil ocean water, burn a city to the ground, flambé fields of crops, vaporize water reserves, and burn unlucky soldiers and civilians to a crisp.

Sounds too good to be true. Or maybe too awful to be true. Either way, the Germans were not expecting this space station to be ready anytime soon. According to captured documents, they were playing the long game—which makes sense, considering they were expecting to be the vanguard of a thousand-year Reich. They had time to get this right, to wait for the necessary technology and scientific development to catch up. The physicists and engineers from Hillersleben were thinking fifty years, a hundred maybe. One day, the world would cower under the might of the Nazi sun gun.

Or not.

The Germans were only off by 988 years.

The Nazis suspended the sun gun project in the spring of 1945 as the Allied armies closed in on both sides. The top German scientists became prime targets for Allied intelligence agencies. Not to kill, but to sweep off the battlefield for use in the impending Cold War. Because Hillersleben was west of Berlin, the Nazi scientists and engineers of the proving ground became guests of the US and UK governments.

AND THEN WHAT?

After the war, Hermann Oberth continued to promote his sun gun concept to anyone willing to listen. Of course, he wasn't advocating for the military use of the system, just its originally intended peaceful applications. He was joined in this advocacy by his former student turned boss Wernher von Braun. But von Braun didn't seem to care all that much about the touchy-feely, save-the-world aspects of Oberth's idea. He wanted to kill Russians. During the height of the Cold War, he lobbied the US military to consider finishing what the Nazis had started, and build a sun gun to use on the Russians.

Our two famous Germans would reunite in 1955 when Oberth moved to the United States to join his former colleague von Braun working for the US Army. Together they helped the fledgling American space program produce a series of rockets capable of reaching outer space. Their collaboration led to the development of the Saturn V rocket, which would eventually bring the crew of Apollo 11 to the moon.

Hermann Oberth stayed in the United States for three years before returning to West Germany in 1958. In his retirement, he continued to work on the theoretical and mathematical side of rocketry and astronautics. He lived just long enough to see the fall of the Berlin Wall, dying a little more than a month later in Nuremberg.

Of course, Oberth wasn't the first person to think of using mirrors as weapons. That was Archimedes, back in 212 BCE.

According to legend, during the siege of Syracuse, famous Greek scientist/inventor/physicist/astronomer/Eureka! exclaimer Archimedes constructed a burning glass to set Roman warships on fire. Lucian of Samosata and Galen of Pergamon, both of the second century CE, are often given as sources of Archimedes' burning mirror. But both simply state, in passing, that Archimedes set fire to the Roman fleet without precisely describing how.

Lucian: "The former [Archimedes] burned the ships of the enemy by means of his science."

Galen: "In some such way, I think, Archimedes too is said to have set on fire the enemy's triremes by means of pyreia."

Maybe this happened. Maybe it didn't. Everyone from French philosopher/mathematician René Descartes to

American philosophers/pyromaniacs the *MythBusters* has dismissed this story out of hand.

But you know what? I don't really care if it's true or not. These two stories are apples and oranges. They shouldn't be considered in the same breath.

Because whatever Archimedes was up to, he definitely wasn't doing it with a mirror three-and-a-half square miles in area ... in space.

PART IV

"FUN" WITH NUCLEAR WEAPONS

THE PLOWSHARE PROGRAM'S STRANGEST IDEA

Just prior to the landfall of Hurricane Irma in September 2017, a Facebook "event" page was created calling for Florida gun owners to shoot at the hurricane in an attempt to either weaken it or change its course. The page exclaimed: "YO SO THIS GOOFY LOOKING WINDY HEADASS NAME IRMA SAID THEY PULLING UP ON US, LETS SHOW IRMA THAT WE SHOOT FIRST" [multiple emojis redacted].

Of course this was a joke (right?), but *more than eighty-five thousand people* indicated that they were "interested" or "going" to the event. Maybe they were joking too, but the (real or faux) interest in shooting at the hurricane felt potentially serious enough that the Pasco County Sheriff's Office tweeted, "To clarify, DO NOT shoot weapons @ #Irma. You won't make it turn around & it will have very dangerous side effects."

What a time to be alive.

I mean, what could possibly be stupider than shooting metal projectiles into a tropical cyclone? There's enough debris already flying around in a hurricane without adding more to the mix. This has to be—*has* to be—the most asinine idea anyone has *ever* had involving launching things into hurricanes. How idiotic.

The *only* thing possibly more astronomically stupid than bullets would be missiles of some kind—hell, let's say nuclear weapons to up the ante—and there's *no way* anyone could be that stupid.

If only that were true.

In the 1950s, a group of scientists and government personnel pushed for a program to test the potential of using nuclear weapons for peaceful purposes. I know that sounds like yet another paradox. How can the world's most destructive weapon be used for "peaceful" applications? But this was new technology, and who knew how it might change the world? Even the Soviets were thinking more broadly about how to use nukes—their Nuclear Explosions for the National Economy program wound up exploring concepts very similar to those tested by the United States.

In 1957, scientists from the Lawrence Radiation Laboratory (remember them from Brilliant Pebbles?), Los Alamos, and Sandia laboratories held a classified conference to discuss the possibilities of using nuclear weapons to produce power, dig out huge excavations, and produce known or then-unknown isotopes for scientific (and perhaps medical) usage.

On June 6, 1958, the Atomic Energy Commission (AEC) publicly announced the establishment of the "Plowshare Program," named for Isaiah 2:4:

> And they shall beat their swords into plowshares, and their spears into pruning hooks; nation shall not lift up sword against nation, neither shall they learn war anymore.

I suppose we should be happy it wasn't called the "Pruning Hooks Program."

Peaceful industrial applications for nuclear weapons were thought to fall into two broad categories: (1) large-scale excavation and quarrying (blowing up and/or moving massive quantities of rock to make things like canals, harbors, highways, and railroad passages through mountains, dams, and so on), or (2) underground engineering (blowing up nukes underground to see what comes loose. Some applications might be stimulation of natural gas production, creation of natural gas and petroleum storage areas, and more). The program ran from 1958 to 1975, and during this time the United States conducted twenty-seven total Plowshare nuclear tests. The first test, Gnome, was conducted in an underground salt bed near Carlsbad, New Mexico. The last, 1973's Rio Blanco, was part of a joint government/industry natural gas experiment held outside Rifle, Colorado. In between, twenty-three of the tests were held at the Nevada Test Site (NTS) sixty miles or so northwest of Vegas.

On top of the twenty-seven executed Plowshare tests, there were a number of proposed projects that were never carried out, and a relatively equal number of ideas that never even made it beyond the conceptual phase. For every Sulky, Templar, Vulcan, Gasbuggy, Cabriolet, Schooner, and Flask-Green (all executed Plowshare tests), there was a Ditchdigger, Carryall, Dogsled, Ketch, Bronco, Thunderbird, and Aquarius. Some of these were extraordinarily ambitious. The Tennessee/Tombigee Waterway project would have excavated three miles of a cut through low hills, connected the Tennessee and Tombigee rivers, and dug a *250-mile-long* canal. In 1962, the United States formally agreed to participate in a joint feasibility study with Australia to see if it made sense to use nuclear weapons to construct an entire harbor on the latter country's northwest coast (it didn't).

But the most interesting—and strangest—project proposed under the umbrella of the Plowshare Program was put forth for consideration by a meteorologist named Jack Reed. Reed began his career at the end of World War II working for what would become the US Air Force. After the war, he served in the Philippines as a military meteorologist and studied the power of hurricanes (called "typhoons" since they were in the Pacific), riding through them on eight missions in a specially modified B29 bomber. Later, he joined the Sandia National Laboratories, and was sent along with his colleagues to study the effects of atmospheric nuclear testing in the Pacific Ocean.

During the first-ever thermonuclear (or hydrogen bomb) test in 1952, code-named "Mike," Reed had an idea. Mike had produced a mushroom cloud more than twenty miles high. That's considerably higher than the top of a hurricane. What if a nuclear explosion like this one could disrupt the central engine of a hurricane? What if we could use a nuke to kill a storm? Or failing that, could we at least mess with it enough to make it less dangerous to the human population on land?

Reed did some calculations. This could work, he thought. To be sure, he knew that no matter how strong a nuclear blast might be, it could never completely blow apart a large hurricane. They're just too big and too powerful. Such a direct approach was a nonstarter. Reed wasn't delusional. He understood the physics of tropical storms as well as or better than anyone.

But what about an *indirect* approach?

Once Reed had his ducks in a row, he set out to convince the world. He presented his plan at two prestigious conferences—first at the 1959 symposium on the Plowshare Program, and then at an American Meteorological Society conference on tropical weather. First the nuke experts. Then the weather people.

Scientists were coming up with ways to do just about anything you could think of with nuclear weapons. Someone must think *this* idea makes sense. Right?

Reed's paper, titled "Some Speculations on the Effects of Nuclear Explosions on Hurricanes," provided two plans of action for hurricane mitigation, literally labeled "Plan A" and "Plan B."

Plan A was the more modest proposal. It worked off what Reed called the "apparent correlation of storm symmetry with direction of motion and acceleration." In English, this means that when storms are symmetrical around the eye, they are not only at their most powerful, but also tend to move east to west—that is, directly at the shoreline of the Caribbean or the eastern seaboard of the United States. When storms get closer to the shore, they begin to become asymmetrical, likely due to the cooler air from the land. This weakens the storm a bit, but it also curves it to the north and northeast.

Just think of all of the storm tracks you've seen over the years. Almost every single one of them tracks west, until it gets close to shore and takes a hard right turn. Hurricane Andrew hit Miami, and then proceeded to turn right to thump New Orleans. So did Katrina. Hurricane Sandy came right at the northern part of the mid-Atlantic region, and then worked its way northeast right up the coast.

Reed's premise: If we can find a way to create asymmetry

in the center of a hurricane, we might be able to weaken it a bit, and—far more important—we might be able to *change its direction,* so that it turns back into the open ocean before hitting populated areas on land.

Pretty cool. If it works.

So how do we create this asymmetry? Reed's answer: a 20megaton thermonuclear explosion. According to his calculations, a nuclear explosion of this size would, "for at least 15 minutes, greatly influence the horizontal circulation of a hurricane." He continues, "If a burst were made on one side of a storm or two bursts on opposite sides of a storm, considerable asymmetry in circulation could result."

All we need is one 20megaton bomb. Or maybe two. Seems a lot more rational than putting up hurricane shutters and buying bottled water …

Plan B was Reed's masterpiece. It was based on what were, at the time, new discoveries about the temperature structure of a hurricane. In particular, scientists had discovered that at about twenty thousand feet above sea level, the eye of a hurricane is nearly ten degrees centigrade warmer than the surrounding storm. Reed's idea was to take advantage of this thermal discrepancy. "It appears," he wrote, "that a megaton explosion in the eye would engulf and entrain a large quantity of this hot 'eye' and carry it out of the storm into the stratosphere." The removed air would rush out and be replaced by a "horizontal convergence of cooler air from the storm walls." In other words, blow its heart out.

Reed wasn't entirely sure about what kind (or kinds) of bombs would make the most sense. Big ones were a possibility, such as the 20megaton bomb proposed in Plan A. But Reed also acknowledges that it might be "more economical to remove air with several smaller shots depending on the cost of devices." It's important when you are nuking natural disasters to remain economically responsible.

At worst, Reed argued, even if a storm couldn't be eliminated entirely, it could be significantly weakened by the cooler air brought into the eye by the expulsion of the higher-temperature air. For example, a 150-knot hurricane could be reduced to about 120-knot maximum winds. This might not sound like a lot, but a 20 percent reduction in wind speeds could have a marked impact on the damage caused by the storm. Even more promising, Reed argued, would be the plan's effect on less powerful storms. A hurricane with 100-knot winds could be reduced to 50. Fifty-knot winds are not even hurricane strength, so if you close one eye, turn your head a little to the left, squint with the other eye, and suspend disbelief, Jack Reed actually figured out a way to use nuclear weapons to eliminate a hurricane.

But how do we get the thermonuclear weapon inside the hurricane in the first place? While acknowledging we could drop it from an aircraft into the eye of the storm, Reed had other ideas:

A more suitable delivery would be from a submarine. It would penetrate a storm eye underwater at least a day in advance and record as many weather data and trends as possible before launching missileborne devices. After diving for protection from the blast, it would resurface and continue recording storm weather and track data to be analyzed for discontinuous reactions.

Looking for "discontinuous reactions" was a very important

part of the plan. Scientists in the United States had been experimenting with weather modification for years by this point—socalled cloud seeding, wherein we tried to use several specific compounds (silver iodide among them) to cause clouds to produce rain. The problem with this from the angle of scientific methodology is that it's tricky to know if your cloud seeding mission caused the cloud to produce rain, or if it was going to anyway (it's a cloud, and clouds sometimes form rain). Some scientists are still arguing today about how to correctly measure correlation versus causality in weather modification experiments. Reed was hoping to nip this in the bud before anyone could claim it was nature— not his nuke—that weakened the hurricane. The submarine's continuous observation would help to prevent this kind of argument.

Something we haven't yet discussed is radioactivity—and for something like this you'd think that would be front and center to the debate. To a degree it was, but not as prevalent as you might think. There is no such thing as a completely clean nuclear weapon, but Reed wasn't wrong when he maintained that the newer fusionbased thermonuclear weapons were far less radioactive than their fissionbased predecessors. To be sure, the radiation effects of a hydrogen bomb would still kill hundreds of thousands (if not millions) in any fullscale nuclear exchange between the United States and the Soviet Union. But in that case, we are talking about thousands (or tens of thousands) of warheads. This operation called for significantly less radioactive potential. Still, Reed understood the potential dangers:

Of course, a submarine should monitor for radioactivity

rained out into the ocean surface and be prepared to submerge between periodic weather observations if high dose rates were encountered. Shielding by the water plus downward settling of radioactive fallout in the water would allow the necessary observations to be made without undue exposure of the submarine crew.

But even those not protected by an advanced submarine shouldn't worry too much about the prospect of launching a nuclear weapon into a hurricane. According to Reed:

A clean device [he means cleaner; remember, there's no such thing] would minimize lingering radioactivity placed in the atmosphere. An airburst [detonating the weapon a set distance from the surface of the water. Probably around a thousand feet] would result in no intense fallout [note the word "intense" rather than "none"] and the cloud would rise well above the storm to avoid rainout [radioactivity falling back to the ground via rainfall]. The majority of fission products [a fission bomb is actually used as the *trigger* for a fusion warhead] would form extremely small particles high in the atmosphere which would fall very slowly [presumably so you can … get out of the way in time?]. There would be no hazard from the few large fallout particles which might form nor would there be an appreciable damage from the blast wave, if the shot were to take place over the open ocean far from civilization [people would be safe, but screw the whales].

To his credit, Reed was willing to put his money where his mouth was. Or at least, put American taxpayers' money. At the end of his proposal, he called for a fullscale test of his idea. It was the only way to be sure.

Alas … no. Not a single person with any kind of authority was willing to even entertain the idea of nuking hurricanes. Later in life, Jack Reed bitterly chalked this up to his idea being "politically incorrect."

It's far more likely that most of the scientists who evaluated his plan realized the immense power of a multimegaton nuclear weapon was still no match for the extraordinary amount of energy inside even a moderately strong hurricane. The Soviet Union's 58megaton Tsar Bomba would barely make a dent.

In addition, the experimentation that would be required to confirm (or more likely refute) Reed's hypothesis would be extremely expensive—multiple nuclear weapons would be needed for testing, each costing millions of dollars.

Finally, the Reed proposal was coming at a time when the United States and the Soviet Union were working on an agreement to limit (and then eventually ban) atmospheric nuclear tests. It would do no good to approve an expensive, dubious operation that could have the unfortunate side effect of ruining years of diplomatic effort aimed at making the world a safer place.

The plan was dead on arrival.

AND THEN WHAT?

The Plowshare Program was discontinued at the end of fiscal year 1975. This was due to several factors, including insufficient public support, nonexistent congressional support, and a feeling that most of the tasks Plowshare was designed to accomplish could be done more cheaply and safely through conventional, nonnuclear means. Even natural gas production, which was the most promising use for peaceful nuclear explosions, could not be justified because of all the effort and technical requirements that would be necessary to reap any kind of tangible benefit. At the same time, alternative (nonnuclear) technologies were in development that could much more efficiently stimulate natural gas production.

Even though the scientific community rejected Jack Reed's idea, it didn't mean that they were ignoring the threat of hurricanes. From 1962 to 1983, the US government engaged in a series of experiments known as Project Stormfury. The program investigated the possibilities of modifying the strength of a hurricane through silver iodide cloud seeding technology. The hope was that they could artificially stimulate the eye wall, making it wider and therefore less powerful. Hurricane modification was tried in four hurricanes over eight different days. On four of those days, it seemed to work: The winds decreased in intensity by up to 30 percent. But don't get too excited. Stormfury suffered from the same problems Jack Reed had identified and tried to mitigate in his proposal. It's nearly impossible to distinguish between results from cloud seeding and those from naturally occurring intensity changes. Hurricane winds ebb and flow on their own, thus making it impossible to accurately measure the impact of the silver iodide.

But what if we wanted to dust off Jack Reed's plan today and give it the old college try?

We couldn't even if we thought it was a good idea. The Peaceful Nuclear Explosions Treaty, an international agreement among nuclear powers, signed and ratified in 1990, limited the yield of nuclear weapons for nonmilitary purposes to a paltry 150 kilotons.

Yet this hasn't stopped wellmeaning citizens from continuing to suggest using nuclear weapons to combat tropical storms. So much so, apparently, that the webpage of the National Oceanographic and Atmospheric Administration (NOAA) has a "Frequently Asked Questions" page that directly addresses this (still ridiculous) question. Whoever is the wonderful and patient person who is tasked with dealing with this nonsense should get a medal:

> Apart from the fact that this might not even alter the storm, this approach neglects the problem that the released radioactive fallout would fairly quickly move with the tradewinds to affect land areas and cause devastating environmental problems. *Needless to say, this is not a good idea.*

That emphasis is mine, but it's an ironic sentence if you think about it. It's obviously *not* "needless to say." Apparently, it needs to be said again and again. The NOAA page itself indicates that "during *each hurricane season,* there always appear suggestions that one should simply use nuclear weapons to try and destroy the storms."

I don't know who keeps sending in these suggestions. But I have a feeling it's someone from Florida.

PROTECTING THE PEACEKEEPER

The last intercontinental ballistic missile deployed by the US Air Force in the twentieth century was ironically named the "Peacekeeper." It was one of the most lethal nuclear weapons ever developed, and could carry up to ten independently targetable reentry vehicles with greater accuracy than any other ballistic missile in history. Each of the Peacekeeper's ten thermonuclear warheads packed a yield of 300 kilotons.

While under development, the Peacekeeper was called MissileX, for "Missile-eXperimental"—or simply the MX. Development began in the early 1970s. Strategic Air Command (SAC) was excited about the prospects of its new missile. It would have increased range and pinpoint accuracy, and the MIRVed system would allow considerable flexibility in targeting and enough destructive power to level multiple major cities.

The MX had a quirky launch procedure called a "cold launch technique." The missile was popped out of the silo (like a cork coming out of a champagne bottle) using steam pressure, then when it reached an altitude of 150 to 300 feet, its first-stage rocket would ignite for liftoff. For just a slight moment—but for what must have felt like three heart-palpi-tating days for those watching the launch—the missile would seemingly hover in the air before blasting off toward its even-tual destination, which could be up to six thousand eight hundred miles away.

But despite its (quite significant) upgrades over its pre-decessors, the MX still had one glaring weakness: It was a landbased missile, and thus a sitting duck for Soviet ICBMs. Unlike the other delivery systems of the US nuclear triad—ballistic missile submarines, which lurk in the ocean depths until ordered to war, or strategic aircraft, which at even the slowest speeds are still moving at hundreds of miles per hour—nuclear missile silos are static, and so make juicy targets for "counterforce" strikes, using nuclear weapons to target the other guy's nuclear weapons. Improvements in the 1960s in Soviet ICBM forces and missile accuracy (like the deploy-ment of the SS9 missile, which was specifically designed to destroy US ICBM launch control centers and their missiles) raised serious concerns over the ability of silo-based ICBMs to survive a dedicated counterforce attack.

So why bother? First and foremost, the nuclear triad was a core component of the American nuclear strategy. Having three options meant that there would still be a way to coun-terattack if the Soviets disabled one or even two legs of the triad. Second, these were really powerful missiles.

One solution to the problem could be to harden the missile silos to make them less vulnerable to damage during an attack. They'd sit there and take the punishment in the hope that they were durable enough to survive the onslaught long enough to punch back.

The other option was to make the MX mobile. To keep

it bobbing and weaving. Floating like a butterfly so it could sting like a bee. Never in the same spot for long, and thus impossible to effectively target.

Not the worst idea, really.

So in the late 1970s, President Carter asked the Department of Defense to study options for helping American Peacekeepers survive the apocalypse. What would be the best way to do this? What method of mobility would keep our missiles safe?

The DoD used eleven criteria, from cost to how long the missile would survive post-attack to the environmental impact to the legality, to evaluate the different options for MX basing.

And, with these in mind, the Pentagon began its search for the best way to protect the Peacekeepers.

The first option considered wasn't really an ICBM basing mode but a reaffirmation of a Cold War nuclear strategy that left much to be desired. Known as Launch Under Attack (LUA), this concept calls for keeping missiles safe by ensuring they are no longer in the ground when Soviet missiles arrive. How do you do this? You get our birds out of the ground as soon as your warning systems (radar and satellites) detect a Soviet missile launch.

This might sound sensible on paper, but comes with considerable downsides. For one, timing. An ICBM launched from the Soviet Union would only take, at most, thirty minutes to reach the United States, a submarine-launched missile as few as five. This gives very little time for the president to determine if the threat is a real attack or a false alarm before he has to order a retaliatory strike. He couldn't take any chances with the survival of the United States on the line, so even false alarms would be likely to spur a full-scale nuclear war. Also, American missiles would need to be pre-aimed at special targets and put on a hair-trigger alert status, since there wouldn't be any time to have a planning and targeting meeting or to prep the missiles before the order to launch. It's hard to imagine that this wouldn't be a recipe for accidents or unintentional or unauthorized launches.

But all this assumes our early warning systems and communications networks are fully operational. The Soviets would surely try to find ways to blind our warning systems or disrupt American command and control communications. This could be accomplished through radar jamming, or through kinetic (physical) attacks on our radar installations, communications platforms, or imagery and sensor-based satellites. In this case, the president would have an excruciating decision to make: He would be forced to decide to launch on the basis—and only on the basis—that our warning systems were not working, rather than on real indications of a Soviet attack. In other words, ordering the deaths of tens (or hundreds) of millions based only on inconclusive evidence.

Another possibility that required sufficient early warning was Orbital Based. The concept behind this idea was to place all or a fraction of the total US nuclear force into orbit, upon warning, or maybe even during a period of increased geopolitical tension. They could stay there for up to fifteen days, or until the missile is deorbited onto Soviet targets, as commanded by the president. If tensions deescalate, or if the warning of a Soviet missile launch was actually a false alarm, the warheads could be deorbited into the open sea. These warheads possibly could even be recovered afterward, although the Pentagon acknowledged that "this is a difficult and complex problem which has not been satisfactorily worked."

The warheads would probably be lost, and those aren't exactly cheap. But it's still a marked improvement over the LUA. The ability to send the missiles up into space based on early warning or increased international tensions would provide decision makers with time to figure out what was going on. Is this a real attack? Is this a false alarm? We can take time to make our decision without actually executing a full-scale apocalypse.

That is, if the Soviets don't misconstrue our orbital pre-positioning as an actual attack. A protective launch into orbit could trigger the Soviets into launching their missiles against the United States. They'd have no way to know the difference between these preparations and the beginning of the end. For the sake of their national survival, the Soviets would have to assume this was the real deal. Sure, we could tell them what it was. But why the hell would they believe us?

Then there was the slight issue of missiles orbiting over the United States every ninety minutes or so, every day, for the duration of the time the ICBMs are in space. The Pentagon was aware of this potential concern. "Safety issues associated with nuclear warheads orbiting the earth with periodic passes over the US are not clear [really?]. Special precautions would be definitely needed."

Finally (and likely what doomed this idea before it really got started), the deployment of nuclear weapons into space is prohibited by the Treaty on Principles Governing Actions of States in the Exploration and Use of Outer Space, Including the Moon and Other Celestial Bodies (the "Outer Space

Treaty"), which the United States signed and ratified in 1967. Remember the legality criterion?

Another idea, less fraught with diplomatic difficulties, was called the Hydra, though I'm surprised it even made the final list. The Hydra system consisted of waterproof missiles with attached flotation devices designed to be launched by remote signal while floating in the water, a bit like a baby with water wings.

The goal of the concept is to create uncertainty as to the location of the missiles (for the Soviets, that is). The US military would secretly drop their MX missiles into the ocean from naval ships or submarines—or maybe even a naval ship disguised as a civilian craft. The missiles would float vertically until launch time. According to the plan, "Only an inconspicuous part of the missile front end is visible above the surface."

Inconspicuous? When's the last time you've gone boating and seen a ballistic missile nose cone bobbing in the water? I think I would notice.

Perhaps others might notice too. Like the Soviets, who could either pre-target the missiles for destruction in case of war, or simply pluck them out of the water whenever they felt like it.

Then there's the terrifying possibility that: "a third-nation, or paramilitary groups, would also be engaged in a hunt for the Hydras. Not under our direct control, any missile can be destroyed or towed away (stolen) at leisure." But even if the missiles weren't located and stolen by Iran, North Korea, or the Aryan Nation, the Hydra would present unprecedented safety problems: "The idea of missiles with nuclear warheads floating unattended in ocean waters introduces an unacceptable hazard to navigation for the world's shipping."

Some of these major problems were solved by another proposal, called Orca. The Orca concept prevents the someone-can-steal-the-missile-if-you-don't-run-into-the-missile-first issues plaguing Hydra by anchoring the MX to the ocean floor. When the missile is needed, a command could be sent via sonar to activate the warhead, release the anchor, and allow the weapon to float to the surface (from where it would be launched). That's the good news.

The bad news: Although Orca would be harder to find than Hydra (really, what wouldn't?), it could still be discovered using sonar from Soviet surface ships or submarines. It would be hard to hide the sonar signature of a massive ballistic missile, even one just sitting quietly. It has a very recognizable profile, and the Soviets would be unlikely to mistake it for frolicking seals or a humpback whale. And if they discovered the missiles, they would be apoplectic. So would the international community, and rightly so. The deployment of nuclear weapons on international seabeds is prohibited by an international treaty signed more than a decade ago before the point we are talking about (the Treaty on Prohibition of Employment of Nuclear Weapons and Other Weapons of Mass Destruction on the Seabed and Ocean Floor and in the Subsoil Thereof).

But potential diplomatic incidents aside, it was a technical issue that made this idea problematic. To maintain the secrecy of its location, the missile needed to be completely dormant—it conceals its location by emitting no signals. Any active communication with the missile risks giving away its location. But this means no one can test the readiness of the missile's systems and mechanics, or, far more important for command and control purposes, test if you can even communicate with the missile in the first place. The missile's operators would have no idea if they could talk to the missile, release the missile from the seabed, or if it would launch when it reached the surface—*until* the president ordered a nuclear strike. That's not the best time to find out whether your missiles work or not.

But what if we kept them on the surface? Another proposal called for putting missiles on barges that would be towed in random directions along American inland and coastal waterways. Ship-Inland called for the use of fourteen hundred barges to tug missiles over fourteen thousand miles of coastal waters, twelve thousand miles in the Mississippi River system, and three thousand miles on other inland waterways.

The problems with this plan were twofold. First, barge locations would be hard to hide. Soviet satellites, or even local human intelligence assets here in the United States, could easily spot the barges chugging up and down the Mississippi. And while they would be a moving target, they wouldn't necessarily be all that hard to sink. Furthermore, "moving so great a number of nuclear weapons on heavily traveled waterways is potentially a severe threat both to public safety and to missile security."

Maybe, then, we could get those missiles far away from the American homeland? The Ship-Ocean concept called for using specialized surface ships to move MX missiles randomly across the high seas. The ships (about sixty-five of them, with forty at sea at any given time) would each carry eight MX missiles, with up to ten warheads apiece.

Unfortunately, command and control of forty ships widely dispersed over the world's oceans could be a nightmare, and since the locations of the ships would be pretty obvious through the Soviets' use of surveillance satellites, trailing ships, and submarines, "the ships are extremely vulnerable to surprise attack by enemy ships, submarines, tankers, aircraft, and missiles." Pretty much everything, in other words. This was also the problem for the Dirigible plan.

Blimps/airships/dirigibles actually had a significant advantage over most every other air-mobility basing concept: endurance. They could float for days, casually moving from place to place at a leisurely pace. They could also carry a *lot* of weight—perhaps up to three hundred thousand pounds of payload, or three MX missiles.

The problem with dirigibles, as you might have guessed, is how ridiculously easy they would be to track and destroy. Another difficulty is the risk factor: "There is much controversy concerning the operational feasibility of dirigibles, particularly in regard to safety and reliability in adverse weather conditions and ground handling."

One way to avoid having our missiles crash, sink, get run over by cruise ships, or stolen by pirates is to keep them safely on land, inside the confines of the continental United States. The Commercial Rail plan called for special trains carrying MX ICBMs to use already existing commercial railroads in less populated parts of the northwestern United States. This wasn't a new idea: The same kind of rail mobile concept had been entertained in the early 1960s for the Minuteman I deployment.

But it was dismissed as impractical and dangerous then. So why would things be any different in the 1980s?

They weren't, per a review of the project, "Public safety and safety of the missiles pose insurmountable problems ... Simultaneous operation of commercial and nuclear missile trains within or near populated areas poses an unacceptable hazard to the civilian population." Not to mention it would be "virtually impossible to conceal train locations from enemy agents." A KGB spy could just sit and watch the railroad tracks, or, if they were really ambitious, recruit someone within the railroad office to provide the train schedules. As a result, "The mobile units would likewise be susceptible to sabotage or paramilitary attack." All an enemy would need is a small explosive placed on the tracks. Can you imagine the public reaction if a train carrying ICBMs derailed outside of Cheyenne, on the outskirts of Las Vegas, or while traveling through Denver?

So commercial trains are out—even a dedicated system would be impossible due to the time and space it would take to build what would be an entire railroad out west. If we've done planes and trains, it must be time for automobiles.

Two plans, known as Off-Road Mobile and Road Mobile (New Missile), proposed bringing the MX to the nation's highways and byways. Off-Road Mobile called for a fleet of 220 tractor-trailers with off-road capabilities. Each vehicle would carry one MX missile, and would continuously travel in seemingly random patterns to confuse Soviet intelligence and to maximize the potential for survival. The vehicles, however, would require *ninety thousand square miles* of dedicated land from which to operate, which is about the size of Great Britain.

The Road Mobile (New Missile) wouldn't need any additional operating space, because it would use the already existing highways that stretch across the country. The trucks would be staged inside American military bases until international tensions prompted their deployment. The plan went this way: Once the United States received strategic warning of an impending Soviet ICBM attack, 375 trucks would depart sixteen military bases and use fortyfive thousand miles of road (traveling at a constant 30 mph) until they were dispersed over an area of three hundred thousand square miles. Security, command and control, and communications personnel and equipment would follow along in a convoy of vans.

One major problem with this proposal was warning. Unless the trucks could be dispersed onto the roads *at least* two hours before an attack, the system was essentially worthless.

But that's not the biggest issue. There were two others that doomed the proposal:

1. "Given sufficient warning, there is also the possibility that traffic jams will delay dispersal." Always a pain in the neck when rush hour gets in the way of mutually assured destruction.
2. The Soviets would obviously know when the assets were being deployed. They watched American military bases anyway, as a part of their broader intelligence collection efforts. If, all of a sudden, hundreds of nuke-carrying trucks rushed out of sixteen of our bases, they would most certainly notice, and the action "might invite an immediate attack because the Soviets would know that they had one to two hours to launch their missiles after which an attack would not succeed." The need to protect the missiles might be the spark that starts World War III.

My favorite of the nearly thirty scrapped MX basing mode proposals was the Ground Effect Machine, or GEM. I don't love it because it was the best idea of the bunch. In fact, it's probably one of the worst. Really, it's one of the least likely to succeed, despite its harsh competition for ineptitude. This plan is so indefensible that the only reason it was included with the others *has* to be because of the military geekiness of the technology itself (GEM is a fancy word for hovercraft).

Instead, they finally decided on a program called the MX/MPS, which stood for Multiple Protective Shelter system. Two hundred MX missiles and their launchers are randomly distributed throughout the country among forty-six hundred shelters. Every so often, the missiles are moved from one shelter to another—or they pretend to move them. It's the classic shell game. Keep the Soviets guessing. They would never be able to target the American nuclear arsenal with the certainty of eliminating all of it in a first strike. For all they knew, they could be targeting empty shelters.

Or even decoy missiles. The construction of the system would even allow them to add an additional layer of deception to the MX deployment scheme. During construction of the shelters, the plan called for the insertion of a mock missile in each one. Upon completion of the shelter, a transporter would bring over an MX and exchange it for the mock-missile … or maybe not. As a result, even if there were Soviet spies nearby, "no observer can tell whether a missile has been moved or not. Most of the time, nothing has happened."

The survivability of the system depends on keeping missile location uncertain. But if you pull that off, the Soviets would be in a tough position. This was the solution.

AND THEN WHAT?

And then the whole thing turned out to be for naught. The MX/MPS concept would cost $37 billion, and require a ridiculous amount of land for the two hundred missiles and fourthousandplus hardened silos (and even when that number was later significantly reduced, the land usage problem remained). When all was said and done, the Reagan administration decided to propose a compromise. Shove the Peacekeepers inside of already existing Minuteman III silos. Congress loved the idea. It was cheap, easy, and they didn't have to think about it all that much.

If *this* was in fact a viable solution to the problem, we could have avoided all this nonsense. But Congress (and Reagan) didn't seem to care. The first four Peacekeepers were delivered to the Strategic Air Command in late 1986. By January 1988, twenty missiles were operational inside converted Minuteman silos, and by the end of that year all fifty budgeted Peacekeepers had been deployed.

Just in time for the Cold War to end.

19

PROJECT ICEWORM

As far as these things go, Camp Century was a pretty good cover. It was nominally designed as an underground military research station, located about 150 miles east of the American air base at Thule, Greenland. The stated purpose of Camp Century was to improve the American defense capability in the Arctic—to develop better survival and transportation techniques, and to obtain more useful knowledge about the harsh climate and the physical properties of the region. In essence, we covered up for a super-secret operation using a slightly less secret one.

The United States had been operating in the area since 1951, when the Thule air base and radar station first opened (it was a key cog in the Distant Early Warning—DEW—Line of radar installations). In 1958, the US Army's Cold Regions Research Engineering Laboratories (CRREL) sent more than two hundred men (the facility was a strictly male society) to be the first team to deploy to Century. Don't let the "Camp" in Camp Century fool you. This wasn't just a bunch of tents in the tundra. This was as close to a modern town as you could get in the middle of nowhere. The thirty-two buildings that comprised Camp Century included power stations, workshops, offices, a radio station, garages, waste management facilities, living quarters, a modern hospital (with an Xray machine and operating room), a fitness center (unlikely anyone would be jogging outside), a hobby shop, barbershop, bathing facilities, canteens, storerooms, a cinema, a library, and, of course—to make *everyone* feel welcome—a chapel and a bar. All built partially or completely underground.

Which is good, because you wouldn't want to spend too much time outside. This is an inhospitable environment to the extreme. Century was located only eight hundred miles from the North Pole. The *average* temperature was just under minus 24 degrees centigrade. The average annual snow accumulation was four *feet,* and it wasn't uncommon to see temperatures plunge into the minus 50, 60, or even 70 degree range when the wind, which could gust to over 125 mph, really got going. This meant that even simple tasks could be incredibly difficult, like basic resupply of the facility. Everything had to be brought in. Sure, you could fly in supplies fairly quickly from Thule, but that's only if the weather cooperated—and that was rare.

The solution was to use what were known as "Swings." These weren't quite as fun as they sound, but they were pretty cool nonetheless. Swings were humongous wagons and sledges dragged over from Thule by even more ginormous tractors. The wheels of the wagon were more than twice as tall as an adult man. Swings were ridiculously slow—about walking pace—but they could go anywhere and everywhere. Nothing the Arctic weather could throw at them could stop them. Camp Century was powered by the world's first portable nuclear reactor, the PM2A ("A" for "Arctic"). Designed as part of the US Army Nuclear Power Program (ANPP), the Camp Century reactor was built by the American Locomotive Company and created to study the capability of generating electrical and spaceheating energy at remote, relatively inaccessible sites. The Army was worried it might cost too much to deliver oil or coal to the facility, and also raised the possibility that some of their distant but vital bases might be cut off altogether in a war. The reactor could be a test model for providing constant power, regardless of geopolitical situation. The PM2A at Camp Century would produce 1.5 megawatts of electricity each year and a huge amount of heat energy. According to scientists, it would take as many as 850,000 gallons of oil per year to run a diesel generator that would turn out as much power and heat.

But why would they need that much power to run a dinky Arctic science facility?

A couple of reasons. First, something needs to keep the movies playing, the hospital Xraying, and the workshops workshopping. But besides that, Camp Century, though primarily a cover for a more secret project, actually hosted some seriously impressive science. Most of this involved deep ice core drilling. In 1961, physicists drilled more than forty-five hundred feet into the ice to reach the bottom of the Greenland Ice Sheet for the first time. This gave the scientific community an ice core representing more than a hundred thousand years of climate history, and so for the first time, ice core samples could be used to study the Earth's climate. Camp Century biologists were also able to observe microscopic organisms and germs that had been frozen for centuries in glaciers and then during the warmer summer months melted off into streams of water to be collected by enterprising science teams.

But of course, the real reason for Camp Century—and all its power—was to serve as a test bed for what came next: Project Iceworm. The nuclear reactor, resupply procedures (through the Swings), and the broader study of the feasibility of the ice as a platform for major military operations, were all designed to see if the deployment of American nuclear weapons to the Greenland Ice Shelf was a possibility.

Iceworm called for the placement of up to six hundred nuclear-armed, medium-range ballistic missiles in a series of underground tunnels. Ultimately the tunnel system would span almost two thousand five hundred miles of the sub-surface, and railroad tracks would connect thousands of individual firing positions. Although you'd only have hundreds of missiles, you could keep the Soviets guessing by having multiple places from which we could launch each missile. The missile itself was a modified version of the US Air Force's primary ICBM, the Minuteman. But this one would be shorter, designed for medium ranges, and renamed the "Iceman."

On its face, it was a great plan. The missiles could hide out under the massive ice sheet, impervious to Soviet strikes, and then pop out when it was time to launch. They would take the most direct path to the Soviet Union—over the Arctic—and end the war before it began.

Iceworm would be a huge undertaking, and it's not altogether clear how anyone expected it to remain a secret. When fully manned (and we are still probably talking about just men), the project called for eleven thousand personnel working in an area of more than *fifty-three thousand* square miles, which is about three times the size of Denmark.

Speaking of Denmark, the bigwigs in the Kennedy

administration loved this idea. It provided them with the flexibility in nuclear weapons development that they preferred.
JFK's administration wanted to have options—not like the
Eisenhower administration, which was committed to the idea
of Massive Retaliation (in essence, when war began America
would launch everything it had). But one major potential
roadblock to the plan was the government of Denmark, the
country that administered Greenland. In the 1950s, when
the United States was working with its European partners
on overseas nuclear weapons deployment, Denmark refused
to allow American weapons to be placed on Danish soil (as
part of a US-Danish defense agreement in 1951). It wasn't that
they didn't want to work closely with the United States and
NATO. Nor was it because they were less worried about the
expansionist threat of the Soviet Union than were the United
States or NATO. In fact, it was because they were *more* afraid
of the Soviets. Denmark is a small country, with significant
strategic importance due to its location at the entrance to the
Baltic Sea. And it's quite close to the border of what was once
the Soviet Union. Even though it was a stalwart American
ally and a member of NATO, Denmark was smart enough
to avoid purposely poking the Soviet bear.

So it's altogether possible that Denmark would have
blocked the use of Greenland for the deployment of hundreds of American nuclear missiles.

That is, if they knew about it.

The most interesting part of the US-Danish alliance was
the *intentional* lack of information transfer that occurred
between these two NATO allies. It all started with the Thule
air base. The United States requested use of Thule as part of
the 1951 joint agreement. It was clear from the get-go that the

PROJECT ICEWORM

US Air Force wanted to use Thule as a launching and staging point for its long-range strategic bombers. But of course, this would violate the provision in the treaty to keep American nuclear weapons off Danish territory.

The solution to the problem was a display of diplomatic contortionism for the ages. When the United States brought up the topic of what "might" be based at Thule, the Danish responded with, "The Danish government does not want to be asked that kind of a question."

We never had this conversation. If you don't ask me, then I don't need to say no. Now please go away and let's pretend this never happened.

This diplomatic philosophy posed tantamount benefits to both sides: The Danish government saves face with the Soviets and strengthens NATO, all while providing the United States with a valuable centerpiece for JFK's nuclear strategy.

But we will never know, because Iceworm never made it to the operational stage. We would just be speculating about the reaction of the Danish government to American missiles deployed in Greenland—and we hate to speculate.

In fact, neither Cold War geopolitics nor Danish domestic policy prevented Project Iceworm from becoming a reality. Instead, it was nature.

You might assume an ice sheet more than twice the size of Texas to be stationary. You'd be wrong. The Greenland Ice Sheet, like all ice masses on the Earth, is in constant (albeit really, really slow) movement. The ice sheet is spreading outward from the center, and from higher elevations to lower ones. If the naturally flowing ice from the ice sheet reaches the sea, it chunks off into ice blocks that turn into icebergs in the sea. We've all seen this happen in nature documentaries.

It's a more or less continuous process: The Greenland Ice Sheet is always moving.

And this was a major problem for Camp Century and Project Iceworm. All your perfectly drilled tunnels, trenches, and caverns won't remain that way. They might narrow, as the ice crunches in around them. They might expand, at which point the ceilings would no longer have the support of the carefully measured walls. By 1962, only a few years into the operation, the ceiling of the room housing the PM2A reactor had dropped precipitously, and had to be raised five feet in order to continue operations.

Government scientists scrambled to determine the ramifications of an ice sheet moving so much faster than had been anticipated. After taking ice core samples, the scientific team presented the bad news: The shifting of the ice sheet would make Project Iceworm unfeasible in just two years. The ballistic missile firing positions would be gone. The tunnels and trenches that allowed personnel to move around the base would be no longer. No more cinema. No more fitness center. No more bar. Everything would be swallowed up by the forces of nature.

Camp Century was cleared of personnel in 1965, and formally closed the following year. Project Iceworm never really got off the ground.

In 1969, a special US Army team traveled to the remnants of Camp Century to survey the damage to the facility. They found significant warping and buckling of the metal arches, steel beams, and wooden timbers in the facility's foundation. The buildings, still furnished and untouched since the day of the final evacuation, were slowly being crushed under the weight of the moving ice. When the team left the facility, they assumed that the secret of Project Iceworm would be permanently hidden under the ice, never to be heard from again.

But they were they wrong.

AND THEN WHAT?

Anthropogenic climate change, that's what.

Climate change is happening, whether we like it or not. More to the point, climate change is happening, whether we *believe* it or not. Science doesn't care what we believe.

Neither does the planet, whose warming trend is bringing us extreme weather, vicious storms, devastating wildfires, rising seas, spreading deserts, deadlier (and more prolific) diseases, and diminishing reserves of vital resources. It's here. It's worldwide. It's man-made. And it's just going to get worse.

No region is more sensitive to climate change than the Arctic. This is not new information—scientists first recognized the Arctic's susceptibility to warming in the nineteenth century. The reason for this is a phenomenon known as albedo feedback, in which an initial warming sets in motion a chain reaction that significantly amplifies the rate of warming. Here's how it works: Most of the Arctic is covered in snow and ice, which is, you know, white. As every schoolchild knows, white surfaces reflect sunlight (and dark surfaces absorb it). "Albedo" is actually a scientific measure of how white (or reflective) a surface is. Snow and ice have an albedo as high as (or higher than) 80 percent, meaning that 80 percent of the sun's energy hitting the surface is reflected back into space. Ocean water, on the other hand, tends to be a much darker color (blue, green, brown), and has an albedo of less than 10 percent. Barely any energy gets sent back to where it came from.

As the Earth gets warmer, more of the Arctic ice melts. And this is, of course, problematic for those who live on coastlines, where a small increase in sea level could be catastrophic. But even if you live in Nebraska, or Germany, or the Himalayas, melting Arctic ice is *your* problem too. Melted ice and snow turns into ocean water. Dark ocean water. Instead of reflecting solar energy, it absorbs it, warming the planet even further.

Melting ice causes dark water. Dark water causes more warming, More warming brings more melting. More melting brings more dark water. The albedo feedback.

The melting Arctic is an economic and security issue. The reason: The Arctic region is the largest unexplored trove of petroleum resources remaining on Earth—ninety *billion* barrels of oil, seventeen hundred *trillion* cubic feet of natural gas, and fortyfour *billion* barrels of liquid natural gas. According to the Office of the Director of National Intelligence, climate change "will raise the risk of increased competition between Arctic and non-Arctic nations over access to sea routes and resources."

Two of those Arctic nations: the United States and Russia.

And if we all somehow survive the new oil rush to the North Pole (and all the other problems caused by a warming planet), climate change has another surprise in store for us. The Greenland icecap is receding, and threatening to uncover the top-secret US government Cold War nuclear project that was assumed to be buried for all eternity.

For decades it had been assumed this covert facility would be covered by ice and snow until the end of time. But a 2016 study published in the *Geophysical Research Letters* argued that within the next seventy-five years, the ice and snow that covers Camp Century will begin to melt faster than it is replaced. Once this happens, it will be only a matter of time before the camp is reintroduced to the public.

But that's not all that will be exposed to the world. When Project Iceworm was abandoned, the US government assumed that the Greenland Ice Sheet would provide the cover (pun intended) not just for their secret facility, but also for all of its physical, chemical, biological, and radioactive waste.

Physical waste (like building material and railroad remnants), chemical waste (thousands of gallons of diesel fuel and PCBs—which we will talk about in a moment), biological waste, and radiological waste (coolant for the reactor) are now likely buried about 120 feet down into the ice—with some liquid wastes perhaps even farther down, maybe as deep as 200 feet.

That sounds deep, but it's not. Because of the rapidity in which climate change is altering the environment, it might only hold out for another couple of decades. And it could happen sooner if the pace of climate change amps up even more.

And regardless of when the actual melting of all the ice on the surface occurs, the waste left over from Century/Iceworm could be swept into the sea by some of the surface ice melting and seeping down through the ice sheet. Once it does, the water can pick up and wash away waste through small crevasses and channels in the solid ice and out into the open ocean. Then it could impact key habitat areas off the coast of Iceland that are used by a multitude of marine animals and birds.

So it's bad if you happen to live in Iceland, but what about the rest of us? Remember when I mentioned the PCBs?

They are particularly nasty. The military used PCBs—more formally known as polychlorinated biphenyl—in a lot of its paints used in the Arctic region during the early Cold War because PCBs are especially resistant to extreme temperatures. They also don't quickly break down once in the environment—which is great for longevity when in use, but it also means they can last a long time cycling among air, water, and soil. They can be carried long distances, and have been found in snow and seawater in areas far from where they were released into the environment. So even though they would be released way the hell up in the Arctic, they could find their way to a neighborhood near you.

PCBs have been shown in multiple peerreviewed studies to cause cancer in animals (and likely humans) as well as a number of serious noncancer health effects in both animals and humans, including harmful effects on the immune system, reproductive system, nervous system, and endocrine system. PCBs can also cause deficits in neurological development, including visual recognition, shortterm memory, and learning.

And it's coming our way.

AIRCRAFT NUCLEAR PROPULSION AND PROJECT ORION

The International Space Station is powered by eight arrays of solar panels, totaling 262,400 solar cells. Each of the arrays (the technical term for a grouping of interconnected solar panels) is 112 feet long and 39 feet wide, and combine to cover an area of nearly 27,000 square feet.

Solar power works brilliantly for anything operating close to (you guessed it) the sun. The Hubble Space Telescope, the Magellan spacecraft to Venus, the Mars Global Surveyor, and the Mars Observer all use (or used) solar power. Vanguard 1, the first solarpowered satellite sent into space (in 1958), transmitted information back to Earth for years. The Juno mission to Jupiter, launched in 2011, broke the record for solar-powered distance in January 2016 when it traveled 493 *million* miles from the sun.

But Juno is the rare exception. In most cases, solar power carries significant limitations. Every other spacecraft that has traveled as far as Jupiter (and there have been eight of them) has used nuclear power instead of solar. Nuclear power, usually in the form of a slowly decaying isotope of plutonium called plutonium238 (nuclear weapons use the much more volatile Pu239), can support spacecraft in the cold and dark void of deep space, places where solar power can rarely do the job.

Among those that operated (or still operate) on nuclear power include:

The Transit Satellite Network—The first satellite powered by plutonium, Transit 4A, was launched into space in 1961.

Apollo 11—The first manned mission to the moon left behind a seismic monitoring system that relied on the Apollo Lunar Radioisotopic Heater, which used Pu238 to keep the system warm during ridiculously cold lunar nights, when the temperature dropped to minus 243 degrees Fahrenheit. Each of the remaining Apollo missions used plutonium as well, but inside nuclear batteries that provided power to surface experiments.

Voyager 1 and Voyager 2—These are the ones with the golden records full of images, audio clips, and information about the planet and its life forms that hopefully won't be interpreted by alien species as a declaration of war. Voyager 1 has traveled nearly 12 *billion* miles on its three Pu238 nuclear batteries. It is now the only human-made object that has reached interstellar space.

The Mars Curiosity rover—About the size of an SUV, Curiosity landed on Mars in 2012. The rover is equipped with a stereoscopic camera (with which it sends back amazing pictures you can see online), a powerful microscope, and an infrared laser it uses to zap Mars rocks. Curiosity is powered by a 125watt nuclear battery that should keep it conducting important scientific experiments well into the mid-2020s.

Most of us have no idea that these spacecraft were filled with radioactive fuel. It wasn't a big deal anyway—if something went wrong with the plutonium, the impact would be confined to areas outside of the atmosphere, or even millions (or billions) of miles into deep space.

But what if you brought that nuclear fuel inside the atmosphere, and used it to power a conventional aircraft? Or what if you decided slowly decaying nuclear material was too weak to do the job in outer space, and you really needed something with more ... punch?

In the 1940s and '50s, the US government attempted to develop two unique programs. One was an aircraft powered by a nuclear reactor. The other, a spacecraft propelled by *nuclear explosions*.

You'd think Enrico Fermi would have had enough on his mind. The theoretical physicist was one of the most important members of the team working to develop the atomic bomb during World War II. But while creating the first artificial self-sustaining nuclear chain reaction at the University of Chicago in 1942, Fermi was thinking big. What if we could use atomic energy for more than building bombs? Specifically, what if atomic energy could be used for the propulsion of aircraft?

These questions would have to wait, however. The development of the desperately needed bomb was the first and only priority. There wasn't any uranium or plutonium to spare for side projects, no matter how potentially beneficial. It was the bomb, only the bomb, and nothing but the bomb.

But when the war ended, the US Air Force (a lot of this story occurs after 1947, so I'll use that name despite the fact that the USAF didn't technically exist until 1947), with support from the newly formed Atomic Energy Commission (AEC), finally began to carry out studies on the feasibility of using nuclear energy to power airplanes. In 1946, the Air Force awarded a contract to the Fairchild Engine and Airplane Corporation to manage the multiple industrial firms brought in to work on the project, thereby officially starting the Nuclear Energy for the Propulsion of Aircraft (NEPA) program. The purpose of NEPA was to test the feasibility of the concept—in other words, can we pull this off? Can our scientists and engineers develop atomic-powered long-range strategic bombers that can influence the global balance of power?

Think about it for a second. American bombers could stay in the air for days, weeks even. No need to refuel. An abundance of power. Always on station and ready to fly into harm's way. It was the kind of thing an Air Force general's dreams were made of. The perfect weapon for a Cold War. It's no wonder why it seemed like such an obvious and tantalizing application to Fermi during World War II.

It just had to be built.

Apparently, the US military thought it could be done. In 1951, the Joint Chiefs of Staff determined that a "military requirement" existed to justify the construction of a nuclear-powered aircraft, at which point the NEPA—which, remember, was created to test feasibility—was replaced by a joint AEC/USAF program known as ANP (Aircraft Nuclear Propulsion). The mandate of the ANP program was to take the NEPA concept and bring it to the next level: the full-scale development of aircraft reactor and engine systems that would propel the Air Force toward the ultimate goal, the deployment of a fleet of nuclear-powered strategic bombers.

The AEC was responsible for designing a nuclear reactor small enough (and safe enough) to install on an airplane. They were also tasked with working out "shielding"—how to protect the crew from the reactor's radiation. The Air Force, in turn, was responsible for building the rest of the plane. The Air Force was ready to go, urging the AEC to move as quickly as possible to make this idea a reality:

> There is a highest priority requirement for an intercon-tinental bomber capable of delivering, with acceptable attrition rates, any of our nuclear weapons on any target from bases within our continental limits. Recent studies performed by the Office for Aircraft Nuclear Propulsion indicate that a nuclear propeller aircraft possibly can be built which may meet this requirement by as early as 1960, providing the Air Force and the Atomic Energy Commis-sion place sufficient priority on the solution of the difficult R&D problems involved.

The AEC replied: It would, within the *limits* of its resources and such funds as *might* be made available within overall program priorities, continue to *explore* ways and means of …

Clearly, the AEC didn't share the Air Force's urgency. Or maybe it did, but had so many competing priorities—like building and maintaining an effective nuclear deterrent—that it could only do its utmost to work with the Air Force "within the limits" of its capabilities.

And there were limits. Plenty of them. Enough so that

the program muddled along throughout the majority of the 1950s without much progress, until the Soviet launch of Sputnik forced the government to take a serious look at what was happening. In October 1957, the Research and Development Subcommittee of the Joint Committee on Atomic Energy (a congressional committee that included members from the US House and the Senate) made a direct appeal to President Eisenhower to put his full weight behind the ANP project. They explained:

> Speaking frankly, Mr. President, the ANP program since its inception has suffered from a lack of incentive and initiative on the part of those who have been charged with the responsibility of conducting the program. It has also been characterized by the lack of any well-defined future objective, including target dates for completion, and has not had the kind of well-coordinated and centralized direction which is necessary for the successful achievement of such an extremely difficult research and development task.

Harsh but fair. Still, it didn't work.

In July 1959, Herbert York, former Manhattan Project physicist and, in July 1959, the first Director of Defense Research and Engineering for the Department of Defense, was brutally honest in his assessment of the ANP:

> The ANP program has been characterized by attempts to find short cuts to early flight and by brute force and expensive approaches to the problem. Thus we find that only a relatively very small fraction of the funds and energies applied to this program has gone into trying to

develop a reactor with a potentially high performance …
As a result of this approach to the problem we are still at
least *four years away* from achieving flight with a reactor-
engine combination *** which can *just barely fly* [emphasis
mine. *** in original].

Finally, in March 1961, the newly inaugurated President
Kennedy took one look at the quagmirical money pit/
flaming pile of rubbish that was the ANP and terminated the
program. By that time, the United States had spent nearly
fifteen years and more than $1 billion on the program (almost
$8.5 billion today), with very little to show for the effort.

So why did this go so badly? What went wrong, and why
didn't someone from the government see this happening and
stop it long before the program had spent *one billion dollars*?
True, the US government spent millions weaponizing bats,
but you'd think when it hit $500 million someone would
have raised a red flag.

But therein lies the problem, not just with the budget but
with the entire program: No one was really paying all that
much attention. Sure, fourteen separate government reviews
of the project were made from 1955 until the cancellation in
1961—but by fourteen *different* review groups, all temporary,
with little continuity in membership among the groups, and
the reviews themselves based on brief visits to the contractors'
plants and briefings and discussions in Washington, rather
than indepth and comprehensive study. Nine of the fourteen
review groups were ad hoc—temporary and hurried.

Not exactly vigorous oversight.

For example, the review group that issued the first report,
in April 1955, based its findings entirely on information

received during an inspection trip on which they spent a single day at the General Electric plant, and a single day at the Oak Ridge National Laboratory. These were followed by a oneday meeting in Washington with the Technical Advisory Panel on Atomic Energy.

The review group that wrote the June 1955 report based its analysis solely on meetings in Washington, and *did not even visit* the contractors' locations. A group that completed its review in April 1957 spent more time both in the field with contractors as well as in meetings in Washington (one day each at GE, Pratt & Whitney, Convair, and Lockheed, and five days in DC), but the overall mission of this group (also ad hoc) was to evaluate the *entire ANP program,* analyze the objectives and soundness of the technical approaches to the problem, *and* advise as to the future of the ANP program.

This was several months-worth of work shoved into a couple of days. No wonder no one knew what the hell was going on.

While the ANP was trying to bring nuclear energy into the wild blue yonder, another extraordinary government program was aiming for the stars. The conceptual basis for Project Orion can be traced to the hallowed laboratories of the Manhattan Project. Polish-American mathematician Stanislaw Ulam, one of the men most responsible for the development of the hydrogen bomb (along with Edward Teller), first conceived of the idea of using nuclear explosions to propel an object through space (a concept known as nuclear pulse propulsion) after witnessing the testing of the atomic bomb in July 1945.

Have you ever bounced on a pogo stick? I know "kids

these days" have their video games and smartphones and Candy Crush, but back in my day if we really wanted to have fun—and a chance to severely injure ourselves—we'd grab the rusty pogo stick from the garage and bounce on it three or four times until we lost control and flew into the bushes. Good times. If you know what I'm talking about, you'll have no problem understanding the concept behind Project Orion. If not, look it up. This story will make a lot more sense.

Orion was a spacecraft that would essentially chuck out nuclear bombs behind it. The bombs would explode, and the resulting shock wave would hit Orion and propel it forward. Do this a couple hundred (or thousand) times, and you can really get your spacecraft moving—enough so that you can quickly and easily visit other planets, or even take a trip to another solar system.

There's a little more to this concept, of course. When the bomb exploded (about fifty meters or so from the ship) it would create a shock wave of highvelocity, highdensity plasma that would hit a massive pusher plate at the stern of the spacecraft (some of the specifics are still classified). The pusher plate would weigh as much as a thousand tons, and would be coated with what's known as an "ablative" plastic (like what is used on a space capsule's heat shield) to protect it from the flurry of nuclear blasts. Each detonation would add about 20 mph to Orion's velocity, and since it would be traveling through the frictionless vacuum of space, this acceleration could continue until Orion ran out of bombs.

But if that's all there was to the pusher plate, it would not keep Orion safe for human occupancy. The reason: The acceleration from the shock wave of a nuclear blast at that distance would be somewhere in the ballpark of ten thousand times the force of gravity (10,000 g). That's a lot—and it would happen over and over again, each time another nuke went off. Most normal humans can only take about 5 g without experiencing serious medical problems. To make it safe for humans, Orion's pusher plate was attached to the body of the spacecraft by gigantic springs that served to absorb the force of the nuclear blast, reduce the acceleration forces to a comfortable 4 g, and then transfer that energy into forward motion—like a nuclear-bomb-powered space pogo stick.

(And yes, physicists, I know I am stretching this comparison. But for the layperson, please continue to play along.)

The idea for this kind of vehicle was codified by Stanislaw Ulam and Cornelius Everett in their 1955 report titled *On a Method of Propulsion of Projectiles by Means of External Nuclear Explosions.* At that point it was just a concept paper, but after Sputnik, esoteric scientific concepts began to move quickly from the minds of scientists to development in the real world. Project Orion was formally proposed as a serious program in 1958 by a team of scientists and engineers at the General Atomics Division of the General Dynamics Corporation. Many of those working on the program were veterans of the Manhattan Project, and looked forward to finding new ways to use their wartime invention toward peaceful pursuits. That same year, governmental support came in the form of funding for a feasibility study from the newly established Advanced Research Projects Agency, which didn't really make a ton of sense since ARPA was a Department of Defense agency and required that all sponsored projects should have a military application. The scientists and engineers working on Orion weren't thinking of their work in terms of military uses, but they were certainly happy to have the financial support. No one was going to look the gift horse in the mouth.

This is especially true considering that no other government agency wanted anything to do with Orion. NASA, which had also been formed in the wake of the Sputnik launch, did not see Orion as a practical means of space exploration. Perhaps it was too forward-thinking. At this time, NASA was still trying to figure out how to get a small satellite and a chimpanzee into space. The US Air Force was not interested either, although it had taken over many (if not all) of ARPA's military space projects. Orion didn't fit squarely in this category, and the Air Force rightly concluded that the program was unlikely to produce any tangible military benefits. Orion was going to take us to Mars, or to the moons of Saturn. Or even to another solar system. Unless there were aliens to fight, this wasn't a military mission.

So it was ARPA or nothing.

One of the benefits of government funding was the ability to start small-scale testing. In 1959, the Orion team began to test some of the theoretical concepts to see if they worked in practice. The initial tests, sarcastically nicknamed "Putt Putt," involved detonating small balls of plastic explosive under jerry-rigged spaceship models made out of things like metal mixing bowls the team had bought from the local grocery shop. By November they had moved on to more realistic testing of a true scale model of what might someday be the Orion spacecraft.

It was called "Hot Rod," and it was 7 feet tall and 3.3 feet in diameter. Just like the real Orion would, Hot Rod was equipped with a pusher plate and a spring shock absorber. In the test, six successive detonations of high-powered plastic explosive pushed the model 184 feet into the air. After twenty-three seconds of flight, the test vehicle parachuted back to the ground. The concept worked, and it was cause for celebration.

At least until 1960, when ARPA decided it had had enough of Orion and dumped the program.

This forced the General Atomics team to go hat in hand to the US Air Force to try to get it to pick up the project. To their relief, the Air Force said yes—the project was just too tantalizing to let go—but this presented both parties with new and particularly tricky complications. For one, the Air Force was prohibited from funding nonmilitary projects, so the Orion team found themselves all of a sudden working on a "military" spacecraft. This was total nonsense, but it meant that those on the project would have to at least nominally try to find a direct military requirement that Orion could fill.

During the Kennedy administration, this was especially difficult. Secretary of Defense Robert McNamara, who controlled the Pentagon's purse strings, was no idiot when it came to evaluating the efficacy of military projects (we won't get into his ability to evaluate Southeast Asian insurgent movements). McNamara could see that Orion was designed solely for interplanetary space exploration, not warfare. To his credit, he didn't order the Air Force to cut the program outright, but he continually refused to allow it to increase Orion's budget or expand the project beyond the small-scale testing stage, which would require experiments with nuclear weapons.

In the end, however, it was a geopolitical consideration that might have contributed most to the demise of Project Orion. In 1963, the governments of the United States, the Soviet Union, and the United Kingdom signed the Treaty

Banning Nuclear Weapon Tests in the Atmosphere, in Outer Space and Under Water, otherwise known as the Limited Test Ban Treaty. Finalized in the wake of the Cuban Missile Crisis, the treaty would, at least temporarily, begin to rein in the Cold War arms race, which was alarmingly spiraling out of control. Which is a noble cause—unless, of course, you need nuclear weapons to propel your cool spaceship.

The Orion team could continue to do Putt Putts and Hot Rods, but not much else. Not without NASA's help, anyway. And NASA had no intention of getting involved.

I should really qualify that statement: There were some in NASA who thought Orion was a great idea. Wernher von Braun, former Nazi rocket scientist and a key member of the brain trust behind NASA's manned space program, in 1964 wrote a report advocating for Orion, called *Nuclear Pulse Propulsion—Its Potential Value to NASA*. Others, particularly within the engineering community at NASA, expressed interest as well.

But it was not enough to save the program, which was formally canceled by the Air Force in June 1965. The leadership of NASA didn't like the nuclear weapons component of the project, nor were they enamored by Orion's increasingly high level of classification. NASA leadership was committed to the Apollo program, which planned to use the Saturn V rocket to send Americans to the moon. They were also shrewd political animals. They understood that the public might be terrified by the idea of using nuclear weapons to propel a spacecraft (even if this might have been an irrational fear, it still had to be taken into consideration). Without public support, NASA could find itself cut off from needed congressional funding.

The game was up.

AND THEN WHAT?

Let's go back to the Aircraft Nuclear Propulsion program for a moment. Despite what I wrote earlier, this program wasn't a complete disaster. Some of the high-temperature materials developed during the project, as well as some key data it produced on radiation shielding, were used later by NASA for the space program.

And despite its failure, the promise of the ANP has inspired some modern scientists to advocate for a reevaluation of the potential benefits of airplanes powered by nuclear energy, particularly as we now know more and more about the environmental impact of fossil fuels.

Let's not get ahead of ourselves, though. The likelihood that we will book a trip to Paris on a nuclear-powered airplane in our lifetime is slim to none. There are still significant problems to overcome, including the question of how to effectively shield the passengers from radiation without adding a huge amount of weight to the airframe. Then there are the flight attendants and the pilots, who would be exposed to higher levels of radioactivity on each and every flight. Finally, terrorism experts would probably have something to say about some of the potential problems associated with flying nuclear reactors.

21

PROJECT A119

Dr. Leonard Reiffel was a true polymath. In his almost ninety years (he died of cancer in 2017 at the age of eighty-nine), he was granted more than fifty patents; was a colleague of Enrico Fermi at the University of Chicago; worked with former Nazi scientists brought back to the United States as part of Operation Paperclip; worked on NASA's Apollo program, rising from the position of an outside consultant to the deputy director of the entire program; authenticated priceless artwork for the Hermitage Museum in St. Petersburg, Russia; won a Peabody Award as a children's broadcaster; wrote science-fiction and thriller novels; and acted as a consultant for Ukraine and Belarus following the Chernobyl disaster. If you're feeling inadequate right now, well … join the club.

But it was a particular program starting in the late 1950s that interests us the most. Reiffel was asked by the US Air Force to be its director. The program never happened (thank whatever higher power you want to thank), but in its planning stages it was officially called "A Study of Lunar Research Flights," and its *beyond* top-secret nomenclature was Project A119.

If it had been carried to fruition, it would have been one of the most ridiculous projects ever envisioned. It had no practical purpose. It had no discernible national security goals. It was solely designed to show the world that America could do something this ~~stupid~~ spectacular.

And Leonard Reiffel was in charge.

The incessant beeping chirped away in the key of Aflat.

Beep. Beep. Beep.

The sound lasted three-tenths of a second. Then came three-tenths of a second of silence. Then the sound again. Over and over.

It was a sound that changed history. The NBC radio announcer on that night, October 4, 1957, understood the ramification of that beeping.

"Listen now," he said, "for the sound that forevermore separates the old from the new."

The object making that incessant sound was not very big—about the size of a beach ball. It only weighed 184 pounds. But it spurred on a revolution in science and technology that prompted the United States to put a new national priority on beating the Soviets at their own game. Through a radical reorganization of how America operated in science, technology, and engineering—from the laboratories of universities, to the factory floors of private industry, to the corridors of power in Washington—American innovation would never be the same. The US would eventually put their own satellites into space (first, Explorer 1, and then later, the Corona reconnaissance satellite), reorganize defense research into a powerful organization (the Advanced Research Projects Agency, now the Defense Advanced Research Projects Agency), and create a civilian space agency (NASA) to fly them into the great beyond.

Eventually.

But at that moment, something needed to be done sooner rather than later. America needed to prove to the world that it hadn't lost the space race before it had even begun. The American people needed a sign to reassure them that the Soviets did not have a permanent upper hand—that Sputnik wouldn't soon be replaced by Soviet ICBMs raining down on the United States. *America* were supposed to be the world's innovators. America invented potato chips, condensed milk, electric light bulbs, photographic film, the phonograph, candy floss, the mousetrap, the airplane, ice lollies, and chocolate chip cookies. America invented sunglasses, nylon, and the microwave.

America invented the atomic bomb.

America needed to show the world they were back in the game.

And they needed something big.

Leonard Reiffel had no desire to leave Chicago. He was a native of the Windy City, and greatly enjoyed his exciting and rewarding job working alongside physics legend Enrico Fermi at the University of Chicago's Institute for Nuclear Studies following the conclusion of World War II. But in 1949 he was given a chance to manage all of the cutting-edge physics research at another Chicago-based institution, the Armour Research Foundation (ARF—now known as the Illinois Institute of Technology). From that year through 1962, Reiffel and his team pushed physics to its limit, working on projects that studied the global environmental effects of nuclear explosions.

Sometime before May 1958 (Reiffel isn't quite sure of the exact date), the US Air Force asked the ARF team to investigate something truly out of the ordinary: "the visibility and effects of a hypothetical nuclear explosion on the Moon." The Air Force wanted to surprise the Soviets and the world. Hey, look at what we can do. We can blow the hell out of the moon.

Reiffel, to his credit, knew that he didn't have the necessary expertise inhouse to do this kind of a study. To supplement his ARF researchers, he brought on Gerard Kuiper, the expert on planetary physics whose name you might recognize from the Kuiper belt, a diskshaped region beyond Neptune that contains hundreds of thousands of icy bodies and a trillion or more comets. To round out the group, Kuiper suggested that Reiffel bring in a young graduate student from the University of Chicago whose name you'll likely also recognize: Carl Sagan. Yes. That Carl Sagan.

Sagan's job was to do maths. Lots of maths. It was important to the project that someone like Sagan could accurately model the expansion of the dust cloud that would be caused by a nuclear explosion on the moon. We needed to know how the moon would react so that we could know if the explosion could be seen from Earth. After all, that was the whole point of the program.

And this brings up two important questions:

1. Why would self-respecting scientists agree to a project to detonate a nuclear weapon on the moon?
2. Would this thing work in the first place? What would a nuclear explosion on the moon look like?

To answer the first question, we need to put ourselves in the shoes of American scientists in the late 1950s/early 1960s. This was a time when American science was (unfortunately) inextricably linked to American Cold War policy. Although the age of McCarthyism had ended, scientists still vividly remembered when Robert Oppenheimer was publicly flogged for taking a position considered antithetical to US national security—opposing the creation of the hydrogen bomb.

But it wasn't just fear that inspired physicists, chemists, biologists, astrophysicists, and others to join university laboratories, private industries, or government institutions that were working on defense research. Most of these scientists were patriots. They believed in what they were doing. This was a fight to the death, or at least for the future of the free world. These men and women (but mostly men because of the times) had a skill set that was integral for the security of their nation. Sometimes it's as simple as that.

But what about this program in particular? Surely nuking the moon just for the public relations win would stretch the limits of what even the most patriotic scientists would willingly accept.

You'd be surprised.

Whether these were serious considerations, or just ways to justify their actions, many of those involved in Project A119 cited the potential for *real and important scientific discovery* that could come out of detonating a nuclear weapon on the surface of the moon. These were exciting times, with the potential to explore new frontiers of science. Carl Sagan, the man who would dedicate his life to searching for evidence of life on other worlds, thought this could be a great way to try to identify the presence of microbes or organic molecules on the moon (this is when we still thought there might be something up there besides dust). Others envisioned experiments centered on lunar chemistry, or the thermal conductivity of the lunar surface. Reiffel's team also wondered if the nuclear blast would produce enough seismic activity to evaluate the makeup of the moon's immediate subsurface structure. According to Reiffel, "A central theme, which runs through many of the projected experimental situations, envisions placing of a maximum of three identical instrument packages at arbitrary locations on the visible face of the moon prior to any possible nuclear detonation. These instrument packages would be equipped to make a variety of measurements."

There were also serious fears that the Soviets would blow up a part of the moon before we got the chance to do it ourselves. On November 1, 1957, United Press International sent out a wire report that claimed that the Soviets planned to detonate a hydrogen bomb on the moon on or about November 7. Headlined "Latest Red Rumor: They'll Bomb Moon," the article states that a "fellow" told UPI he talked to "a guy 'high in US intelligence'" who said that the Soviets were timing the launch to coincide with the November 7 fortieth anniversary of the Bolshevik Revolution. Although the article exclaimed, "If that's true—look out!" it also warned that the rocket carrying the nuke was just as likely to miss the moon entirely and boomerang back to Earth. "If the rocket contained an Hbomb," the article surmised, "the best hope of earth would be that the whole thing would burn up harmlessly in the atmosphere before it impacted, as the missile men say."

No one is really sure where this rumor started, but it is indicative of the kind of panic in the United States in the wake of the launch of Sputnik.

Now to the most important question: Would this work?

First, let's get the basics out of the way. By 1959, the Soviet Union had already crashed a probe into the moon. The United States followed this less than three years later with a kamikaze probe of their own. So, in a general sense, the world knew that launching something on a rocket and sending it to the surface of the moon was feasible. We still don't know some of the specific technical details of early American ballistic missile technology (some things are still classified), but during an interview Reiffel gave later in life, he insisted we had the capability to hit a target on the moon with an accuracy of within two miles. That's pretty good, given that the Moon has a diameter of 2,159 miles.

That leaves us with the most important question: where would you detonate the bomb on the moon? You'd want to detonate the bomb on the edge (known as the terminator) of the dark side of the Moon, so that the sun's light would silhouette the trademark mushroom cloud from behind. It would look incredibly cool.

Except … that wouldn't happen.

Mushroom clouds from a nuclear explosion are caused by the movement of dust and debris kicked up in a *dense* atmosphere. The explosion also releases a massive amount of heat very rapidly, which interacts with the cooler surrounding air and makes it *less dense*. (You don't need a nuclear explosion to make a mushroom cloud. Really anything that causes a rapid release of heat, like a volcano or even a major forest fire, can cause a mushroom cloud to form.) The hot air in the center of the blast rises, creating a vacuum that is immediately filled by the surrounding air (which also expands and starts to rise). Eventually the rising air runs smack into the air on top of it,

271

which had been just hanging around in the atmosphere—like on any normal day—helping birds and planes fly. The atmospheric air pushes down on the rising column of smoke, dust, debris, superheated and notsosuperheated air and flattens out the top. Voilà, a mushroom cloud.

Then we have to factor back into the equation the atmospheric air. A lot of it is busy applying pressure to the top of the cloud, but some of it doesn't have much choice and gets blown out of the way by the rapidly rising heat. This air, which is at much lower temperature than the air in the center column, does what cooler air does: It descends. But it doesn't get far. The cooler air gets sucked back into the vacuum created by the explosion, and back up again it goes. This is why you see that swirly pattern at the edges of a mushroom cloud.

The moon, however, is essentially a vacuum already. It has *some* gases hanging around on its surface, but it really doesn't have an atmosphere like we do on Earth. Without the weight of a dense atmosphere, there would be no resistance to the expansion of the nuclear-produced dust and debris. They would just keep on going and going, instead of curling back to the surface. No big plume, no sound or shock wave, and no mushroom cloud. Just a lot of dust.

This doesn't mean there wouldn't be a hell of a show. The people of Earth would see a visible flash from the detonation. And maybe the sun would shine through the dust and debris in such a way as to give the world a pretty view.

But it's really not the same.

AND THEN WHAT?

You might have noticed I skipped over the when, how, and

why this program was ultimately scrapped. It's not because we don't know the when; we do: January 1959. It's not because we don't know the how; we also do: The US Air Force decided it was time to mothball Project A119.

The reason I waited until now to discuss the cancellation of the program—and part of what makes it so fascinating—is I've yet to see anyone provide a convincing reason for *why* it was canceled. Multiple sources have weighed in. All are operating on speculation. There's a lot of using words like "apparently" and "seemingly" in references to the end of the project. *Apparently* the Air Force canceled the program because of the potential danger to people on Earth (in case the mission catastrophically failed the way so many of the early US attempts at spaceflight sadly—and sometimes humorously—failed). *Apparently* the scientists were concerned about contaminating the moon with radioactive material, preventing any future mission to land a man on the surface (or even lunar colonization). The mission was scrapped *seemingly* out of a worry that the best-laid PR plans of the Air Force would be thwarted when the public saw this as an abhorrent defacement of the moon's beauty instead of a demonstration of American scientific prowess. *Maybe* we realized landing a man on the moon was possible, and more impressive?

Who the hell knows? If Reiffel did, he wasn't telling.

When Reiffel went public and acknowledged his role on the project in 2000, he also claimed he didn't know the precise reason for the cancellation of the project. But that didn't stop him from providing his own speculation:

> As these things go, this was small. It was less than a year and never got to the point of operational planning. We

showed what some of the effects might be. But the real argument we made, and others made behind closed doors, was that there was no point in ruining the pristine environment of the moon. There were other ways to impress the public that we were not about to be overwhelmed by the Russians.

Are you convinced the US Air Force, at the height of the Cold War, in the wake of the shocking launch of Sputnik and the fear left in its wake, scrapped A119 because it might make a bit of a mess on the moon?

Neither am I.

One of the most interesting components to this whole story is why Leonard Reiffel, after all those years maintaining his silence, decided to go public. He did it because of Carl Sagan, and a conviction that Sagan broke the law.

Many of us remember Carl Sagan as the man who authored, coauthored, or edited more than twenty books, like the extraordinary *Pale Blue Dot,* or the much-better-than-the-movie *Contact*. Others might remember him as the popular television personality, who brought the universe into American households through the 1980 series *Cosmos*.

But if Leonard Reiffel is correct, Carl Sagan should have been known more for his unauthorized disclosure of classified nuclear secrets. Sagan seems to have included his role in the project on his application for an academic scholarship at the University of California, Berkeley, in 1959—just after the cancellation of the program. On his application forms, Sagan listed his qualifications and accomplishments … which happened to include two classified papers from A119: *Possible Contribution of Lunar Nuclear Weapons Detonations to the Solution of Some Problems in Planetary Astronomy* and *Radiological Contamination of the Moon by Nuclear Weapons Detonations.*

It didn't take a rocket scientist to ferret out what those papers were talking about. (Although it's likely several actual rocket scientists were evaluating his application …)

So what did Sagan have to say about all of this security breach hubbub? He died three years before it became public, and would never get a chance to clear his name.

But what about the rumors of a Soviet plan to nuke the moon that surfaced just after Sputnik? Those rumors were totally unfounded, and based on God only knows what information, likely someone's vivid imagination. The crazy part is, they were right. Sort of. There was no Soviet plan to nuke the moon in November 1957. Yet that doesn't mean the Soviets *never* intended to do just that. In fact, not long after the rumored November launch, the Soviets actually decided to begin planning for their quest to conquer the moon. It was called the "E-series" of programs. E-1 had the mission to hit the moon, and accomplished this on September 14, 1959, when the spacecraft Luna 2 became the first man-made object to reach the moon. E2, launched on October 4, 1959, as Luna 3, sent back the first pictures of the far side of the moon. E3 had a similar "flyaround" mission, but failed to achieve orbit.

E4 was the doppelgänger of Project A119: Explode a nuclear device on the moon's surface. Fortunately, this idea was dismissed along with its American counterpart. The Soviets were afraid of a failure to launch, which could drop the nuclear warhead back onto Soviet soil. Or even worse, a partial launch failure, which might drop the warhead on *someone else's* soil, causing (in wonderful Russian understatement) "a highly undesirable international incident."

Hard to argue with that.

CONCLUSION

AND THEN WHAT?

What *were* these people thinking? The million-dollar question. What inspired intelligent, accomplished, and serious men* to put forth the absurd ideas highlighted in this book? Projects and programs that ran the gamut from wacky, to inexplicable, to downright certifiable. Brilliant scientists and engineers. Savvy world leaders. Decorated military officials. Seasoned agency directors. People not usually taken to flights of fancy or wild propositions. What caused world governments and their military and intelligence agencies to take them seriously enough to devote vast resources to developing them? Why were they willing to entertain these particularly outlandish proposals?

Historical context is key, of course. These ideas don't exist in a vacuum. They are the products of the times in which they exist—from the carnage of World War II to the fear that resulted from the uncertainty and tension of the Cold War. These people were terrified. They held the future of their countries, even humanity, in their hands.

---

*You might be wondering why I haven't said 'people' here. The answer is that, while some of the plans discussed in this book were the work of brilliant women, they tended to be quite good plans.

They were desperate. And these programs were the result.

But how would these programs fare today? Could ideas as absurd, dangerous, and outright abominable be funded and explored now? The imminent threats of Nazi Germany and the Soviet Union are no longer present, but that doesn't mean we have less capacity for demonizing, dehumanizing, and killing one another. We are just as vicious. Just as inhumane. Equally as likely to vilify our neighbors as to welcome them. We are still capable of horrible things, and just as capable of rationalizing those actions with the justification of "national security."

We are no better than our ancestors. Just a little less desperate.

Yet that could change in an instant. It's altogether possible we are *more* susceptible today to acts of desperation, even without the menace of a true existential threat. The reaction to the September 11, 2001, attacks and the extremes to which people across the globe were willing to allow their governments to go to in their names, is testament to this fact. Nearly the same number of Americans died on 9/11 as in the attack on Pearl Harbor. That's bad enough. But imagine if Al Qaeda had the wherewithal to pull off a followon attack, or a series of attacks on the United States. Or, God forbid, what if Al Qaeda was able to deploy a weapon of mass destruction in an American city. And imagine what that would mean for the rest of the world.

I'm not confident we wouldn't embrace ideas in the vein of some of the more egregious ideas in this book. Are you?

In fact, we have no way to know what ideas might be getting tossed around at this very minute; what scientific and technological schemes might be under development by our governments today. It's a secret—for now at least.

The good news is that none of the ideas in this book ever came to fruition. Logic, rationality, sometimes the sheer luck of superseding events prevailed. In some cases, the better angels of our nature intervened on our behalf. "And we call ourselves the human race," JFK is thankfully said to have declared in disgust after hearing one particularly aggressive nuclear plan. If history is our guide (and hopefully it can be), any outlandish ideas currently under scrutiny will be scrapped before they get off the drawing board.

But you never know. If the neighborhood stray cat suddenly takes an unnatural interest in your private conversations, don't say I didn't warn you.

SOURCES AND FURTHER READING

The case studies in this book come from stories that I have either read or heard about over the years as part of (1) conducting my own research on separate topics, (2) my job as historian and curator of the International Spy Museum, or (3) chatting with my friends and colleagues in the business—and sometimes this means swapping fun stories, usually late at night, while trying to oneup each other with the most crazy, outrageous thing we can think of. "Have you heard the one about …" or "This thing is totally insane …" or "You'll never *believe* what I read in the archives last week …"

It's nerdy, but it's fun.

So while I came in knowing the broad outlines of each chapter, I turned to a range of sources to fill in the specifics (and make sure things actually happened the way people told me they happened): primary and secondary source literature, archival research, archival literature, expert interviews, and broad-ranging scientific, intelligence, foreign policy, and national security policy perspectives.

In this section, I will try to provide you with the sources I used for specific references within the chapters (direct quotes, statistics, budgetary numbers, factoids, and so on). I don't expect most of you to have the time (or the inclination) to schlep to an archive to hunt down a government document. That's okay, because other kind and enterprising people have put a lot of these docs online. Where they are available, I will provide you a link. Sources are listed in order of importance to the chapter.

I am also hoping that these chapters will ignite your curiosity to learn more about history—or at least the history of these extraordinary projects. So in addition to listing the sources I've directly referenced in this book, I have also included suggestions for further reading that might be of interest. This will *not* be all-encompassing. This isn't a comprehensive bibliography. It's just a taste of what is out there.

(I will almost certainly leave out your favorite book/article/document. The one you swear by. The *only one that matters*. And it's *totally* the one Wikipedia used. I didn't forget to include it. And it's not like I don't know it exists. I just left it out because I knew it would annoy you.)

I hope this gives you a little insight into what else is available for each of these amazing projects should you choose to keep digging.

Chapter 1: Acoustic Kitty

Robert Wallace and H. Keith Melton. *Spycraft: The Secret History of the CIA's Spytechs, from Communism to AlQaeda*. New York: Dutton, 2008.

Victor Marchetti and John Marks. *The CIA and the Cult of Intelligence*. New York: Knopf, 1974.

Jeffrey Richelson. *The Wizards of Langley: Inside the CIA's Directorate of Science and Technology*. New York: Basic Books, 2001.

Emily Anthes. *Frankenstein's Cat: Cuddling Up to Biotech's Brave New Beasts*. New York: Scientific American/Farrar, Straus & Giroux, 2013.

"Views on Trained Cats." Redacted CIA memorandum. National Security Archive. https://nsarchive2.gwu.edu//NSAEBB/NSAEBB54/st27.pdf.

"Hair Cells and the Mechanoelectrical Transduction of Sound Waves." In *Neuroscience,* 2nd ed., edited by Dale Purves et al. Sunderland, MA: Sinauer Associates, 2001. www.ncbi.nlm.nih.gov/books/NBK10867/.

Kat Eschner. "The CIA Experimented on Animals in the 1960s Too. Just Ask 'Acoustic Kitty.' " *Smithsonian Magazine,* August 8, 2017. www.smithsonianmag.com/smart-news/ciaexperimentedanimals-1960s-too-justaskacoustickitty180964313/.

"IsraelRelated Animal Conspiracy Theories." Wikipedia. https://en.wikipedia.org/wiki/Israelrelated_animal_conspiracy_theories.

United States Senate (95th Congress, first session). "Project MKUltra, The CIA's Program of Research in Behavioral Modification: Joint Hearing Before the Select Committee on Intelligence and the Subcommittee on Health and Scientific Research of the Committee on Human Resources." Washington, DC: Government Printing Office, 1977. www.nytimes.com/packages/pdf/national/13inmate_ProjectMKUL TRA.pdf.

Chapter 2: Operation Capricious

Stanley Lovell. *Of Spies and Stratagems: Incredible Secrets of World War II Revealed by a Master Spy*. Englewood Cliffs, NJ: Prentice Hall, 1963.

Jeffrey Lockwood. *SixLegged Soldiers: Using Insects as Weapons of War*. New York: Oxford University Press, 2008.

Mary Roach. *Grunt: The Curious Science of Humans at War*. New York: Norton, 2017.

Benjamin B. Fischer. "The Central Intelligence Agency's Office of Technical Service, 1951–2001: Celebrating Fifty Years of Technical Support to US Foreign Intelligence Operations." 2001 (released in 2007). www.cia.gov/library/readingroom/docs/DOC_0001225679.pdf.

Chapter 3: Project X-Ray

Jack Couffer. *Bat Bomb: World War II's Other Secret Weapon*. Austin: University of Texas Press, 1992.

Hal K. Rothman. "A Stronger Federal Presence: Depression, New Deal, and World War II." Chapter 7 of *Promise Beheld and the Limits of Place: A Historic Resource Study of Carlsbad Caverns and Guadalupe Mountains National Parks and the Surrounding Areas*. Washington, DC: Department of the Interior, National Park Service, 1998. www.nps.gov/parkhistory/online_books/CarlsbadCav/pdf/7.pdf.

Dr. Patrick Drumm and Christopher Ovre. "A Batman to the Rescue." *Monitor on Psychology* (American Psychological Association) 42, no. 4 (April 2011). www.apa.org/monitor/2011/04/batman.aspx.

James O'Donnell. "Air PickUp." *Enroute* (National Postal Museum) 9, issue 1 (January–March 2000). https://postalmuseum.si.edu/research/articles-from-enroute/air-pickup.html.

Patents by Lytle S. Adams. Google Patents. https://patents.google.com/?inventor=Lytle+S+Adams.

Marshall Gates. "Louis Frederick Fieser, 1899–1977." *Biographical Memoir*, 161–75. Washington, DC: National Academy of Sciences, 1994. www.nasonline.org/publications/biographical-memoirs/memoir-pdfs/fieser-louis.pdf.

SOURCES AND FURTHER READING

Chapter 4: Project Fantasia

Robert Kodosky. *Psychological Operations American Style: The Joint United States Public Affairs Office, Vietnam and Beyond.* New York: Lexington Books, 2007.

Jules Archer. *Frontline General: Douglas MacArthur: America's Most Controversial Hero.* New York: Sky Pony Press, 2017.

Colonel Alfred Paddock Jr. "Psychological and Unconventional Warfare, 1941–1952: Origins of a 'Special Warfare' Capability for the United States Army." Carlisle Barracks, PA: US Army War College, 1979. https://fas. org/man/eprint/paddock.pdf.

"Edgar Salinger, 83, Aided War Victims." *New York Times*, February 26, 1971. www.nytimes.com/1971/02/26/archives/egarsalinger-83-aided-war-victims.html.

"The Office of Strategic Services: Morale Operations Branch." *News and Information* (CIA), July 29, 2010. www.cia.gov/news-information/ featured-story-archive/2010-featured-story-archive/oss-morale-operations. html.

"A Look Back … Barbara Lauwers: Deceiving the Enemy." *News and Information* (CIA), August 19, 2009. www.cia.gov/news-information/ featured-story-archive/barbara-lauwers.html.

William Donovan. "Psychological Warfare." Speech, New York, December 12, 1942. Wikimedia. https://upload.wikimedia.org/wikipedia/ commons/c/c1/Donovan_on_PW.pdf.

Linda Lombardi. "Kitsune: The Divine/Evil Fox Yokai." *Tofugu*, September 9, 2014. www.tofugu.com/japan/kitsune-yokai-fox/.

Chapter 5: Blue Peacock

Frank Barnaby and Douglas Holdstock, eds. *The British Nuclear Weapons Programme, 1952–2002.* London: Routledge, 2003.

Richard A. Bitzinger. "Assessing the Conventional Balance in Europe, 1945–1975." Santa Monica, CA: RAND Corporation, 1989. www.rand. org/content/dam/rand/pubs/notes/2007/N2859.pdf.

Matthew Gault. "The Ultimate Weapon of War: Nuclear Land Mines?" *The Buzz* (blog), *National Interest,* September 20, 2015. https:// nationalinterest.org/blog/the-buzz/the-ultimate-weapon-war-nuclear-land-mines-13890.

Jeremy Bender. "In the 1950s, the UK Had Serious Plans to Use Live Chickens to Help Keep Nuclear Land Mines in Working Order." *Business Insider*, May 15, 2015. www.businessinsider.com/ukdevelopedchickenwarmed-nuclear-landmines-20155.

John Finney IV. "A NATO Nuclear Strategy." *New York Times*, December 2, 1973. www.nytimes.com/1973/12/02/archives/anato-nuclear-strategy-use-ofoutsideamerican-atomic-forcesis.html.

"List of Rainbow Codes." Wikipedia. https://en.wikipedia.org/wiki/List_of_Rainbow_Codes.

University of Kentucky, College of Agriculture & Kentucky Poultry Federation. *Poultry Production Manual*. Chapter 7, "Air Temperature." https://afs.ca.uky.edu/poultry/chapter7air-temperature.

Chapter 6: Operation Foxley

Mark Seaman. *Operation Foxley: The British Plan to Kill Hitler*. London: Public Record Office, 2001.

British National Archives, "Hitler Assassination Plan." https://nationalarchives.gov.uk/documents/education/foxley.pdf, retrieved February 10, 2019.

Internet Archive, "Files for WorldWarIIOperationFoxley," https://archive.org/download/WorldWarIIOperationFoxley, retrieved December 20, 2018.

Chapter 7: Operation Northwoods

A massive trove of government documents can be found at the Mary Ferrell Foundation: www.maryferrell.org/pages/Operation_Northwoods.html.

Another set can be found at the National Security Archive of George Washington University: https://nsarchive2.gwu.edu/news/20010430/northwoods.pdf.

Brig. Gen. Edward Lansdale. "Meeting with the President, 16 Mar 1962." Mary Ferrell Foundation. www.maryferrell.org/showDoc.html?docId=236#relPageId=21&tab=page.

Chapter 8: Felix and His Rifle

Felix Rodriguez. *Shadow Warrior: The CIA Hero of a Hundred Unknown Battles*. New York: Simon & Schuster, 1989.

SOURCES AND FURTHER READING

Don Bohning. *The Castro Obsession: US Covert Operations Against Cuba, 1959–1965*. Washington, DC: Potomac Books, 2005.

Ted Shackley and Richard Finney. *Spymaster: My Life in the CIA*. Washington, DC: Potomac Books, 2005.

Marita Lorenz. *Marita: The Spy Who Loved Castro*. New York: Pegasus Books, 2017.

Alleged Assassination Plots Involving Foreign Leaders: An Interim Report of the Select Committee to Study Governmental Operations with Respect to Intelligence Activities (the Church Committee). Washington, DC: Government Printing Office, 1975. www.intelligence.senate.gov/sites/default/files/94465.pdf.

Don Bohning. "Fidel Castro and the 'Secret War' Waged by CIA." *Miami Herald*, November 26, 2016. www.miamiherald.com/news/nation-world/world/americas/fidelcastroen/article117202083.html.

Documents pertaining to JM/WAVE from the Mary Ferrell Foundation: www.mary ferrell.org/php/cryptdb.php?id=JMWAVE.

Justin F. Gleichauf. "A Listening Post in Miami." *Studies in Intelligence* (CIA) 44, no. 5 (May 8, 2007). www.cia.gov/library/center-for-the-studyof-intelligence/kent-csi/vol44no5/html/v44i5a06p.htm.

Documents pertaining to Operation Mongoose from the Mary Ferrell Foundation: www.maryferrell.org/pages/Operation_Mongoose.html.

"Program Review by the Chief of Operations, Operation Mongoose (Lansdale)." *Foreign Relations of the United States, 1961–1963*, vol. 10, *Cuba, January 1961–September 1962*. Edited by Louis J. Smith. Washington, DC: Government Printing Office, 1997. https://history.state.gov/historicaldocuments/frus1961-63v10/d291.

Tim Elfrink. "CIA Considered Bombing Miami and Killing Refugees to Blame Castro." *Miami New Times*, October 27, 2017. www.miaminewtimes.com/news/jfk-docs-cia-plotted-to-bomb-miami-kill-refugees-and-blame-castro-9782696.

Chapter 9: Project Seal

T. D. J. Leech. *The Final Report of Project "Seal."* School of Engineering, Auckland University College, Ardmore, New Zealand (Department of Scientific and Industrial Research, Wellington, New Zealand), December 18, 1950.

Jerry Smith. *Weather Warfare: The Military's Plan to Draft Mother Nature*. Kempton IL: Adventures Unlimited Press, 2006.

Matthew Gault. "The Ultimate Weapon: Nuclear Tsunami Bombs?" *War Is Boring,* March 5, 2015. https://medium.com/war-is-boring/no-iran-can-t-trigger-a-nuclear-tsunami-that-wipes-out-israel-76258b6e5f69.

Ray Waru. *Secrets & Treasures: Our Stories Told Through the Objects at Archives New Zealand*. Auckland: Random House, 2012.

W. G. Van Dorn, B. Leméhauté, and LiSan Hwang. *Final Report: Handbook of Explosion Generated Water Waves (Vol. 1: State of the Art)*. Pasadena, CA: Tetra Tech Inc., October 1968. www.dtic.mil/dtic/tr/fulltext/u2/845485.pdf.

Becky Oskin. "Japan Earthquake & Tsunami of 2011: Facts and Information." *Live Science*, September 13, 2017. www.livescience.com/39110-japan-2011-earthquake-tsunami-facts.html.

Dave Mosher. "A New Russian Video May Show a 'Doomsday Machine' Able to Trigger 300-Foot Tsunamis—but Nuclear Weapons Experts Question Why You'd Ever Build One." *Business Insider*, July 24, 2018. www.businessinsider.com/russia-doomsday-weapon-submarine-nuke-2018-4.

Sara Malm. "Russian 'Doomsday Machine' Nuke Could Wipe Out Coastal Infrastructure with 300ft Tsunamis." *Daily Mail,* April 24, 2018. www.dailymail.co.uk/news/article-5652239/Russian-doomsday-machine-nuke-wipe-coastal-infrastructure-300ft-tsunamis.html.

Chapter 10: Operation Monopoly

Thomas Boghardt. "Operation Monopoly: Digging for Secrets in Washington, D.C." *Spy Museum Background Briefings.* www.spymuseum.org/education-programs/news-books-briefings/background-briefings/operation-monopoly/.

United States of America vs. Robert Philip Hanssen. United States District Court for the Eastern District of Virginia (Alexandria Division), May 16, 2001. https://fas.org/irp/ops/ci/hanssen_indict.html.

James Risen with Lowell Bergman. "US Thinks Agent Revealed Tunnel at Soviet Embassy." *New York Times,* March 4, 2001. www.nytimes.com/2001/03/04/us/us-thinks-agent-revealed-tunnel-at-soviet-embassy.html.

John Kelly. "What Lies Beneath: FBI Tunnel in Glover Park Heated Up the Cold War." *Washington Post*, February 27, 2016. www.washingtonpost.com/local/what-lies-beneath-fbi-tunnel-in-glover-park-heated-up-the-cold-war/2016/02/27/d722abc6-d9b9-11e5-81ae-7491b9b9e7df_story.html?utm_term=.ffba660d045c.

Matt Soniak. "How a Gift from Schoolchildren Let the Soviets Spy on the US for 7 Years." *Atlas Obscura*, June 21, 2016. www.atlasobscura.com/articles/how-a-gift-from-schoolchildren-let-the-soviets-spy-on-the-us-for-7-years.

William Safire. "Essay; Who Lost Mount Alto?" *New York Times,* September 22, 1985. www.nytimes.com/1985/09/22/opinion/essay-who-lost-mount-alto.html.

Chapter 11: Operation House Party

Michael Howard. *British Intelligence in the Second World War*, Volume 5, *Strategic Deception*. London: H.M. Stationery Office, 1990.

Ben MacIntyre. *Double Cross: The True Story of the D-Day Spies*. London: Bloomsbury Publishing, 2012.

R. V. Jones. *Most Secret War: British Scientific Intelligence, 1939–1945*. London: Penguin Books, 2009.

Richard Aldrich. *The Hidden Hand: Britain, America, and Cold War Secret Intelligence*. London: John Murray, 2001.

Tatiana Zerjal et al. "The Genetic Legacy of the Mongols." *American Journal of Human Genetics*, Vol. 72, No. 3 (2003), 717–21.

John Zambri. "Why Chinghis Khan Matters: Reflections on the Mongol Way of Intelligence," https://smallwarsjournal.com/jrnl/art/why-chinghis-khan-matters-reflections-on-the-mongol-way-of-intelligence, retrieved February 4, 2019.

Huw Dylan. "Super-weapons and Subversion: British Deterrence by Deception Operations in the Early Cold War," *Journal of Strategic Studies*. Vol. 38, No. 5 (2015), 704–728.

Stephen Twigge and Len Scott. "Strategic Defence by Deception," *Intelligence and National Security*, Vol. 16, No. 2 (2001), 152–157.

NUKING THE MOON

Chapter 12: Project Habakkuk

Henry Hemming. *The Ingenious Mr. Pyke: Inventor, Fugitive, Spy.* New York: PublicAffairs, 2015.

John Bryden. *Deadly Allies: Canada's Secret War, 1937–1947.* Toronto: McClelland & Stewart, 1989.

L. D. Cross. *Code Name Habbakuk: A Secret Ship Made of Ice.* Victoria, BC: Heritage House Publishing, 2012.

M. F. Perutz. "A Description of the Iceberg Aircraft Carrier and the Bearing of the Mechanical Properties of Frozen Wood Pulp upon Some Problems of Glacier Flow." *Journal of Glaciology* 1, no. 3 (1948): 95–104. https://doi.org/10.3189/S0022143000007796.

Jamie Hyneman. "Can You Build Ships Out of Ice? The Mythbusters Investigate." *Popular Mechanics,* April 30, 2009. www.popularmechanics.com/science/a4101/4313387/.

Sir Charles Goodeve, F. R. S. "The Ice Ship Fiasco." *Evening Standard* (London), April 19, 1951. www.chem.ucl.ac.uk/resources/history/people/goodeve_cf/habakkuk.html.

Ford Class Aircraft Carriers (official website). www.thefordclass.com/.

Chapter 13: Tagboard

Clarence "Kelly" Johnson and Maggie Smith. *Kelly: More Than My Share of It All.* Washington, DC: Smithsonian Books, 1985.

Ben Rich and Leo Janos. *Skunk Works: A Personal Memoir of My Years at Lockheed.* New York: Little, Brown, 1994.

Roadrunners Internationale (a resource dedicated to "preserving the history of the aviation pioneers and programs that developed the U2, A12 and YF12 during the Cold War"). http://roadrunnersinternationale.com/.

David Robarge. *Archangel: CIA's Supersonic A12 Reconnaissance Aircraft.* Center for the Study of Intelligence Publications (CIA), April 10, 2014. www.cia.gov/library/center-for-the-study-of-intelligence/csi-publications/books-and-monographs/a-12.

Peter Garrison. "Head Skunk." *Air and Space,* March 2010. www.airspacemag.com/history-of-flight/head-skunk-5960121/.

Tom Demerly. "The Time I Found a Formerly Top Secret D21 Supersonic Drone in the Arizona Desert." *The Aviationist,* June 8, 2018. https://theaviationist.com/2018/06/08/

288

the-time-i-found-a-formerly-top-secret-d-21-supersonic-drone-in-the-arizona-desert/.

"Lockheed D21B Drone." Museum of Flight. www.museumofflight.org/aircraft/lockheed-d-21b-drone.

"Senior Bowl D21: Tagboard." Federation of American Scientists, Intelligence Resouce Program. https://fas.org/irp/program/collect/d-21.htm.

"Lockheed D21B." National Museum of the US Air Force. www.nationalmuseum.af.mil/Visit/Museum-Exhibits/Fact-Sheets/Display/Article/195778/lockheed-d-21b/.

"SR71 Sistership, the MD21 Blackbird Accident." YouTube. Posted by Blackbird 101, November 14, 2007. www.youtube.com/watch?v=GMyC2urCl_4.

"Blackbird Losses." SR71 Online. www.sr-71.org/blackbird/losses.php.

Ralph Vartabedian. "Now It Can Be Said—He Has the Right Stuff." *Los Angeles Times*, September 29, 1989. http://articles.latimes.com/1989-09-29/news/mn-249_1_test-pilots.

/NSAEBB439/.

Chapter 14: The X--20 and the MOL

Tom Wolfe. *The Right Stuff*. New York: Farrar, Straus & Giroux, 1983.

Amy Shira Teitel. *Breaking the Chains of Gravity: The Story of Spaceflight Before NASA*. New York: Bloomsbury Sigma, 2018.

"X20 DynaSoar Space Vehicle." Boeing. www.boeing.com/history/products/x-20-dyna-soar.page.

"Dynasoar." *Encyclopedia Astronautica*. www.astronautix.com/d/dynasoar.html.

Greg Goebel. "[1.0] Prelude: The X15, Dyna-Soar, & The Lifting Bodies." *The Space Shuttle Program*, v1.2.0, January 1, 2017. Vectors. http://vc.airvectors.net/tashutl_c01.html.

Robert F. Dorr. "X20 DynaSoar Spaceplace Was Decades Ahead of Its Time." Defense Media Network, September 3, 2011. www.defensemedianetwork.com/stories/what-might-have-been-x-20-dyna-soar/.

James D. Outzen, ed. *The Dorian Files Revealed: A Compendium of the NRO's Manned Orbiting Laboratory Documents*. National Reconnaissance Office, Center for the Study of National Reconnaissance. Washington, DC:

Government Printing Office, 2015. www.nro.gov/Portals/65/documents/
history/csnr/programs/docs/MOL_Compendium_August_2015.pdf.

Elizabeth Howell. "Manned Orbiting Laboratory Declassified: Inside a
US Military Space Station." Space.com, March 4, 2017. www.space.
com/34661-manned-orbiting-laboratory-declassified-photos.html.

Al Hallonquist. "The MOL-Men Come Into the Light." *Air and
Space*, December 4, 2015. www.airspacemag.com/daily-planet/
mol-men-come-light-180957353/.

"Manned Orbiting Laboratory." National Museum of the United States Air
Force. www.nationalmuseum.af.mil/Visit/Museum-Exhibits/Fact-Sheets/
Display/Article/195891/manned-orbiting-laboratory/.

"Model, Manned Orbiting Laboratory, 1:30." Smithsonian National Air
and Space Museum. https://airandspace.si.edu/collection-objects/
model-manned-orbiting-laboratory-130-0.

"Spacesuits Open Doors to MOL History." NASA, July 13, 2017. www.nasa.
gov/centers/kennedy/about/history/molsuits.html.

Philip Richardson. "Da Vinci's Observations of Soaring Birds." *Physics
Today*, November 2017. https://physicstoday.scitation.org/doi/
abs/10.1063/PT.3.3773?journalCode=pto.

Ben Wright McGee. "The Curious Case of MOL's Missing Mission."
Astrowright, June 20, 2018. https://astrowright.wordpress.com/?s=mol.

Chapter 15: Brilliant Pebbles

Ashton Carter and David Schwartz, eds. *Ballistic Missile Defense.*
Washington, DC: Brookings Institution Press, 1984.

Office of Technology Assessment. *Ballistic Missile Defense Technologies.*
Honolulu: University Press of the Pacific, 2002.

Edward Reiss. *The Strategic Defense Initiative.* Cambridge, UK: Cambridge
University Press, 1992.

Office of the Secretary of Defense and Joint Staff. *Brilliant Pebbles
Experiment Program.* Washington, DC: Government Printing Office,
2013.

Ronald Reagan. "Address to the Nation on Defense and National Security."
Washington, DC, March 23, 1983. www.reaganfoundation.org/ronald-
reagan/reagan-quotes-speeches/address-to-the-nation-on-defense-and-
national-security/.

SOURCES AND FURTHER READING

"Strategic Defense Initiative (SDI), 1983." US Department of State (archive). https://2001-2009.state.gov/r/pa/ho/time/rd/104253.htm.

Donald R. Baucom. "The Rise and Fall of Brilliant Pebbles." *Journal of Social, Political and Economic Studies* 29, no. 2 (Summer 2004): 143–90. http://highfrontier.org/oldar chive/Archive/hf/The%20Rise%20and%20 Fall%20of%20Brilliant%20Pebbles%20-Baucom.pdf.

William J. Broad. "What Next for 'Star Wars'? 'Brilliant Pebbles.' " *New York Times*, April 25, 1989. www.nytimes.com/1989/04/25/science/what-s-next-for-star-wars-brilliant-pebbles.html?pagewanted=all.

Edward L. Rowny. "What Brilliant Pebbles Could Do." *Washington Post,* no date given. www.washingtonpost.com/archive/opinions/1990/03/10/what-brilliant-pebbles-could-do/61a839e6-0c2d-45c4-b624-677f4d697131/?noredirect=on&utm_term=.7c4832953337

"Strategic Defense Initiative." GlobalSecurity.org. www.globalsecurity.org/space/systems/sdi.htm.

James Gattuso. "Brilliant Pebbles: The Revolutionary Idea for Strategic Defense." Heritage Foundation Report, January 25, 1990. www.heritage.org/defense/report/brilliant-pebbles-the-revolutionary-idea-strategic-defense.

United States General Accounting Office. "Strategic Defense Initiative: Estimates of Pebbles' Effectiveness Are Based on Many Unproven Assumptions." Report to the Chairman, Committee on Armed Services, US Senate. March 27, 1992. http://archive.gao.gov/d31t10/146232.pdf.

Patrick E. Tyler. "How Edward Teller Learned to Love the Nuclear-Pumped XRay Laser." *Washington Post*, April 3, 1983. www.washingtonpost.com/archive/opinions/1983/04/03/how-edward-teller-learned-to-love-the-nuclear-pumped-x-ray-laser/6df462e5-26e0-428c-a90b-c39bb8075210/?utm_term=.304272a6a2b9.

Ashton B. Carter. "Section 3: Directed Energy Weapons for Boost-Phase Intercept." *Directed Energy Missile Defense in Space*—A Background Paper. Washington, DC: US Congress, Office of Technology Assessment, OTA-BP-ISC-26. April 1984. www.princeton.edu/~ota/disk3/1984/8410/841005.PDF.

United States Department of Defense and Joint Chiefs of Staff. "Report to Congress: Declaratory Policy, Concept of Operations, and Deployment

Guidelines for Left-of-Launch Capability." May 2017. bhttps://fas.org/man/eprint/left.pdf.

Chapter 16: The Sun Gun

"The German Space Mirror: Nazi Men of Science Seriously Planned to Use a ManMade Satellite as a Weapon for Conquest." *Life*, July 23, 1945. https://books.google.com.au/books?id=3okEAAAAMBAJ&pg=PA78&dq =german+space+mirror&hl=en&ei=s2vVTI-pDo_4sAP9qZGNCw&sa= X&oi=book_result&ct=result&redir_esc=y#v=onepage&q=german%20 space%20mirror&f=true.

Alan Bellows. "The Third Reich's Diabolical Orbiting Superweapon." *Damn Interesting,* February 9, 2008. www.damninteresting.com/ the-third-reichs-diabolical-orbiting-superweapon/.

Joe Pappalardo. "The Very Real History of Death Stars." *Popular Mechanics,* February 14, 2018. www.popularmechanics.com/military/research/ a15928734/real-history-death-stars/.

"Hermann J. Oberth." International Space Hall of Fame at the New Mexico Museum of Space History. www.nmspacemuseum.org/halloffame/detail. php?id=21.

"Hermann Oberth." NASA. www.nasa.gov/audience/foreducators/rocketry/ home/hermann-oberth.html.

"Hermann Julius Oberth." Barron Hilton Pioneers of Flight Gallery. Smithsonian National Air and Space Museum. http://pioneersofflight. si.edu/content/hermann-julius-oberth-0.

Chapter 17: The Plowshare Program's Strangest Idea

Scott Kaufman. *Project Plowshare: The Peaceful Use of Nuclear Explosives in Cold War America*. Ithaca, NY: Cornell University Press, 2012.

Florida stories from Twitter handle @_FloridaMan.

Michael Edison Hayden. "Sheriff Warns Against People 'Shooting' Hurricane Irma." ABC News, September 10, 2017. https://abcnews. go.com/US/sheriff-warns-people-shooting-hurricane-irma/ story?id=49741491.

Lawrence Radiation Laboratory (Livermore) and US Atomic Engery Commission (San Francisco Office). *Proceedings of the Second Plowshare Symposium. May 13–15, 1959. San Francisco, California. Part V: Scientific*

SOURCES AND FURTHER READING

Uses of Nuclear Explosions (Plowshare Series: Report No. 2). Includes Jack Reed's "Some Speculations on the Effects of Nuclear Explosions on Hurricanes" (pp. 78–88). https://babel.hathitrust.org/cgi/pt?id=mdp.3901 5077324005;view=1up;seq=1.

United States Department of Energy. "Executive Summary: Plowshare Program." www.osti.gov/opennet/reports/plowshare.pdf.

NOAA, Hurricane Research Division. "Frequently Asked Questions." Version 4.10, June 1, 2017. www.aoml.noaa.gov/hrd/tcfaq/tcfaqHED.html.

Mark Strauss. "Nuking Hurricanes: The Surprising History of a Really Bad Idea." *National Geographic*, November 30, 2016. https://news.nationalgeographic.com/2016/11/hurricanes-weather-history-nuclear-weapons/.

"Could the Pressure of a Nuclear Explosion Disrupt a Hurricane?" Bradbury Science Museum, November 2015. www.lanl.gov/museum/news/newsletter/2016-11/science-question-nuke-hurricane.php.

"Nuking Hurricanes." *Atomic Skies,* September 26, 2013. http://atomic-skies.blogspot.com/2013/09/nuking-hurricanes.html.

John Fleck. "Scientist: Hurricanes Can Be Nuked." *Albuquerque Journal*, September 18, 2004. www.abqjournal.com/news/metro/225048metro09-18-04.htm.

"The Man Who Wanted to Nuke a Hurricane." *War Is Boring*, August 19, 2015. https://medium.com/war-is-boring/the-man-who-wanted-to-nuke-a-hurricane-c47aa37b0181.

Chapter 18: Protecting the Peacekeeper

MX Missile Basing Advisory Panel (Office of Technology Assessment). *MX Missile Basing*. September 1981. http://ota.fas.org/reports/8116.pdf.

Office of the Deputy Under Secretary of Defense for Research and Engineering (Strategic and Space Systems). *ICBM Basing Options: A Summary of Major Studies to Define a Survivable Basing Concept for ICBMs*. December 1980. www.dtic.mil/dtic/tr/fulltext/u2/a956443.pdf.

Jeffrey G. "Insuring Survivability: Basing the MX Missile." Heritage Foundation, May 27, 1980. www.heritage.org/defense/report/insuring-survivability-basing-the-mx-missile.

Art Hobson. "The ICBM Basing Question." *Science and Global Security* 2 (1991): 153–98. http://scienceandglobalsecurity.org/archive/sgs02hobson.pdf.

Lauren Caston et al. "The Future of the US Intercontinental Ballistic Missile Force." RAND Project Air Force (RAND Corporation), 2014. www.rand.org/content/dam/rand/pubs/monographs/MG1200/MG1210/RAND_MG1210.pdf.

Chapter 19: Project Iceworm

Todd Tucker. *Atomic America: How a Deadly Explosion and a Feared Admiral Changed the Course of Nuclear History.* New York: Free Press, 2009.

"Camp Century, Greenland, Project Iceworm: 'City Under the Ice' R&D Progress Report 6 1963 US Army." YouTube. Posted by Jeff Quitney, August 8, 2012. www.youtube.com/watch?v=x0c9ykqe2Xs.

Elmore Clark. "Technical Report: Camp Century Evolution of Concept and History of Design Construction and Performance." Hanover, NH: US Army Materiel Command Cold Regions Research & Engineering Laboratory, October 1965. www.dtic.mil/dtic/tr/fulltext/u2/477706.pdf.

Marie Eriksen Dyekjær. "The City Under Ice." Part 7 of *Who, What, When* series, *Willi Dansgaard.* Niels Bohr Institute (University of Copenhagen). www.nbi.ku.dk/english/www/willi/dansgaard/byen-under-isen/.

"Camp Century." Atomic Heritage Foundation. www.atomicheritage.org/history/camp-century.

Frank Leskovitz. "Camp Century, Greenland." *Science Leads the Way.* http://gombessa.tripod.com/scienceleadstheway/id9.html.

Julia Rosen. "Mysterious, IceBuried Cold War Military Base May Be Unearthed by Climate Change." *Science,* August 4, 2016. www.sciencemag.org/news/2016/08/mysterious-ice-buried-cold-war-military-base-may-be-unearthed-climate-change.

Ben Panko. "A Radioactive Cold War Military Base Will Soon Emerge from Greenland's Melting Ice." *Smithsonian,* August 5, 2016. www.smithsonianmag.com/science-nature/radioactive-cold-war-military-base-will-soon-emerge-greenlands-melting-ice-180960036/.

Mark Serreze. "Why Is the Arctic So Sensitive to Climate Change and Why Do We Care?" Pacific Marine Environmental Laboratory (NOAA). www.pmel.noaa.gov/arctic-zone/essay_serreze.html.

SOURCES AND FURTHER READING

"The Arctic and Antarctica." *Global Trends* (National Intelligence Council). www.dni.gov/index.php/the-next-five-years/the-arctic-and-antarctica.

Chapter 20: Aircraft Nuclear Propulsion and Project Orion

R. W. Bussard and R. D. Delauer. *Fundamentals of Nuclear Flight.* New York: McGraw-Hill, 1965.

Herbert York. *Race to Oblivion.* New York: Simon & Schuster, 1970.

George Dyson. *Project Orion: The True Story of the Atomic Spaceship.* New York: Henry Holt, 2002.

Joseph Campbell (Comptroller General of the United States). "Report to the Congress of the United States: Review of Manned Aircraft Nuclear Propulsion Program, Atomic Energy Commission and Department of Defense." United States General Accounting Office, February 1963. https://fas.org/nuke/space/anp-gao1963.pdf.

C. B. Ellis, ed. "The Aircraft Nuclear Propulsion Program and General Reactor Technology. General Progress Report for Period Ending November 30, 1949." Oak Ridge National Laboratory, January 10, 1950. http://moltensalt.org/references/static/downloads/pdf/ORNL-0528.pdf.

Karen A. Frenkel. "Resuscitating the Atomic Airplane: Flying on a Wing and an Isotope." *Scientific American,* December 5, 2008. www.scientificamerican.com/article/nuclear-powered-aircraft/.

Freeman J. Dyson. "Death of a Project." *Science,* new series, vol. 149, no. 3680 (July 9, 1965): 141–44. http://citeseerx.ist.psu.edu/viewdoc/download?doi=10.1.1.691.3128&rep=rep1&type=pdf.

"The Atomic Spaceship." www.oriondrive.com/index.php.

United States Department of Commerce, National Technical Information Service. "Nuclear Pulse Vehicle Study Condensed Summary Report (General Dynamics Corp.)." Huntsville, AL: NASA, January 1964. https://ntrs.nasa.gov/archive/nasa/casi.ntrs.nasa.gov/19760065935.pdf.

Thaine W. Reynolds. "Effective Specific Impulse of External Nuclear Pulse Propulsion Systems." Washington, DC: NASA, September 1972. https://ntrs.nasa.gov/archive/nasa/casi.ntrs.nasa.gov/19720025114.pdf.

G. R. Schmidt, J. A. Bonometti, and P. J. Morton. "AIAA 2000-3856: Nuclear Pulse Propulsion—Orion and Beyond." From the 36th AIAA/ASME/SAE/ASEE Joint Propulsion Conference and Exhibit, July 16–19,

2000. Huntsville, AL: NASA Marshall SFC, 2000. https://ntrs.nasa.gov/archive/nasa/casi.ntrs.nasa.gov/20000096503.pdf.

George Dyson. "The Story of Project Dyson." TED Talk, February 2002. www.ted.com/talks/george_dyson_on_project_orion?language=en.

"Propulsion Test Vehicle, Project Orion." Smithsonian National Air and Space Museum. https://airandspace.si.edu/collection-objects/propulsion-test-vehicle-project-orion.

Chapter 21: Project A119

Leonard Reiffel. *A Study of Lunar Research Flights*, vol. 1. Kirtland Air Force Base, NM: Air Force Special Weapons Center Air Research and Development Command, June 19, 1959. https://nsarchive2.gwu.edu//NSAEBB/NSAEBB479/docs/EBB-Moon02.pdf.

Bob Goldsborough. "Leonard Reiffel, Inventor of Telestrator Used to Show NFL Replays, Dies at 89." *Chicago Tribune,* April 20, 2017. www.chicagotribune.com/news/obituaries/ct-leonard-reiffel-obituary-20170420-story.html.

Richard Sandomir. "Leonard Reiffel, Who Studied Lunar Nuclear Bomb, Dies at 89." *New York Times,* April 26, 2017. www.nytimes.com/2017/04/26/us/obituary-leonardreiffel-nuclear-bomb-moon.html.

"Sputnik: The Fiftieth Anniversary." NASA. October 10, 2007. https://history.nasa.gov/sputnik/index.html.

Paul Dickson. "Sputnik's Impact on America." *Nova* (PBS), November 6, 2007. www.pbs.org/wgbh/nova/space/sputnik-impactonamerica.html.

Leonard Reiffel. "Sagan Breached Security by Revealing US Work on a Lunar Bomb Project." *Nature* 405, no. 13 (May 4, 2009). www.nature.com/articles/35011148.

Aleksandr Zheleznyakov. "The E4 Project—Exploding a Nuclear Bomb on the Moon" (translated from the Russian). Sven's Space Place. www.svengrahn.pp.se/histind/E3/E3orig.htm.

Joseph L. Myler. "Latest Red Rumor: They'll Bomb the Moon." *Pittsburgh Press,* November 1, 1957. https://news.google.com/newspapers?id=5kUqAAAAIBAJ&sjid=Bk4EAAAAIBAJ&pg=5584,131807.